FROM
**EVERYDAY
MEALS** TO
**CELEBRATION
CUISINE**

GCHI'S

BIG BOOK
OF KOREAN
COOKING

MAANGCHI **WITH**
MARTHA ROSE SHULMAN
PHOTOGRAPHS BY MAANGCHI

A RUX MARTIN BOOK   HOUGHTON MIFFLIN HARCOURT   BOSTON   NEW YORK

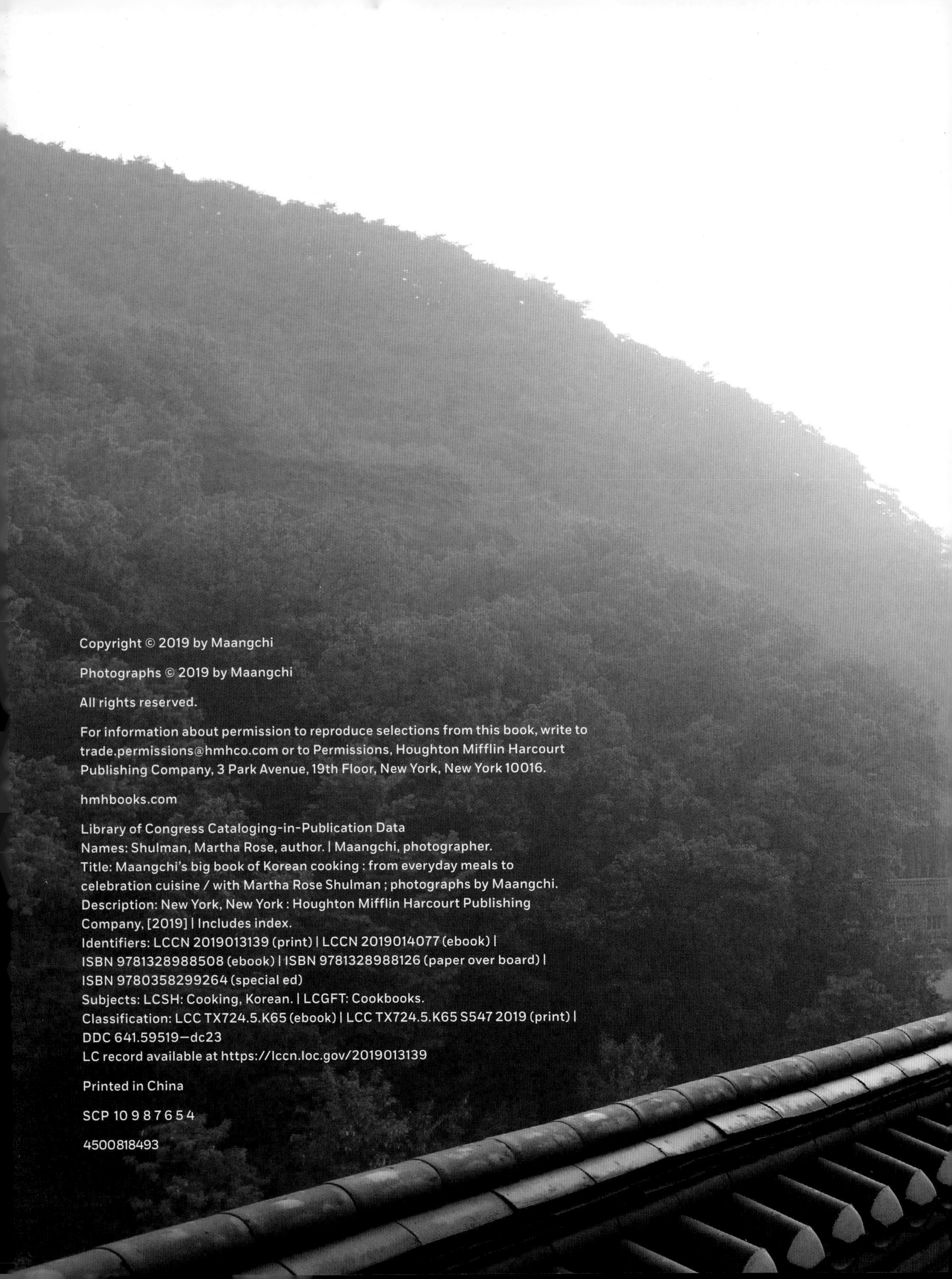

For information about permission to reproduce selections from this book, write to
trade.permissions@hmhco.com or to Permissions, Houghton Mifflin Harcourt
Publishing Company, 3 Park Avenue, 19th Floor, New York, New York 10016.

hmhbooks.com

Library of Congress Cataloging-in-Publication Data
Names: Shulman, Martha Rose, author. | Maangchi, photographer.
Title: Maangchi's big book of Korean cooking : from everyday meals to
celebration cuisine / with Martha Rose Shulman ; photographs by Maangchi.
Description: New York, New York : Houghton Mifflin Harcourt Publishing
Company, [2019] | Includes index.
Identifiers: LCCN 2019013139 (print) | LCCN 2019014077 (ebook) |
ISBN 9781328988508 (ebook) | ISBN 9781328988126 (paper over board) |
ISBN 9780358299264 (special ed)
Subjects: LCSH: Cooking, Korean. | LCGFT: Cookbooks.
Classification: LCC TX724.5.K65 (ebook) | LCC TX724.5.K65 S547 2019 (print) |
DDC 641.59519—dc23
LC record available at https://lccn.loc.gov/2019013139

Printed in China

SCP 10 9 8 7 6 5 4

4500818493

FOR MY CHILDREN, CHAN AND HWANHEE
You inspire me in everything I do, every day. Writing this book
reminded me of all the food I used to make for you when you
were young. Now you are both grown up, and I couldn't be prouder
or happier. So much of this book is about you two.

ACKNOWLEDGMENTS

We did it, **Dave**! Thanks for your help, again!

Thank you, **Wonhae**, of Goun Temple in Korea, for all your kindness and generosity, and for giving me the experience of a lifetime. Thanks also to **Ms. Youngji Suk** and **Mr. Kwangjin Kim** at the Korean AgroTrade Corporation in New York for organizing my trip to the temple.

This book wouldn't exist without the vision of my super editor, **Rux Martin**, who convinced me that it needed to be written and that I was the person to write it. I couldn't have done this book without the help of **Martha Rose Shulman**. Thanks for hours and days and weeks and months of testing, tasting, writing, and rewriting. I also owe a lot to the guidance and help of my agent, **Janis Donnaud**, and a special thanks to **Paul Brissman**, who photographed the covers of both of my cookbooks.

And thanks to my **mom**, who always worries when she sees me working late at night on my website, videos, and cookbook. She's concerned about my health even though she's much older than me and I'm supposed to be concerned about hers! She tells me: "I'm praying for your health whenever I go to church," which warms my heart every time I hear it.

CONTENTS

HELLO EVERYBODY!

Welcome to my big, delicious book.

When I uploaded my first video to YouTube more than a decade ago, Korean food was just beginning to take hold in the United States. My early followers were those who already were familiar with it, and the recipes they requested were mostly standbys like kimchi and bulgogi. But soon, people who had never even tried this cuisine began to discover all kinds of lesser-known dishes, from chicken ginseng soup to steamed dumpling, making and garnishing them so that they looked exactly like mine.

I could never have imagined the stories my readers and viewers have shared with me over the years. I've heard from a group of young people who regularly have kimchi-making parties, where they get together to chop and salt the vegetables, eat, and drink. I've talked to couples who have huge Korean barbecue parties for their weddings and then give away the heavy traditional grill pans to their guests. I've met people who started watching my videos and ended up falling in love with Korean culture, learning the language, and moving to Korea to work and live.

Koreans who were adopted as children and had never experienced their native country's food tell me they have used my recipes to get in touch with their heritage and the essence of who they are. When they tasted the food they made, they say they felt whole for the first time in their lives. Koreans who have lost their mothers have followed my recipes and brought their families back together over meals. Some of my readers who aren't Korean have started businesses or restaurants with my recipes and support their entire families with the profits.

Millions more use my recipes to make Korean food for their family and friends once a month or once a week or every day, with no special story at all; they just like doing it.

It took the invention of the internet to spread our food far and wide, not just through my website and videos, but also thanks to Korean TV dramas and online videos that demonstrate and explore our cuisine, as well as the thousands of photos that people snap with their phones and share on social media. Now grocery stores all over carry Korean barbecue-flavored potato chips, and kimchi is in nearly every supermarket. No one asks me what it tastes like anymore! American cooks have started to spice up their favorite dishes with Korean hot pepper paste (gochujang), and chefs are turning to the vegan cuisine

of Buddhist temples for inspiration.

For me, the biggest change has been that my love for the cooking of my homeland has become my full-time job, totally by accident! It's been wonderful to see all these changes, but I think it's just the beginning of the story of my country's food emerging into the world. I'm proud to help it go forward, which is part of what this book is about.

From spicy to mild, from meat-centric to vegan, from bubbling hot to icy cold, and with textures ranging from soft to chewy to noisily crunchy, Korean cuisine offers choices for every season, time of day, taste, and mood. Some recipes take seconds to make, and a few take days. There are dishes that are older than recorded time, and others that are as contemporary as a ten-minute-old Instagram post.

Romanization of Korean Words

The anglicization of Korean words in this book follows the Revised Romanization of Korean system developed by the National Academy of the Korean Language and made official Korean policy in 2000. The system allows for the use of hyphens to be added at the author's discretion in order to clarify pronunciation. In general, this book follows the hyphenation patterns set by the *Korean Food Guide*, published by the Korea Foundation.

There is no accurate way to show the exact pronunciation of Korean using the English alphabet, but pronouncing the syllables as they sound can usually get you close.

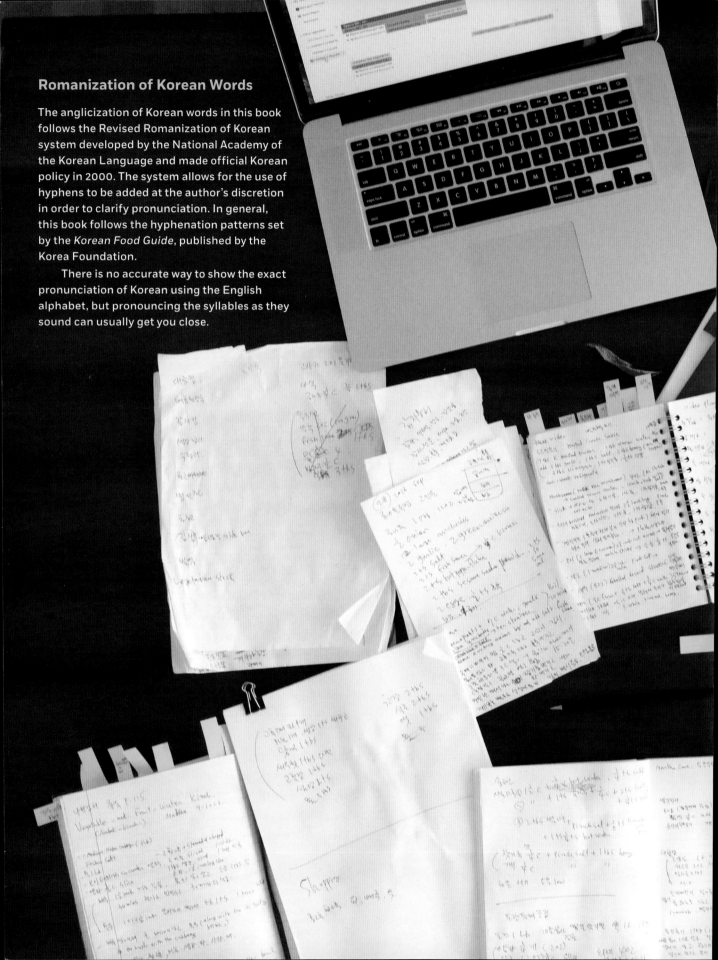

FOR AS LONG AS I CAN REMEMBER, food was one of the most important things to me. Before I was old enough to wield a knife, I pretended to cook. When I was about eleven, I began cooking for real for my siblings, and then for my own family after I got married. I never read a single cookbook. Instead, I learned from the people around me—my mom, my aunts and grandmother, women in the market and vendors on the street, fishermen and farmers, friends— more people and places than I can count or remember. This has never stopped; I continue to learn new dishes and techniques, anywhere and everywhere.

After my first cookbook, many people wrote to me asking for more recipes. When my editor asked me to write a second book, I said I'd think about it. When she asked me again, I said, "Maybe later." But the more I thought about it, the more I realized that my first book was only the beginning. There was so much more to say! Although I eat Korean food at nearly every meal every day, I'm still amazed by its diversity and complexity (though most of it is so simple). Cooking videos are great for demonstrating techniques, but they can't show the larger picture of how all the recipes fit together to make up our cuisine, which for us food-obsessed Koreans is the foundation of our culture.

I wanted to expand on dishes I already knew, like the sides called banchan and mitbanchan that are the cornerstones of Korean cuisine,

which you can combine in various ways to make countless different meals, and the traditional lunchboxes known as dosirak that I've been making for my family for decades.

I also came up with dozens of new dishes. I developed a vegetarian kimchi, something my readers and viewers have been asking about for years. I created three variations of the mega-popular and easily customizable soft tofu stew sundubu-jigae, and a homemade fish cake recipe that steams instead of being deep fried and includes much more seafood than anything store-bought.

I also reworked some of my most popular recipes, improving and simplifying them. Sweet Potato Starch Noodles with Vegetables and Meat (japchae), for instance, went from being a lengthy preparation to an easier but even tastier one-pot meal. Other recipes were inspired by the constant feedback I get from my readers and viewers, like my new rendition of Sweet and Sour Chicken (dak-tangsuyuk), a dish that

is traditionally made with pork. I've given you directions for traditional fermented alcohol as well as modern cocktails, plus nibbles to eat with them, such as Sweet, Spicy, and Sour Baby Back Ribs (dwaeji-deunggalbi-jorim), and other party food.

YOU MAY THINK YOU'VE TRIED everything already, but I guarantee you that there's something in this book that you've never tasted, or some corner of Korean cuisine that will surprise you. Even I didn't know much about the unique dishes of Buddhist temple food, so I traveled deep into the mountains to meet and cook with a group of nuns at a monastery and have devoted a chapter to their recipes.

So much of Korean food is about tradition, with recipes passed down from mothers and mothers-in-law to daughters and daughters-in-law. Yet there is also a lot of intuition and flexibility. Nowhere is that more evident than on the city streets of Korea, where vendors are always adapting new methods and ingredients to make the most alluring dishes to tempt their customers. For this book, I returned to the streets of Seoul to taste the best and latest versions so I could re-create them for you.

Reproducing authentic Korean food begins with getting the right ingredients. For that reason, I've provided a photographic guide to help you shop in Korean grocery stores and online, with information on produce, rice and noodles, spices and other seasonings, and dried, canned, and frozen items, so you'll know exactly what to buy and where to find it in a typical market. I also give you details about some of the basic cooking techniques that I have been using for decades, like cleaning fresh mackerel and freezing them for later use, cleaning and opening fresh clams, handling unfamiliar ingredients like dried taro stems, dried fernbrake, and dried sea cucumber, and even working with a whole octopus. I've taken hundreds of step-by-step photos, along with closeups of ingredients and finished dishes, to show you exactly how to prepare and serve them.

FAMILY FRIENDLY

I'm not a big fan of fussy-looking food or tiny portions on big plates. I prefer the traditional Korean manner of serving food mountain style, in a large, gently sloping mound. It reflects our most important value—generosity. You see it in our markets, where many ingredients and dishes are displayed this way to draw in passers-by; you see it in our ceremonial food meant to please the gods and our ancestors; and you see it in our homes. This is how families share food together.

Above all, I want this to be a user-friendly book that will satisfy all your cravings.

"I feel like some Korean barbecue this weekend! Let's check out the meat chapter."

"I want seafood—let's see what's here."

"Friends are coming over for drinks; what shall I serve with them?"

"I want to make a beautiful, healthy lunch that my kids will love; what are some easy options?"

"Are there any side dishes that I can make ahead and eat during the week?"

You'll find answers to all these questions and many more as I guide you into the heart of Korean cooking, as if you were part of my family. You'll discover that this cuisine has a lot to offer beyond its wonderful flavors. It embodies generosity, innovation, patience, compassion, frugality, practicality, flexibility, and resourcefulness. It shows respect and love for the natural world and good, in-season ingredients. I've tested the recipes with love, again and again, until I was absolutely sure that they were right. I've tried to explain what makes each dish unique and to give you the keys to achieving beautiful, tasty results. All you have to do now is follow the directions step by step, and you'll make the best food I know.

MAANGCHI

New York City

SHOPPING FOR KOREAN INGREDIENTS AND KITCHENWARE

Use this guide to help you find what you need to make the recipes in this book. Don't be intimidated or afraid if you've never been to a Korean grocery store before! I'll be there with you. Open the door with confidence and go in.

Once you enter, you'll find the produce section on the side of the store. The fish and meat counters are usually at the back, and the pastes, powders, sauces, oils, beans, grains, dried foods, cans, and jars are on shelves in the middle. The refrigerated and frozen sections can be found in the middle or somewhere on the perimeter. Many Korean grocers keep the big bags of rice right near the front door so customers can carry them out easily, or they stack them outside in front. You'll often also find prepared food sections, where you can get premade side dishes. Larger supermarkets often have full restaurants inside.

The staff may not speak perfect English, but I guarantee they will be happy to see you and will assist you the best they can. If you get stuck, just find someone wearing a store uniform—the people who stock the shelves are usually very helpful—and show them the ingredient in this book, or a photo of the book page on your phone. If it's a tiny one-person store, show the cashier at the front.

To find a Korean grocery store near you, check the list on my website, Maangchi.com/shopping, as submitted by my readers from all around the world. There are thousands, and the list is constantly updated as stores close and open.

You can also find many of the products you'll need for Korean cooking on Amazon.com. Be sure to read and compare listings carefully there, as different suppliers can offer the same products at wildly different prices, or in too-big or too-small quantities. On my site, I keep an up-to-date list of the best deals and products. In most cases, shopping at a Korean grocery store is cheaper than shopping online and also offers more variety and options. And of course, it's much more fun to do!

Fresh Produce

ASIAN CHIVES / CHINESE CHIVES / GARLIC CHIVES
BUCHU 부추

These are sold in generous bunches in Korean markets. Choose bunches with no blemishes. They dry out and go bad easily, so once I bring them home, I wrap them in a paper towel and then in a plastic bag before refrigerating. Stored that way, they will last a week. Scallions can be substituted if you can't find Asian chives.

BURDOCK ROOT
UEONG-PPURI 우엉뿌리

These roots have an herbal taste, and Koreans make tea with them, braise them, or eat them raw (see Spicy Burdock Root Salad, page 346). When shopping for burdock root, choose smooth ones that have no blemishes and aren't dried out at all. In Korean markets, they are sold cut into sections.

Observe the cross section to see how fresh the root is: It should be a light tan color, not dark brown. In Chinatown, burdock roots are sold whole, so they're hard to inspect.

CHESTNUTS
BAHM 밤

Fresh chestnuts can be found in the refrigerated produce section in late fall, when they are in season. They should be plump, not dried, and shiny, with no wrinkles or small holes from bugs or worms. Canned chestnuts, found with the canned goods, or frozen chestnuts, in the frozen section, can be substituted. *For how to shell and skin them, see page 418.*

CHINESE YAM
MA 마

These long, cylindrical tubers, with light brown skin and white flesh, are usually sold cut and packaged. The yams can be eaten raw or cooked. Many Koreans grind and eat raw ma for its health benefits. The texture is slimy this way. When cooked, ma is a bit like a potato, but a little crisper, sweeter, and less starchy (see Pan-Fried Chinese Yam Slices, page 348). Peel with a potato peeler before cooking, but put on gloves first, because ma can irritate the skin. Choose tubers that are white, unblemished, and juicy looking inside.

CHRYSANTHEMUM GREENS
SSUK-GAT 쑥갓

These pretty greens, sometimes called edible chrysanthemum, have a mild, refreshing herbal flavor. They are eaten raw or lightly blanched for side dishes and are essential for Spicy Fish Stew (page 184). You can substitute a few sprigs of basil or mint.

ENOKI MUSHROOMS
PAENGI-BEOSOT 팽이버섯

These clumps of small mushrooms, with thin, 4- to 5-inch-long stems, are called for in many Korean dishes. They are easy to find in the refrigerated produce section at Korean and Asian markets, some supermarkets, and whole-foods stores. Make sure they are a milky-white color and not slimy.

GINKGO NUTS
EUNHAENG 은행

A late-fall delicacy, ginkgo nuts enrich and garnish sweet and savory dishes. I usually buy them shelled since they are too easily crushed when you shell them yourself. When cooked, ginkgo nuts turn a beautiful jade color. You'll find them in the refrigerated produce section in season or in the freezer section year-round. *For how to shell and cook ginkgo nuts, see page 419.*

FRESH GINSENG ROOT
SUSAM 수삼

Essential in Chicken Ginseng Soup (page 140) and Ginseng Milkshake (page 386), this bitter, herbal-tasting, fleshy root of a perennial is widely used as both food and medicine. It's found packaged in the refrigerated produce section. Choose roots with the fewest blemishes. Do not substitute dried ginseng.

GREEN CHILI PEPPERS
CHEONG-GOCHU 청고추

These green chilis, usually 3 to 4 inches long, look like long jalapeños, but they are pointier. They have a sweet flavor, and their spiciness can range from very mild (asagi gochu 아삭이고추) to very spicy (cheong-yang gochu 청양고추). Koreans usually chop the pepper with the seeds and use both. Jalapeños or serranos can be substituted.

KING OYSTER MUSHROOMS / KING TRUMPET MUSHROOMS
SAESONGI-BEOSEOT 새송이버섯

These long, thick, white-stemmed mushrooms have a meaty texture, which is why I use them as a substitute for raw fish in Avocado, Mushroom, and Vegetable Bibimbap (page 54). Found in the refrigerated produce section, they are common in stir-fries and pan-fries. Choose mushrooms with thick, white stems and no blemishes.

KOREAN EGGPLANT
GAJI 가지

Korean eggplants are long, thin, and light to dark purple. Their skin is thin and their texture softer and less spongy than Western globe-shaped eggplants. They also have a sweeter, milder flavor. You can find them at many Asian markets and also at some farmers' markets and regular supermarkets, where they are often called Asian eggplants or Japanese eggplants. Ordinary eggplant can be substituted.

KOREAN PEAR
BAE 배

Good-quality Korean pears are sweet, juicy, and crispy. They have a light yellowish-brown skin and are nearly white inside, with a nice aroma. They are in season in the fall and are sold individually, in packs of three, and in large boxes that are meant to be given as gifts. Around festival days, Korean grocery stores will have boxes of different kinds at different price points. You can skin them and eat them on their own, make Steamed Pear with Honey (page 358), or use them to lend sweetness to recipes like Bulgogi with Noodles (page 157) and Grilled Beef Short Ribs (page 159). They also act as meat tenderizers in these recipes. Choose round, firm pears with no blemishes. Ripe but not too soft Bosc or Anjou pears can be substituted.

KOREAN RADISH
MU 무

This large, heavy, bulbous radish is used in many dishes, from Diced Radish Kimchi (page 116) to soups to stews. It is similar to daikon, but shorter, fatter, and heavier. The tops are pale green, and the rest of the radish is cream colored. The flesh is sweet, juicy, and crisp, especially in late fall, which is peak season. Look for radishes that are smooth, firm, and heavy. As soon as I bring a radish home, I wrap it in a paper towel, put it in a plastic bag, and refrigerate it. This prevents it from drying out and becoming spongy. It will last for 2 weeks this way. Daikon can be substituted.

KOREAN RED CHILI PEPPERS
HONG-GOCHU 홍고추

These ripe green chili peppers have a sweet, spicy, and tangy flavor. If you can't find them and need a bright red garnish, substitute chopped or shredded red bell pepper.

LARGE GREEN ONION
DAEPA 대파

This onion resembles a thin leek, except its green leaves are hollow and slightly slimy inside, like a scallion. In Korean cuisine, they're used in soups and stews because they have a mild, sweet, rich flavor.

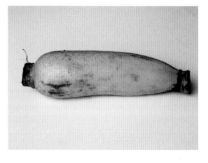

LOTUS ROOT
YEON-GEUN 연근

These roots have a wonderfully distinct pattern of holes when you slice them. They have a crisp texture and a sweet flavor. You can find whole lotus root in Korean and Chinese markets, and sometimes also sliced and packaged in the refrigerated produce section.

MUNG BEAN SPROUTS
SUKJUNAMUL 숙주나물

Mung bean sprouts add crispness and sweetness to dishes. They can be found in most supermarkets these days. Choose sprouts with the plumpest, whitest stems. It's best to use them right after buying them, but you can also refrigerate them for a couple of days. Wash just before using.

MUSTARD GREENS
GAHT 갓

These greens are easy to find in Asian markets and many supermarkets. They are thick, juicy, and green, perfect for Mustard Greens Kimchi (page 122). Be sure to choose greens with thick stems. You can substitute red mustard greens.

NAPA CABBAGE
BAECHU 배추

Napa cabbage is the type of cabbage used for making the traditional kind of kimchi (page 112). Today you can find it in almost any grocery store and in farmers' markets, although the cabbages sold at a Korean grocery store are always cheaper, bigger, and better tasting. In the kimchi-making season of late fall, when napa cabbages are at their best, Korean grocery stores sell them by the huge box. A good cabbage for kimchi is green and leafy with no blemishes. The cabbage should be heavy and dense, and the leaves should be thin so they

don't add too much water to your kimchi as they ferment. If you don't make kimchi with them right away, wrap in a dish towel, put in a plastic bag, and keep in the refrigerator for up to 10 days.

PERILLA LEAVES
KKAENNIP 깻잎

Fresh green perilla leaves are popular in Korean cuisine. Their flavor is somewhere between that of basil and mint. We use them whole in ssam wraps (see page 48) and Korean barbecue, or shredded to add a bit of minty flavor to many other dishes. We also pickle them and make kimchi with them. When cooked, they are often pan-fried in dishes like Pepper and Perilla Leaf Pancakes (page 352). Choose perilla with bright, fresh-looking leaves that are free of blemishes and aren't at all wilted. The stems should also be green; if they're brown, that means they're old. Perilla leaves don't keep for very long in the refrigerator, so to preserve them as best you can, wrap them in a paper towel and then put them in a plastic bag before refrigerating. They should be eaten within a couple of days. They are also very easy to grow in your garden; the seeds are sold in some Korean grocery stores and online.

PINE NUTS
JAHT 잣

Pine nuts are used to garnish many Korean dishes and desserts. They are smaller and nuttier tasting than those available in American groceries and are considered precious (and thus are usually pricey). They are often sold in transparent packaging. Choose pine nuts that have no spots of discoloration and no variation in color from nut to nut. Put them in the freezer as soon as you bring them home, then take out what you need and thaw at room temperature. For aesthetic reasons, I like to remove the tips of the nuts (see page 421).

SHISHITO PEPPERS
KKWARI-GOCHU 꽈리고추

These 2- to 3-inch-long, wrinkled, thin-skinned peppers are milder than usual Korean green chili peppers, so you can eat them whole. If you like spicy food, you can substitute any mild green chili pepper, or serrano or jalapeño peppers.

SOYBEAN SPROUTS
KONGNAMUL 콩나물

Don't confuse these with mung bean sprouts; the beans of soybean sprouts are much bigger. They are a Korean staple and used in Soybean Sprout Soup (page 87), one of our most popular soups. They are sold in the produce section, usually in 12-ounce packages, but also sometimes in 1-pound bags. Soybean sprouts always need to be cooked, because they smell a bit fishy when raw. When cooked, they are crisp and have a nutty flavor. Choose sprouts with no blemishes, nice yellow beans, and white stems. Store in the fridge and use them within a week. *For how to clean soybean sprouts, see page 421.*

TARO ROOT
TORAN 토란

This fuzzy, stringy root has a thick skin and a white interior. Raw taro roots are toxic, so my first step when I get them home is to blanch and peel them. They taste a bit like a potato, but softer and

creamier. Choose roots that are about 2 inches long and are firm, fresh, and heavy, which means they haven't dried out. You can find them in many Asian markets.

WATER DROPWORT
MINARI 미나리

Minari tastes a little like parsley. Its leaves resemble parsley and cilantro leaves, but its stems are a little reddish and thicker. Choose minari with plump stems and leaves that are fresh looking and green, not brownish at all. It should be used within a few days of purchasing. Wrap in paper towels, seal in plastic bags, and refrigerate until ready to use. Parsley can be substituted.

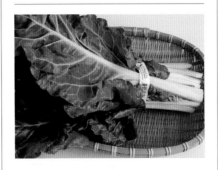

WHITE-STEMMED CHARD
GEUN-DAE 근대

Chard with white stems has a mild taste and becomes soft when blanched, which makes it a good substitute for napa cabbage to make Soybean Paste Soup with Cabbage (page 88).

Grains, Flours, Noodles, and Thickening Starches

BARLEY MALT POWDER / MALT (OR MALTED) BARLEY FLOUR OR FLAKES
YEOTGIREUM-GARU 엿기름가루

This powder has a sweet, malty flavor and is an important ingredient in Homemade Rice Syrup (page 376), which is a traditional sweetener in Korean cuisine. The enzyme amylase in barley malt powder converts the starch in rice into sugar at warm temperatures in water.

BLACK RICE
HEUKMI 흑미

This beautiful, nutty-flavored black rice imparts a purple hue when cooked. Just a little bit, 1 or 2 tablespoons, will give your Multigrain Rice (page 44) a beautiful color. The rice grains contain phytonutrients called anthocyanins that are known for their antioxidant properties. Black rice is found in most Asian markets, whole-foods stores, and some supermarkets.

BROWN SWEET RICE / BROWN GLUTINOUS RICE
HYEONMI-CHAPSSAL 현미찹쌀

This short-grain brown sweet rice has a stickier, more glutinous texture than regular brown rice. It is often used in Multigrain Rice (page 44) and is a healthier choice than white rice.

DRIED RAMYEON
라면

Packaged dried instant ramyeon (called ramen in Japanese) is very popular in Korea, where there's no tradition of making it from scratch. It comes prepackaged with seasoning pouches, but you can take out the dried noodles and use them in Spicy Rice Cakes in Broth with Ramyeon Noodles (page 392) and Army Base Stew (page 396).

GLUTINOUS RICE / SWEET RICE
CHAPSSAL 찹쌀

Sometimes referred to as sweet rice, glutinous rice is not sweet at all, nor does it contain gluten. It's called glutinous rice because it's much stickier and chewier than regular short-grain rice, which makes it perfect for Steamed Rice in Lotus Leaf Wrap (page 334). After opening, seal the package well and store in a cool, dry spot.

GLUTINOUS RICE FLOUR / SWEET RICE FLOUR
CHAPSSAL-GARU 찹쌀가루

Despite its name, this flour is gluten-free. Made from glutinous rice, it is known as mochiko in Japan and often labeled that way. It's an essential ingredient in kimchi (page 112) and Rice Cakes Dusted with Soybean Powder (page 373).

HULLESS BARLEY
TONGBORI 통보리

Hulless barley is a rustic, unprocessed barley with only the outer hull removed. It's chewy, nutty, rich in fiber, and very nutritious. You can find it in Korean grocery stores, as well as some large grocery stores, whole-foods stores, and online. You can substitute other kinds of barley, including pearl barley, which is much more refined, softer, faster to cook, and sold everywhere.

KOREAN BREAD CRUMBS
PPANG-GARU 빵가루

These flaky, crunchy bread crumbs are similar to Japanese panko, which can be substituted. You can find them in Korean markets. They add a long-lasting crunchiness to dishes.

MUGWORT POWDER
SSUK-GARU 쑥가루

This has long been used by Koreans as a healthy natural green food coloring. It adds a nice aroma and gentle herbal flavor to dishes and rice cakes. Keep mugwort powder in the freezer so that it doesn't lose its flavor.

MUNG BEAN STARCH
CHEONGPOMUK-GARU 청포묵가루

Sometimes incorrectly labeled as mung bean flour, this is a fine-grained starch extracted from mung beans. It is used to make noodles and side dishes like Mung Bean Jelly with Soy-Scallion Seasoning Sauce (page 222). With one small package, you can make a huge amount of jelly. Use what you need, then store the rest in the pantry, well sealed.

POTATO STARCH
GAMJA-JEONBUN 감자전분

I always have potato starch on hand because it's essential for achieving the supreme crunchiness for fried dishes like Sweet, Crunchy Fried Chicken (page 150) and Sweet and Sour Chicken (page 148). I also use it as a thickener. I've never found any potato starch that worked better than Korean brands for this purpose. Seal the package well and store in a cool place.

SHORT-GRAIN WHITE RICE
MEP-SSAL 멥쌀

Short-grain white rice (aka sushi rice) is Korea's staple rice. It is stickier and starchier than long-grain rice or Arborio rice (do not confuse the two), but not as sticky as sweet rice (glutinous rice). It's best to buy it in 10-, 15-, or even 20-pound bags at Korean or Asian markets, where it is much less expensive than at Western supermarkets. Seal the package well and store in a cool place.

STARTER CULTURE
NURUK 누룩

Nuruk is made from grains—wheat, rice, or barley—that are moistened, formed into a block, and fermented. You'll need this starter culture to make the Korean clear rice liquor called Yakju (page 296). It is usually sold next to the malt powder and mung bean starch. Seal the package well and store in a cool place for up to 3 months.

SWEET POTATO STARCH NOODLES
DANGMYEON 당면

These are a kind of glass noodle made from sweet potato starch. When cooked, they are shiny, a little chewy, and nearly transparent. They are the signature ingredient in Sweet Potato Starch Noodles with Vegetables and Meat (page 323) and also add springy texture to Bulgogi with Noodles (page 157). Substitute other cellophane or glass noodles like Chinese vermicelli, which are similar but made with mung bean starch. Seal the package well and store in a cool place.

THIN WHEAT-FLOUR NOODLES
SOMYEON 소면

These wheat noodles are very thin and white. When prepared properly, they are surprisingly chewy. Generally, it's best to get everything else ready and cook the noodles last so you can enjoy them at their peak chewiness before they go soggy. You can find them in Korean, Japanese, and Chinese markets. Seal the package well and store in a cool place in the pantry.

Spices and Seasonings

BLACK BEAN PASTE
CHUNJANG 춘장

Salty, slightly sweet, and earthy, this black paste is made with a mixture of soybeans, flour, and caramel and then fermented. It's essential for making Noodles and Black Bean Sauce Platter (page 398). After opening, store in the refrigerator for up to 3 months.

FISH SAUCE
AEKJEOT 액젓

Fish sauce has a salty, pungent flavor that's a little fishy (in a good way). I use it in place of homemade soup soy sauce to add a savory richness to many Korean soups. My favorite brand is Three Crabs because it tastes like the well-aged fermented soup soy sauce my grandmother used to make.

KOREAN FERMENTED SOYBEAN PASTE
DOENJANG 된장

Doenjang is a signature ingredient in Korean cooking. This fermented seasoning is used in classic soups and stews and in dipping sauce. Today most Koreans use commercially made soybean paste (it may not be labeled "fermented"), but traditionally we make it at home. The process takes several months. It's sold in brown tubs at the Korean grocery store. Keep in the fridge and use within 3 months. The top of the paste may oxidize a bit and turn brown, but it's still edible.

KOREAN HOT PEPPER FLAKES
GOCHU-GARU 고춧가루

Korean hot pepper flakes are an essential ingredient in Korean cooking, used in many side dishes, soups, and stews, and in the most important Korean side dish of all, kimchi. They come in mild (deol-maewoon gochu garu 덜매운 고춧가루) and hot (mae-woon gochu-garu 매운 고춧가루) versions. For dishes like kimchi, I use the milder flakes so that I can add a lot for color without making the dish too spicy. My readers often ask me if they can use chili powder or other crushed chili flakes as a substitute, but they won't work with Korean dishes because they have a different flavor and are too spicy. Sometimes Korean hot pepper flakes may be mislabeled on the package as "powder," but all packages will be at least partially transparent, so look inside and make sure they are coarse flakes. Beautiful bright red is best; avoid any that are purplish or brownish. When the flakes go bad, they become a yellowish-red and the flavor goes off. After opening, store the pepper flakes in a zipper-lock plastic bag in the freezer for up to 6 months, and keep a small amount in a jar in the refrigerator for everyday use.

KOREAN HOT PEPPER PASTE
GOCHUJANG 고추장

A staple in Korean cooking, this fermented red paste adds heat, color, and some sweetness to many Korean dishes. Traditionally gochujang was made at home, but today most people buy it at Korean grocery stores. The packaging may be confusing if you don't read Korean, but it's usually sold in a red plastic tub. Refrigerate after opening and use within 3 months. The top of the paste may become darker or dry out a bit, but it's still edible.

MIRIM
미림

This sweet wine (called mirin in Japanese) is not an everyday seasoning for me, but it comes in handy to add sweetness to meat dishes like Grilled Beef Short Ribs (page 159) and Braised Beef Short Ribs (page 163). It also balances the strong fish aroma in Pan-Fried Seasoned Spanish Mackerel (page 176). Store in the pantry.

PERILLA SEED POWDER
DEULKKAE-GARU 들깨가루

Powder made from ground perilla seeds is used to thicken and add a nutty, herbal flavor and creamy texture to many soups and stews, as well as vegetable dishes. Remove all the air in the package after opening, seal it well, then put it in another bag and store in the freezer.

RICE SYRUP / BROWN RICE SYRUP
SSAL-JOCHEONG 쌀조청

This thick, viscous syrup has a rich, earthy, subtly grainy flavor, much more distinctive than sugar or corn syrup. It adds a shiny glaze to dishes like Sweet, Spicy, and Sour Baby Back Ribs (page 326) and can be used as a dipping sauce for rice cakes. Sugar or honey can be substitutes, but they are much sweeter. You can buy it or make it at home (page 376).

SHREDDED DRIED RED PEPPER
SILGOCHU 실고추

Thin and pretty, with a subtle spiciness, this red pepper is used mostly as a garnish for vegetable side dishes and pancakes.

SMALL DRIED RED CHILI PEPPERS
JAGEUN-MAREUN-GOCHU 작은 마른고추

These peppers are not very spicy, and along with garlic and ginger, are usually used to infuse the oil of Korean-Chinese dishes like Spicy Garlic Fried Shrimp (page 311). They can be bought at most Asian markets. Store in the freezer.

SOUP SOY SAUCE
GUK-GANJANG 국간장 /
JOSEON-GANJANG 조선간장

For thousands of years, Koreans traditionally made their own soup soy sauce at home as a byproduct of making doenjang (fermented soybean paste). It is much stronger, saltier, and lighter in color than the soy sauce most Westerners are familiar with. I've never found a commercially made soup soy sauce that has the deep flavor of homemade, and commercially made is often too dark, so I use fish sauce or my own homemade soup soy sauce. But I have given commercial soup soy sauce as an option in some of my recipes.

SOY SAUCE
GANJANG 간장 / JIN-GANJANG 진간장

Soy sauce was introduced to Korea through Japan and is relatively new compared to traditional Korean soup soy sauce. I have been using the Sempio brand for decades.

TOASTED PERILLA SEED OIL
DEULGIREUM 들기름

Perilla seed oil has a unique herbal flavor and aroma. It is added to Korean vegetable side dishes and used in many Korean temple cuisine dishes. It breaks down at high temperatures, so you shouldn't cook it for a long time; rather, add it at the last minute so it will keep all its flavor. It oxidizes easily, so always keep it in the refrigerator. You can substitute toasted sesame oil.

TOASTED SESAME OIL
CHAMGIREUM 참기름

A signature ingredient in Korean cooking, this deeply nutty oil has a rich, distinctive toasty flavor. Korean cuisine often calls for just a little added at the end to make a dish come alive. Don't confuse it with the plain (untoasted) sesame oil sold in large bottles with the vegetable oils in supermarkets. Toasted sesame oil has a very different flavor profile. Keep it in a dark place at room temperature.

TOASTED SESAME SEEDS (TAN AND BLACK)
BOKKEUN-KKAE 볶은깨

Toasted sesame seeds add a nutty dimension and a little crunch to many dishes. I usually sprinkle tan sesame seeds on a dish at the last minute before serving, and use black sesame seeds on white fluffy rice in lunchboxes (dosirak) for contrast and flavor. Always choose the seeds with the latest expiration date. Keep some in a glass container or jar in a cool, dry place and the rest in a zipper-lock plastic bag in the freezer for up to 3 months.

TOASTED YELLOW SOYBEAN POWDER
BOKKEUN-KONGGARU 볶은 콩가루

This toasty powder made from soybeans is an essential ingredient in Rice Cakes Dusted with Soybean Powder (page 373). Check the date on the package to be sure that the powder is very fresh, as it loses its nuttiness over time. Use what you need and put the rest in a zipper-lock plastic bag, squeezing out the excess air. Freeze for up to 1 month.

Dried Roots, Seeds, Beans, Vegetables, and Fruits

ADZUKI BEANS / AZUKI BEANS
PAT 팥
These small red beans are used in many Korean rice and porridge dishes and also as a sweet filling for many desserts. They are sometimes called red beans and are sold in many other Asian markets, as well as whole-foods stores and many supermarkets. Buy beans that are the brightest red you can find, not dark and purple.

DRIED BELLFLOWER ROOTS
MAREUN DORAJI 마른 도라지
These herby white roots smell like ginseng and taste slightly bitter. Tea made with bellflower roots has medicinal properties for treating sore throats and coughs in the wintertime. Choose roots that are

white and plump, not brown and thin. After opening the package, keep it in a cool, dry place.

DRIED FERNBRAKE / BRACKEN
MAREUN GOSARI 마른 고사리
Fernbrake is a wild green gathered in the springtime in the mountains of Korea. Fresh fernbrake is similar to fiddleheads, which can be substituted once the papery outer coating is removed and they are blanched in boiling water. Fernbrake is also blanched and dried for use out of season. You can find packaged dried fernbrake, often labeled "bracken," with the other dried vegetables in Korean markets. It will keep for up to 6 months if stored in a cool, dry place. These expand quite a bit once soaked, so a little goes a long way. *For how to soak dried fernbrake, see page 422.*

DRIED JUJUBES
MAREUN DAECHU 마른 대추
These red dried fruits, with pits that resemble date pits, have a wrinkled skin and a sweet-tart flavor. Jujubes have medicinal properties, and they have many uses in Korean cuisine as a sweetener and garnish. When boiled with ginseng for a long time, jujube becomes a healthy tea. Store in a zipper-lock plastic bag in the freezer. *For how to pit dried jujubes, see page 423.*

DRIED LOTUS LEAVES
YEONNIP 연잎
Korean Buddhist temple cuisine uses fresh, frozen, or dried lotus leaves for Steamed Rice in Lotus Leaf Wrap (page 334). The leaves, which smell a little like cooked kale when steamed, give the rice an earthy, leafy flavor. You can find them more easily in Chinese markets than in Korean markets, sold in large plastic bags. Choose clean leaves with no blemishes. They will keep for 6 months if stored in a cool, dry place.

DRIED OMIJA
MAREUN OMIJA 마른 오미자

Omija, or five-flavored fruits, are small red berries from the schisandra plant, prized in Korea for their nutritional value and for having five flavors at once—sweet, sour, bitter, salty, and pungent. Koreans believe they boost your immune system and prevent all kinds of modern diseases. Choose the brightest red omija you can find, not brownish ones that have been on the shelf for a long time. Keep them in the refrigerator for up to 1 year to prevent them from going brown.

DRIED PERSIMMONS
GOT-GAM 곶감

Dried persimmons are sweet and chewy like jelly candies. In Korea the fresh fruit is harvested in the fall, tied with string, and hung to air-dry. A whitish bloom on their surface indicates that they are dry and sweet. You can eat them by themselves as a snack or in Persimmon Punch Slush (page 380). Choose large,

plump persimmons that are not discolored. They will keep in the freezer for a few months.

DRIED SHIITAKE MUSHROOMS
MAREUN PYOGO-BEOSEOT 마른 표고버섯

Dried shiitake mushrooms have an intense savory flavor and a delightful chewy texture when soaked, so they are used in many vegetarian dishes instead of meat. They are also used to make Vegetable Stock (page 78). They are easy to find in Asian markets and many supermarkets. Choose mushrooms with thick, sturdy tops and an earthy aroma. Keep in a cool, dry place.

DRIED TARO STEMS
MAREUN TORANJULGI 마른 토란줄기

Koreans harvest taro stems in peak season, then blanch and dry them to use throughout the year until the next harvest. Before they are used, the stems must be blanched and soaked to rid them of calcium oxalate, which can irritate the mouth and throat.

They taste a little like cooked celery; celery can be substituted for the soaked stems. Keep in a cool, dry place for up to 6 months. *For how to soak and prepare them for cooking, see page 424.*

DRIED WOOD EAR MUSHROOMS
MAREUN MOGI-BEOSEOT 마른 목이버섯

Wood ear mushrooms are popular in Korean and Chinese cuisines and can be found in both Korean and Chinese markets. They have a chewy texture and savory flavor when rehydrated. Keep in a cool, dry place.

DRIED YELLOW SOYBEANS
MEJU-KONG 메주콩

Dried yellow soybeans are the main ingredient in doenjang and soy sauce. You can find them in Korean markets and whole-foods stores. Store in a cool, dry place.

Dried Seaweed and Seafood

DRIED KELP
MAREUN DASIMA 마른 다시마

Kelp (called kombu in Japanese) is a nutritious sea vegetable used in many Korean dishes. It's also a key ingredient in Anchovy-Kelp Stock (page 74) and Vegetable Stock (page 78). Kelp is sold in huge sheets in many Asian markets, as well as most whole-foods stores. Choose the thickest you can find. Store in a cool, dry place.

DRIED MIYEOK
MAREUN MIYEOK 마른 미역

This sea vegetable (called wakame in Japanese) is widely used in Korean cuisine, particularly in Seaweed Soup (page 92) and salads. A small amount will expand when rehydrated, so you don't need too much for a dish. You can find it many Asian markets and whole-foods stores.

DRIED SEA CUCUMBERS
MAREUN-HAESAM 마른 해삼

Used to make Chinese-Korean dishes like Eight-Treasure Seafood and Vegetables (page 320), dried sea cucumbers are sold in Chinese markets rather than Korean stores. You can also find presoaked sea cucumbers in the Chinese markets, but they don't have the crispy texture of the ones I soak myself, so I always buy them dried and then soak at home (see page 430). Keep in an airtight container or zipper-lock plastic bag in a cool, dry place for up to 1 year.

SEAWEED PAPER
GIM 김

Pressed seaweed paper (called nori in Japanese) is used in rice rolls, for snacks, to garnish soups, stews, and other dishes, or just oiled, salted, and toasted to make a side dish (Traditional Toasted Gim, page 216). The sheets are made by grinding and drying seaweed in a process similar to making paper. We toast the sheets directly over a flame for rice rolls or to crumble for a garnish onto stir-fries, soups, and stews. Store in a zipper-lock plastic bag in the freezer for up to 6 months. *For how to toast, crush, and shred seaweed paper, see page 425.*

Canned Items

CANNED CHESTNUTS
BAHM-TONGJORIM 밤통조림

Cooked chestnuts packed in syrup are used in many Korean sweets and also in sweet and savory dishes such as Braised Beef Short Ribs (page 163). You can find them in Korean and gourmet markets.

CANNED SWEET RED BEANS
PAT-TONGJORIM 팥통조림

Made from adzuki beans, these are used in many Korean desserts like Shaved Ice with Sweet Red Beans and Fruits (page 382). You can substitute them for dried to save time.

CANNED TUNA
CHAMCHI-TONGJORIM 참치통조림

Canned tuna is an everyday ingredient in Korean cuisine, so most Korean grocery stores will have at least one shelf devoted to yellow cans of Korean oil-packed tuna.

Refrigerated and Frozen Products

BEEF BONES
SAGOL 사골

Leg bones, joints, and knuckles are sold precut in the frozen meat section of the store. Use them to make Beef Bone Broth (page 80).

BEEF SHORT RIBS
SO-GALBI 소갈비

Choose the freshest ribs with the most meat attached to the bone for Grilled Beef Short Ribs (page 159) or Braised Beef Short Ribs (page 163). The ribs are sold precut at Korean grocery stores and are 2 to 3 inches long, and either square or rectangular.

BUTTERFISH
BYEONGEO 병어

Popular in Korean cuisine, nutty-tasting butterfish (aka pompano or silver pomfret) is smooth and soft. Choose the freshest fish you can find, with clear eyes and firm flesh that doesn't smell too fishy, more like the refreshing smell of the ocean. They can be found in Korean markets and many other fish markets.

CYLINDER-SHAPED RICE CAKES
GARAETTEOK 가래떡 / TTEOKBOKKI-YONG-TTEOK 떡볶이용떡

These rice cakes are made with short-grain rice flour and pressed into cylinders of various lengths and widths. Thaw them in the refrigerator overnight and cut them into bite-size pieces. Some Korean grocery stores sell them freshly made.

DRIED ANCHOVIES
MAREUN MYEOLCHI 마른멸치

Dried anchovies are sold in plastic bags or boxes, sorted by size. Smaller anchovies (mareun janmyeolchi 마른 잔멸치) are used in stir-fries (page 241) and toasted whole with soy sauce and chili paste to serve, bones and all, as a side dish with rice or as a snack. Large anchovies (gukmul-yong mareunmyeolchi 국물용 마른멸치), around 3½ inches long, are used to flavor soups and make Anchovy-Kelp Stock (page 74). Store in the freezer for up to 1 year. *To clean large dried anchovies, see page 427.*

DRIED WHOLE POLLOCK
BUGEO 북어

Dried pollock is very hard, almost as hard as wood, although it's also sold presoftened. It's used to make Seasoned Grated Dried Pollock (page 246). The best is dried by sea breezes, which makes it more flavorful and flaky. Choose pollock that looks thick, meaty, and a little flaky, with a yellowish color. Store in the freezer for up to 1 year.

DUMPLING SKINS
MANDU-PI 만두피

These small, round wheat-flour wrappers are used to make Steamed Dumplings (page 305). Large skins are 4½ inches wide and medium are 3½ inches. Defrost overnight in the refrigerator or on the kitchen counter before using.

FISH CAKES
EOMUK 어묵

Commercial fish cakes are made of starch, flour, sugar, and ground fish, squid, or shrimp, then fried or steamed and sold frozen. You can buy packs of assorted cakes that have a variety of shapes, textures, and fish content in one convenient package (jonghap-eomuk 종합어묵), which are great for Fish Cake Soup (page 394). You can also buy fish cakes that are shaped into flat, thin, pancake-like rectangles (sagak-eomuk 사각어묵). They are used in stir-fries for lunchboxes (see Stir-Fried Fish Cake, page 248). If using packaged fish cakes, store what you don't use in a zipper-lock plastic bag in the freezer for up to 3 months. Some of the larger Korean grocery stores sell fish cakes freshly fried, and you can also make your own steamed fish cakes at home (page 182).

FROZEN CHESTNUTS
NAENGDONG BAM 냉동 밤

Frozen chestnuts are a good option when you can't get fresh. They are sold vacuum packed so you can keep them frozen until you need them, then thaw them in the refrigerator.

FROZEN OYSTERS
NAENGDONG-GUL 냉동굴

Imported from Korea, frozen oysters are safe to eat raw and a better choice if you do not have access to high-quality fresh oysters. You can also use frozen or fresh American oysters.

FROZEN SEA SQUIRTS/ SEA PINEAPPLES

NAENGDONG-MEONGGE 냉동멍게

Sea squirts are sea invertebrates like clams, which they resemble in flavor and texture. You can't find fresh sea squirts in markets in America, but you can find them frozen in Korean grocery stores. Fresh, they look a little like small pineapples (hence the name), with a bumpy yellow and orangey-red surface. I usually use frozen, vacuum-packed sea squirts, which have been shelled, cleaned, and cut into pieces.

JJAJANGMYEON NOODLES

JJAJANGMYEON-YONG GUKSU 짜장면용 국수

Often mislabeled as Asian or oriental-style noodles or vermicelli, these thick, chewy wheat noodles are sold frozen and used in Noodles and Black Bean Sauce Platter (page 398). Thaw if using immediately or store in the freezer in a zipper-lock bag and let them thaw before using. Frozen noodles will keep for up to 3 months.

KOREAN FROZEN SHORT-GRAIN RICE FLOUR

NAENGDONG MEPSSAL-GARU 냉동 멥쌀가루

Short-grain rice flour is usually found in the frozen section next to the dumpling skins and rice cakes. It's sold frozen to maintain its moisture. There are no substitutes when making Fluffy Pine Nut Rice Cake (page 366) and Rice Cakes Steamed on Pine Needles (page 368). Be sure not to buy the glutinous rice version—that's for a different kind of rice cake and won't work in those recipes. Always store in the freezer.

SALTY FERMENTED SHRIMP

SAUEJEOT 새우젓

Salty fermented shrimp has a deep flavor, so it's used to season many Korean dishes in place of salt. We add it to the paste for many kimchis. It's sold in jars and will keep for 6 months in the refrigerator.

SHREDDED DRIED SQUID

JINMICHAE 진미채 / MAREUN OJINGEOCHAE 마른 오징어채

Thick, soft, and moist, shredded dried squid are eaten straight from the package—they make a good accompaniment to beer. They can be seasoned to make Spicy Shredded Dried Squid (page 244).

SLICED RICE CAKES

TTEOKGUK-YONG-TTEOK 떡국용떡

These oval, thinly sliced rice cake disks are sold in plastic bags in the refrigerated section or sometimes in vacuum-sealed packages in the frozen section of Korean markets. I use them in Rice Cake Soup with Bone Broth (page 62) and Fire Chicken with Cheese (page 402). Store in the freezer for up to 3 months.

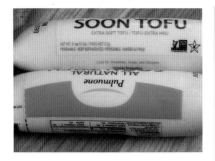

SOFT TOFU
SUNDUBU 순두부

Usually sold in plastic tubes, this soft, white, creamy tofu is the essential ingredient in soft tofu stews. Store in the refrigerator if not using immediately.

TOFU
DUBU 두부

Koreans use medium-firm or firm tofu when pan-frying, in dishes like Pan-Fried Tofu with Soy-Scallion Seasoning Sauce (page 207). Store in the refrigerator. If you use only half the package, submerge the remaining half in cold water and cover before refrigerating. It should be used within a few days of opening.

YELLOW PICKLED RADISH
DANMUJI 단무지

Sold in plastic packages, pickled radish is easy to recognize because of its bright yellow color. Sweet, salty, crisp, and sour, it is an essential ingredient in Seaweed Rice Rolls (page 267). Stored in its pickling liquid, it will keep for a few months in the refrigerator.

Alcohol

SOJU
소주

Soju is traditionally made from rice, though the most popular Korean brands are made from all kinds of starches. It's slightly sweet and usually about 17 percent ABV. Soju usually comes in a 375-milliliter green bottle and is drunk in shot glasses, always with food. These days it's made in different fruit flavors, too. Depending on your local laws, it may or may not be sold in the Korean grocery store. If not, check your local liquor store.

Kitchenware

BAMBOO GIMBAP MAT
GIMBAL 김발

This simple mat made of thin slats of bamboo threaded together is used to roll gimbap and also to shape Steamed Fish Cake (page 182). Wash in soapy water after using. Scrub it with a kitchen brush, rinse it, and dry it out with a kitchen towel.

CLOTH STOCK POUCH / SOUP STRAINER
GUKMUL-BAEG 국물백 / GUKMUL-MANG 국물망

Korean grocery stores offer many options for straining stocks and soups, from pouches made with something like a coffee filter to hemp pouches in different sizes to stainless-steel soup strainers. You can also use cheesecloth.

COTTON CLOTH
MYEONBO 면보

Cotton cloths are useful for straining and for steaming rice cakes. They are sold in different sizes. Wash right away after using, then hang dry. In most recipes you can substitute cheesecloth, folded into a few layers.

KOREAN GRILL PAN AND BUTANE GAS BURNER
BARBECUE GRILL-PAEN 바베큐 그릴팬
BUTAN-GASEU-BEONEO 부탄가스버너

You can make Korean barbecue like Grilled Beef Short Ribs (page 159) on any stove, in any pan, but this is the handy setup Koreans use at home. The advantage of the butane burner is that it can sit on the kitchen table, indoors, and everyone sits around, talks, and eats as the meat cooks in the grill pan. You can find them in Asian grocery stores. The pan is usually round and slightly domed, with a gutter around the edge for catching the fat that runs off the meat as it cooks.

EARTHENWARE ONGGI
ONGGI 옹기

Korean earthenware bowls, pots, and crocks are sold at reasonable prices in many Korean grocery stores. Onggi bowls and pots are slow to heat and slow to cool down, so they are great in the wintertime because they keep your soup or stew hot until you finish it (for more about onggi, see page 110). Onggi jars are often used for fermentation because they are microporous and allow gases to escape. When picking onggi, choose those that are not very shiny, without cracks. Don't clean with soapy water, as the soap will get stuck in the microscopic holes. Instead, use a scrubber with coffee grounds and warm water.

MORTAR AND PESTLE
JEOLGU-WA-JEOLGUGONGI
절구와 절구공이

I find a mortar and pestle handy for quickly pulverizing small amounts of ingredients, pounding rice cakes, and crushing garlic.

RICE SCOOP
BAPJUGEOK 밥주걱

Usually made from thick plastic or wood, with a short handle and wide scoop, these are very handy for scooping rice and can double as a wooden spoon for mixing ingredients.

GRAINS AND ONE-BOWL MEALS

RICE AND HEARTY BOWLS

Any Korean cookbook must begin with rice. It has been at the center of every Korean breakfast, lunch, and dinner for thousands of years. Even our most elaborate dishes, like Braised Beef Short Ribs (page 163), are considered side dishes to accompany a perfect bowl of rice. So, before you begin to make the other recipes in this book, it's important that you master fluffy white rice. Follow my recipe on page 41, and you will understand how properly made Korean rice should look, feel, and taste.

At its most basic, a Korean meal is a bowl of rice accompanied by a bowl of soup, kimchi, and a few side dishes. When times were tough, we mixed the rice with other grains like barley to make it last longer. Today we do this because Barley Rice and Multigrain Rice are healthy, tasty, and beautiful.

We usually don't salt rice, since the dishes we serve with it are usually salty, which brings out the rice's subtle nuttiness. Soupy dishes offset the dry stickiness of Korean short-grain rice. We love to serve colorful dishes with rice as well, to contrast with its gentle whiteness. In this chapter, you will find one-dish meals like bibimbap, porridge, and soup that have rice at their core. We even make cakes out of rice—and alcohol, too (Yakju, page 296).

But Koreans have also loved wheat noodles for centuries, and they are at the heart of some of our favorite meals. I've included some hearty dishes like Spicy Knife-Cut Noodle Soup and Kimchi Hand-Torn Noodle Soup, in which wheat noodles stand in for rice.

Fluffy White Rice

SSALBAP 쌀밥

Makes 4 rice bowls

No matter how many cookbooks I publish, this recipe and the one for Multigrain Rice (page 44) will always be the most important and cherished recipes in the book. You will see that almost every other recipe is meant to be served as a side dish with rice.

When rice is perfectly cooked, the grains are plump and fluffy, sticky enough so that they hold together without being mushy. Even though the grains are sticky, they should separate easily, and you should be able to feel each individual grain in your mouth. Good Korean rice should be soft and airy, shiny white, and a little translucent. It should always be served warm.

Although rice is inexpensive today, when I was young, it was a luxury. I am grateful that now I can buy a huge bag of short-grain white rice at a very reasonable price and eat fluffy rice at every meal if I want to. I don't take it for granted, though; when I wash my rice, I'm careful not to lose a single grain, and I eat every bit of rice in my bowl. Many Koreans are like me: We believe that losing one grain brings bad luck and you will lose whatever fortune you have. Rice defines who we are.

2 cups short-grain white rice

1. Put the rice in a heavy saucepan and cover with cold water. Tilt the pan and slowly pour out the water, taking care not to pour out any rice (you can also drain the rice through a strainer and return it to the pan). Swish the wet rice around in the pan with one hand, then fill the pan with cold water again, swish, and drain. Do this a few more times, changing the water each time, until the water runs clear. Drain as much water as you can. The rice will still be wet.

2. Add 2 cups water to the rice. Cover the pan and let the rice soak for 30 minutes.

3. Place the pan, still covered, over medium-high heat and let the water come to a boil. This should take 7 to 8 minutes. The cover will shake and the water will begin to boil over. As soon as this happens, remove the lid to allow steam to escape. Stir the rice with a wooden spoon or rice scoop to make sure that none is sticking to the bottom of the pan.

4. Partially cover the pan, leaving the lid just a little bit ajar so that the rice won't boil over again. Boil for 1 minute, then cover tightly and turn the heat down to low. Simmer for 7 to 8 minutes.

5. Uncover the rice and test for doneness. Take a small bite (be careful not to burn your tongue!); the rice should be soft. If it is still slightly crunchy, cover and steam for a couple of minutes more, until it is fully cooked. Even if it looks as though all the water has evaporated, the rice will continue to steam and soften.

6. Gently fluff the rice with a wooden spoon or rice scoop and serve.

NOTE

If not serving right away, fluff the rice and leave uncovered until it has stopped steaming. Cover until ready to serve. You can refrigerate the rice in an airtight container for up to 1 week. To reheat, place each serving in a microwave and heat for 1 minute. Or reheat in a steamer.

Scorched Rice and Scorched Rice Tea

NURUNGJI 누룽지 AND SUNGNYUNG 숭늉

One of the best reasons to choose a pan over a rice cooker for cooking rice is that when you cook rice in a pan you get a special bonus, nurungji, the layer that sticks to the pan, which we cook a little longer, until it is toasty and crispy.

When we make scorched rice, we always make scorched rice tea as well, by simmering water in the pan after we've removed the nurungji. The residue stuck to the pan infuses the simmering water with a smoky, grainy flavor.

TO MAKE SCORCHED RICE (NURUNGJI)

1. Once the rice is done, scoop the cooked rice out of the pan, leaving the thin layer that is stuck to the bottom.

2. Cover the pan and place over low heat for 2 minutes. You should smell the rice layer beginning to toast.

3. Open the lid and sprinkle a few drops of water over the rice. Cover and continue to cook for 1 more minute, until brown and crunchy.

4. Scrape out the nurungji, slipping a spoon under it at the outside edges. It should come away from the surface of the pan easily.

TO MAKE SCORCHED RICE TEA (SUNGNYUNG)

1. After removing as much nurungji from the pan as you can, pour in 2 cups water.

2. Bring to a boil over low heat. Scrape the bottom of the pot with a wooden spoon to release any remaining nutty rice residue and serve.

Multigrain Rice

JAPGOKBAP 잡곡밥

Serves 4

Multigrain rice is white rice with various grains mixed in to give it different colors, textures, and tastes. The beautiful purple hue comes from the black rice. It takes only 2 tablespoons to color the white and brown rice when you cook the grains together. These days many Koreans prefer multigrain rice to white, as it is a healthier choice.

Be sure to soak the grains in advance for at least 3 hours, or as long as overnight. Since brown rice, barley, and black rice take longer to cook than white rice, the soaking is required because you will be cooking all the grains together. If you are using a pressure cooker or a multicooker, check to see if it has a setting for multigrain rice. If it does, you can skip the soaking. Just add the washed ingredients and water and turn it on. (For a regular rice cooker, you'll need to soak the grains before using it to cook the rice.) The whole grains will have a coarser texture than white rice even when they are cooked through.

1 cup short-grain white rice

²/₃ cup brown sweet rice or brown glutinous rice

¹/₃ cup hulless barley or pearl barley

2 tablespoons black rice or black glutinous rice

1. Combine the white rice, brown sweet rice, barley, and black rice in a heavy saucepan and cover with cold water. Tilt the pan and slowly pour out the water, taking care not to pour out any rice (you can also drain the rice through a strainer and return it to the pan). Swish the wet grains around in the pan with one hand, then fill the pan with cold water again, swish, and drain. Do this a few more times, changing the water each time, until the water runs clear. Drain as much water as you can. The grains will still be wet.

2. Add 2½ cups cold water to the grains. Cover the pan and let the grains soak for 3 hours.

3. Place the pan, still covered, over medium-high heat and let the water come to a boil. This should take 7 to 8 minutes. The cover will shake and the water will begin to boil over. As soon as this happens, remove the lid to allow steam to escape. Stir the grains with a wooden spoon or rice scoop to make sure that none is sticking to the bottom of the pan.

4. Cover, reduce the heat to low, and simmer for 10 minutes. Taste (be careful not to burn your tongue!) to see if the rice is fully cooked and fluffy. If it is still slightly hard, cover and steam for 3 to 5 minutes more, until the rice is fully tender. Even if it looks as though all the water has evaporated, the rice will continue to steam and soften.

5. Gently fluff the rice with a wooden spoon or rice scoop and serve.

NOTE

If not serving right away, fluff the rice and leave uncovered until it has stopped steaming. Cover until ready to serve. You can refrigerate the multigrain rice in an airtight container for up to 1 week. To reheat, place each serving in a microwave and heat for 1 minute. Or reheat in a steamer.

Barley Rice

BORIBAP 보리밥

Serves 4

Barley rice is white rice mixed with grains of barley. It was originally devised as a way to make white rice go farther, but now that Korea is more developed and most people can afford white rice every day, many people prefer barley rice for its health benefits. The mixture has a soft, pleasantly chewy texture and a bit of an oatmeal flavor.

In this recipe, I show you how to make barley rice the way my aunt made it at my grandmother's when I was a child. The white rice and barley are cooked together but kept separate in the pot, in layers.

| 1 cup short-grain white rice | 1 cup hulless barley or pearl barley, washed and drained |

1. Put the rice in a medium bowl and cover with cold water. Tilt the bowl and slowly pour out the water, taking care not to pour out any rice (you can also drain the rice through a strainer and return it to the bowl). Swish the wet rice around in the bowl with one hand, then fill the bowl with cold water again, swish, and drain. Do this a few more times, changing the water each time, until the water runs clear. Drain as much water as you can. The rice will still be wet.

2. Add 1 cup cold water to the rice. Cover the bowl and let the rice soak for 30 minutes while you prepare the barley.

3. Put the barley in a heavy pot and cover with cold water. Tilt the pot and slowly pour out the water, taking care not to pour out any barley (you can also drain the barley through a strainer and return it to the pot). Swish the wet barley around in the pan with one hand, then fill the pot with cold water again, swish, and drain. Do this a few more times, changing the water each time, until the water runs clear. Drain as much water as you can.

4. Add 3 cups water to the barley. Place the pot, uncovered, over medium-high heat and cook for 10 minutes. Reduce the heat to low and simmer, uncovered, for another 10 minutes.

5. Place a strainer over a bowl and strain the barley. Measure the barley water into a 4-cup measuring cup or bowl and add enough water to make 2½ cups.

6. Return the barley to the pot and spread in an even layer. Drain the rice and spoon it in an even layer on top of the barley.

7. Slowly add the 2½ cups barley water, being careful not to mix the barley and rice. Cover the pot, place over medium-high heat, and bring to a boil, which should take 7 to 8 minutes. The cover will shake and the water will begin to boil over. As soon as this happens, remove the lid to allow steam to escape.

8. Gently insert a wooden spoon or rice scoop between the edge of the pot and the rice and barley. Move it around the edge of the mixture and lift the mixture up a little bit from the bottom, but be careful not to mix the grains together.

9. Cover the pot, reduce the heat to low, and simmer for another 10 minutes, or until the liquid has been absorbed and the rice and barley are tender. Fluff with a wooden spoon or rice scoop and serve right away with side dishes. Or, after fluffing the rice, transfer to an airtight container, cool, and refrigerate for up to a week. To reheat, place each serving in a microwave and heat for 1 minute. Or reheat in a steamer.

NOTE

If you want to keep the grains separate, fluff the white rice layer gently without disturbing the barley, serve it, then fluff the barley, or fluff the remaining rice and barley together.

Leaf Wraps and Rice

SANGCHU-SSAMBAP 상추쌈밥

Serves as many as you wish

Ssam is a popular, traditional style of eating, where you wrap one ingredient in another and eat the wrap right away, usually in one bite. Lettuce, sometimes stacked with a perilla leaf, is the most common kind of ssam (*ssam* means "wrap something" and *sangchu* means "lettuce").

I always have soybean paste dipping sauce and lettuce in my refrigerator. When I'm too busy to make stew, soup, or side dishes, I make rice and take out the lettuce and dipping sauce. I spoon the warm rice onto lettuce leaves, top it with a little sauce, wrap it up, and eat.

Green and/or red lettuce leaves, washed

Fluffy White Rice (page 41), Multigrain Rice (page 44), or Barley Rice (page 46), kept warm

Soybean Paste Dipping Sauce (page 134)

Green chili peppers, cut crosswise into ⅓-inch slices (optional)

For each roll, top a lettuce leaf with a spoonful of warm rice and add about 1 teaspoon dipping sauce and some green chili pepper if desired. Roll up with both hands and enjoy.

MY AUNT'S SECRET

When I was young, I used to visit my grandmother's house in the countryside during summer and winter vacations. Following Korean tradition, my uncle, his wife, and his children lived with my grandmother because it was the responsibility of the first-born son to look after his parents. When I visited, every meal was delicious and varied.

My grandmother was a strong lady. She wasn't rich, but she was the head of the household because my grandfather had passed away. She had a key for the small barn where she kept all her precious commodities, such as rice, barley, dried fish, sesame seeds, toasted sesame oil, and seaweeds. She kept her grains in large earthenware crocks. Every morning she gave my aunt enough rice and barley to use for the day's meals, but she kept the rest locked up in the barn.

At mealtimes my aunt set two tables: one for my uncle and grandmother and the other for herself and the rest of the family. I couldn't help but notice that while we all had barley rice, my grandmother and uncle had mostly white rice in their bowls. Sometimes my grandmother didn't finish her rice and said to me: "Come and eat it." I never rejected her offer. The white rice was so soft and delicious!

But what I couldn't figure out was how their rice was whiter, when we were all served from the same pot. How could this be?

I discovered the secret one day while watching my aunt scoop everyone's rice: There were actually two layers in the cauldron, a layer of cooked barley on the bottom with a layer of cooked rice on top. When she filled the rice bowls, she first fluffed up the white rice on top without disturbing the barley below. The first bowl of rice went to my grandmother, almost all white. The second was for my uncle, mostly white rice too. Then she mixed up everything in the cauldron and filled everyone's bowls with grayish barley rice. She put the leftovers in a large basket with a lid, which she hung in a cool place.

Barley Rice Bibimbap

BORIBAP-BIBIMBAP 보리밥비빔밥

Serves 1

I make this meal for my family all the time on hot summer days. It's one of many good reasons to have barley rice on hand. It's served cool, so it's easy to eat.

1 cup warm Barley Rice (page 46)

½ cup Soybean Paste Stew with Beef (page 90)

½ cup Sweet, Sour, and Spicy Lettuce Salad (page 196)

Korean hot pepper paste (gochujang) to taste

2 teaspoons toasted sesame oil

Combine the barley rice, soybean paste stew, and lettuce salad in a large bowl. Add hot pepper paste to taste. Drizzle on the toasted sesame oil, mix everything together well with a spoon, and serve.

Bibimbap
with Sliced Raw Fish

HOE-DEOPBAP 회덮밥

Serves 2

Hoe-deopbap is a perfect one-bowl meal that I make whenever I can find sashimi-quality fish. I love the combination of the fish, crispy vegetables, rice, and sweet, sour, and spicy sauce mixed with sesame oil—you get an array of flavors and textures in every spoonful. I always serve hoe-deopbap with a clear soybean paste soup, which adds another dimension of flavor.

Since most fishmongers don't sell fish that is fresh enough to eat raw, you should always let them know that you are going to serve it that way before you buy it. A better, though more expensive, option is a Japanese market, where you can find very fresh, well-packaged fish like tuna, salmon, flounder, and orange capelin roe. Large Korean markets often have aquariums that stock flounder and red snapper. Ask them to fillet the fish for you.

2 ounces mixed baby salad greens or lettuce (about 2 cups), washed, drained, and patted dry (if using large lettuce leaves, cut into bite-size pieces)

½ small onion, thinly sliced (about ¼ cup), soaked in cold water for 5 minutes, drained, and patted dry

1 small carrot, cut into thin matchsticks (about ¼ cup)

1 green chili pepper, thinly sliced crosswise

1 small seedless cucumber (or ¼ English cucumber), thinly sliced crosswise

1 to 2 red radishes, thinly sliced crosswise

4 cherry tomatoes, halved

6 perilla leaves or a few mint sprigs, stacked, rolled, and very thinly sliced

½ recipe Fluffy White Rice (page 41), kept warm

8 ounces sashimi-grade raw fish, such as tuna or flounder, cut into ½-inch cubes

2 tablespoons capelin roe (masago in Japanese; optional)

4 teaspoons toasted sesame oil

1 sheet seaweed paper (gim; aka nori), toasted and shredded (see page 425)

2 teaspoons toasted sesame seeds

Vinegared Soy–Hot Pepper Paste Seasoning Sauce (page 131)

Clear Soybean Paste Soup (page 84; optional)

1. Divide all the ingredients into 2 equal portions. Arrange each portion of the salad greens, onion, carrot, chili pepper, cucumber, radish, cherry tomatoes, and perilla leaves nicely in a large, shallow bowl, leaving room in the center for the rice.

2. Scoop each portion of rice in the center of the vegetables.

3. Arrange each portion of fish on top of the rice. Top the fish with the fish roe, if using.

4. Drizzle the sesame oil over the rice and vegetables in each bowl, top with the gim, and sprinkle with the sesame seeds.

5. Spoon some seasoning sauce over the rice and vegetables, mix well with a spoon, and eat along with the soup, if using.

Avocado, Mushroom, and Vegetable Bibimbap

AVOCADO BEOSEOT YACHAE BIBIMBAP
아보카도 버섯 야채 비빔밥

Serves 2

I created this vegetarian version of the one-dish meal Hoe-Deopbap (page 52). The combination of rice, vegetables, and sweet, sour, and spicy sauce is tasty with the rich, creamy avocado and meaty king oyster mushrooms.

4 ounces king oyster mushrooms, cut into ½-inch cubes

¼ teaspoon kosher salt

1 teaspoon vegetable oil

1 ripe avocado

2 ounces mixed baby salad greens or lettuce (about 2 cups), washed, drained, and patted dry (if using large lettuce leaves, cut into bite-size pieces)

½ small onion, thinly sliced (about ¼ cup), soaked in cold water for 5 minutes, drained, and patted dry

1 small carrot, cut into thin matchsticks (about ¼ cup)

1 green chili pepper, thinly sliced crosswise

1 small seedless cucumber (or ¼ English cucumber), thinly sliced crosswise

1 to 2 red radishes, thinly sliced crosswise

6 cherry tomatoes, halved

6 perilla leaves or a few mint sprigs, stacked, rolled, and very thinly sliced

½ recipe Fluffy White Rice (page 41), kept warm

4 teaspoons toasted sesame oil

1 sheet seaweed paper (gim; aka nori), toasted and shredded (see page 425)

2 teaspoons toasted sesame seeds

Vinegared Soy–Hot Pepper Paste Seasoning Sauce (page 131)

Clear Soybean Paste Soup (page 84; optional)

1. In a medium bowl, combine the mushrooms and salt and toss together. Let stand for 10 minutes.

2. Heat a skillet over medium-high heat and add the vegetable oil. Add the mushrooms and stir-fry for 1 minute. Remove from the heat.

3. Halve the avocado lengthwise and remove the pit. Use a knife to cut a grid into the flesh on both avocado halves, cutting to the skin but not through it.

4. Divide all the ingredients into 2 equal portions. Arrange each portion of the salad greens, onion, carrot, chili pepper, cucumber, radish, cherry tomatoes, and perilla leaves nicely in a large, shallow bowl, leaving room for the rice in the center.

5. Scoop each portion of rice into the center of the bowl.

6. Arrange the stir-fried mushrooms on top of the rice.

7. Using a large spoon, scoop out each avocado half and arrange the diced avocado on top of the mushrooms.

8. Drizzle the sesame oil over the rice and vegetables in each bowl, top with the gim, and sprinkle with the sesame seeds.

9. Spoon some seasoning sauce over the rice and vegetables, mix well with a spoon, and eat along with the soup, if using.

Bibimbap
with Seafood Soup

BIBIMBAP-GWA TANGGUK 비빔밥과 탕국

Serves 4 generously

There are many variations on bibimbap, the classic Korean meal of rice mixed with a variety of cooked vegetables. The vegetables provide an array of tastes and textures to go with the soft, warm rice. With such an abundance of produce, bibimbap is not only delicious, but also healthy.

The version that I'm introducing to you with this recipe is special, because in addition to the vegetables (soybean sprouts, spinach, zucchini, Korean radish, fernbrake), it's always served with a soup called tangguk, which is made with beef, seafood (clams here), and little pieces of tofu. It's customary to mix some of the tangguk into the bibimbap just before you dig in—not too much, just enough to moisten the rice and get a taste of it throughout.

Bibimbap-gwa tangguk comes from my father's hometown of Namhae, an island located off the southern coast of Gyeongsang province. When I was still in elementary school, my whole family—twenty to thirty of us—used to go to my grandmother's house on the anniversary of my grandfather's death, to honor and memorialize him in a ceremony called a jesa. At midnight the adults would all participate in the jesa while we children were asleep. Afterward, my aunt would wake us up and give us a bowl of this bibimbap. It was a small bowl, with white fluffy rice and a few different kinds of vegetables, topped with the delicious tangguk.

The recipe is easy to scale up for a larger crowd, just like my grandmother used to do. The gochujang and fried egg are not traditional for this particular version of bibimbap, but I enjoy them.

FOR THE SOUP

1 teaspoon toasted sesame oil

4 to 5 ounces (8 to 10 topneck or littleneck) shelled and cleaned clams (see page 428), chopped

8 ounces beef brisket, chopped

8 ounces Korean radish or daikon, peeled and cut into ⅛-inch-thick pieces (about 2 cups)

2 tablespoons fish sauce

8 ounces medium-firm tofu, cut into ½-inch cubes (about 1 cup)

½ daepa (large green onion) or 2 to 3 scallions, sliced diagonally

FOR THE BIBIMBAP

12 ounces soybean sprouts (about 4 cups), cleaned (see page 421) and drained

2½ teaspoons kosher salt

5 teaspoons toasted sesame oil, plus more for serving if desired

8 ounces spinach, roots trimmed, bunches split in half or quartered to facilitate cleaning, and rinsed

2 small zucchini, cut into matchsticks (about 2 cups)

2 tablespoons plus 1 teaspoon vegetable oil

1 pound Korean radish or daikon, peeled and cut into matchsticks (about 4 cups)

8 ounces soaked fernbrake (see page 422; from 0.8 ounce dried)

2 teaspoons soy sauce

½ teaspoon sugar

FOR SERVING

1 recipe Fluffy White Rice (page 41), kept warm

Korean hot pepper paste (gochujang; optional)

4 sunny-side-up eggs (optional)

MAKE THE SOUP

1. Heat a large, heavy pot over medium-high heat. When it's hot, add the sesame oil, clams, and beef. Stir with a wooden spoon until the beef is no longer pink, about 3 minutes.

2. Add 6 cups water and the radish pieces. Cover and cook for 10 minutes, until boiling vigorously. Uncover and skim off the foam with a large spoon or ladle.

3. Cover, reduce the heat to medium, and cook for 20 minutes, until the soup is flavorful, the radish is well cooked, and the beef is tender. Stir in the fish sauce and add the tofu.

Recipe Continues

4. Increase the heat to medium-high. Cover and cook for 5 more minutes, until the tofu softens. Stir in the daepa or scallions, cover, and cook for another minute. Remove from the heat.

MAKE THE BIBIMBAP

1. Place the soybean sprouts, ½ teaspoon of the salt, and 1 cup water in a large saucepan. Cover and cook for 10 minutes over medium-high heat, until the sprouts smell nutty.

2. Drain, transfer to a bowl, and allow the sprouts to cool for 5 minutes. Mix by hand with ½ teaspoon of the salt and 1 teaspoon of the sesame oil. Arrange in a pile on a large platter.

3. Bring 2 quarts water to a boil in the same saucepan. Add the spinach and cook for 30 seconds, stirring with a wooden spoon. Drain and rinse in a few changes of cold running water to remove any remaining dirt and stop the cooking. Drain, squeeze out the excess water, and transfer to a cutting board. Cut into bite-size pieces and transfer to a bowl. Toss by hand with ½ teaspoon of the salt and 1 teaspoon of the sesame oil. Pile onto the platter.

4. Toss the zucchini matchsticks with ½ teaspoon of the salt in a bowl. Let sit for 5 minutes. The zucchini will be moist, but you don't have to squeeze out the excess water.

5. Heat 1 teaspoon of the vegetable oil in a large skillet over medium-high heat. Add the zucchini and stir with a wooden spoon for 2 to 3 minutes, until the zucchini is translucent and cooked through. Remove from the heat and stir in 1 teaspoon of the sesame oil. Pile onto the platter.

6. Heat 1 tablespoon of the vegetable oil in the same skillet over medium-high heat. Add the radish matchsticks, remaining ½ teaspoon salt, and ¼ cup water. Stir, cover, and reduce the heat to medium. Cook for 10 minutes, or until the radish is fully cooked. Uncover, stir in 1 teaspoon of the sesame oil, and remove from the heat. Pile onto the platter.

7. Drain the fernbrake and cut into 2-inch pieces. Heat the remaining 1 tablespoon vegetable oil in the same skillet over medium-high heat. Add the fernbrake and stir with a wooden spoon or wooden chopsticks for 2 minutes, or until it is soft. Add the soy sauce and sugar and stir gently for 2 to 3 minutes, until the fernbrake is shiny and fragrant. Remove from the heat and stir in the remaining 1 teaspoon sesame oil. Pile onto the platter.

SERVE THE BIBIMBAP AND SOUP

1. **If using large, shallow bowls:** Divide the warm rice evenly among four large, shallow bowls. Arrange some of each vegetable on top. If desired, top the vegetables with 1 to 2 tablespoons of hot pepper paste and an egg.

If serving in earthenware bowls: Put a few drops of sesame oil in the bottom of each bowl and top with rice. Arrange some of each vegetable on top. If desired, top the vegetables with 1 to 2 tablespoons of hot pepper paste and an egg. Place each bowl directly over medium-high heat for 4 to 5 minutes, until you hear the rice begin to crackle. Remove from the heat.

2. Reheat the soup and ladle into four bowls. Give each person a spoon for mixing and eating the bibimbap. Diners should add about 3 spoonfuls of the soup to the bibimbap and mix it all together. Have a spoonful of soup in between bites of bibimbap. Serve with additional sesame oil and hot pepper paste on the side if desired.

Octopus Porridge

MUNEO-JUK 문어죽

Serves 2

Porridge is one of the staples of Korean cuisine. We eat it as a snack or for breakfast. There are many different kinds, made with various vegetables, meats, nuts, and seafood. All are soft, mild tasting, light and, easy to swallow and digest, which is one reason porridge is so good for people recovering from illness. It's also a great diet food, as it's very filling but calls for just a bit of rice.

    The process for making any porridge is similar. First you soak the rice and drain it, then stir-fry it with the ingredient of your choice, add water, and cook until the rice is tender.

    Packaged cooked octopus is available in the fish section in Korean and Japanese markets. If you prefer another type of seafood, you can replace the octopus with mussels, scallops, or shrimp. You can also make this porridge with ground beef.

8 ounces cooked octopus (see page 432)

2 scallions, chopped

1 tablespoon plus 1 teaspoon toasted sesame oil

½ cup short-grain white rice, washed and soaked in cold water for 1 hour

2 garlic cloves, minced

⅓ carrot, chopped (¼ cup)

4 cups octopus broth (see page 432) or water

1 teaspoon fish sauce

2 large eggs (optional)

Kimchi

Kosher salt (optional)

1. Divide the octopus into 2 portions. Chop 1 portion and set aside. Thinly slice the other portion on the diagonal and transfer to a bowl. Add the scallions and 1 teaspoon of the sesame oil and mix well with a spoon. Set aside.

2. Drain the rice. Heat a large saucepan over medium heat. Add the rice, remaining 1 tablespoon sesame oil, and garlic. Stir for 1 minute with a wooden spoon until the garlic smells fragrant. Stir in the chopped octopus and carrot and cook, stirring, for 1 minute. Add the octopus broth. Cover and cook for 5 to 7 minutes, until the mixture is boiling and the rice is cooked. If it boils over, crack the lid.

3. Reduce the heat to low and simmer for 10 minutes, until the rice is smooth and tender.

4. Stir in the fish sauce. Crack the eggs, if using, on top of the simmering porridge. Do not stir. Increase the heat to medium-high and cook for 2 to 3 minutes, until the eggs are set. Remove from the heat.

5. Ladle the porridge into two bowls with an egg on top of each serving. Add the sliced seasoned octopus and serve right away with kimchi. If desired, season with a little salt.

VARIATION

If substituting other seafood for octopus, do not divide into 2 portions. Chop it all, mix with the scallions and 1 teaspoon of the sesame oil, and add in Step 2.

Rice Cake Soup
with Bone Broth

SAGOL-TTEOKGUK 사골떡국

Serves 2 generously

Rice cake soup is made with thinly sliced round or oval white rice cakes. In addition to being a delicious one-bowl meal, the soup has special meaning as the first dish of the year for all Koreans. It's traditionally served for breakfast on New Year's Day, both January 1 and Korean New Year's Day (Seollal, see page 71). The coin-shaped rice slices symbolize purity and wishes for prosperity during the upcoming year. These days the rice cakes in Korean supermarkets are more oval, but the sentiment is the same.

If you are making bone broth and intend to use it right away for this soup, you can save 2 hours by soaking the beef while you are simmering the broth, then cooking it in the broth during the last 2 hours of simmering (you can store the shredded beef in a covered container overnight in the refrigerator). Instead of bone broth, you can use any tasty broth, such as Anchovy-Kelp Stock (page 74), Vegetable Stock (page 78), or even commercial chicken broth.

5 cups Beef Bone Broth (page 80) or other broth

8 ounces beef brisket, rinsed and soaked in cold water for 10 to 20 minutes

1 pound sliced rice cakes (about 3 cups)

1½ teaspoons kosher salt

½ daepa (large green onion) or 2 to 3 scallions, sliced diagonally

Yellow Egg Paper Strips (optional; page 136)

Ground black pepper

Kimchi (optional)

1. Bring the broth to a boil in a heavy pot over medium-high heat. Drain the beef and add to the boiling broth. Reduce the heat to medium-low, cover, and cook for 1½ to 2 hours, until the beef is very tender. Remove from the heat.

2. Remove the beef from the broth and transfer to a cutting board. Let cool until you can handle it easily. Pull the beef into thin shreds by hand and set aside.

3. Separate the rice cake slices and soak in cold water for 20 to 30 minutes, until softened and pliable.

4. Reheat the broth over medium-high heat. If the broth is more or less than 4 cups, add more or pour some out to make 4 cups. Stir in the salt.

5. Drain the rice cakes and add to the boiling broth. Cover and cook for 4 to 5 minutes, until they float. Add the daepa or scallions and cook for 2 to 3 minutes.

6. Ladle the soup into two bowls. Garnish with beef and yellow egg paper strips, if using. Set the pepper on the table for seasoning the broth. Serve with kimchi if you wish.

Noodle Soup
with Kimchi Seasoning

KIMCHI-GUKSU 김치국수

Serves 2 generously

This is my all-time favorite noodle soup. Since I always have kimchi in my refrigerator, I make it often. Kimchi adds a sour element to the broth, as well as a crisp contrast to the soft noodles. The idea of adding it came from one of my friends whose hometown is Busan, in Gyeongsang province, in southeast Korea.

Be sure to use fermented sour kimchi rather than freshly made, and don't cook the noodles until just before you serve the soup. Otherwise they will get too soft, and you want them chewy.

4 ounces fermented kimchi, preferably Traditional Napa Cabbage Kimchi (page 112), chopped

1 tablespoon Korean hot pepper paste (gochujang)

½ teaspoon sugar

2 teaspoons toasted sesame oil

1 teaspoon toasted sesame seeds

5 to 6 cups Anchovy-Kelp Stock (page 74) or Vegetable Stock (page 78)

1½ teaspoons kosher salt

8 ounces thin wheat-flour noodles (somyeon)

1 sheet seaweed paper (gim; aka nori), toasted and shredded (see page 425)

2 scallions, chopped

1. Combine the kimchi, hot pepper paste, sugar, sesame oil, and sesame seeds in a small bowl and mix well.

2. In a small saucepan, bring the stock to a boil. Stir in the salt. Cover and remove from the heat.

3. In a large pot, bring 3 quarts water to a boil over medium-high heat. Add the noodles and stir them with a wooden spoon so that they don't stick together. Cover and cook for a few minutes, until the water begins to bubble over. Uncover the pot and stir. The noodles will float to the surface. Cook for 1 to 2 minutes, uncovered. Taste one or two noodles. They should be chewy but soft all the way through. If they are slightly hard in the middle, cook them a little longer.

4. Drain the noodles through a strainer and rinse them under cold running water, rubbing with both hands to remove excess starch. Continue to rinse, strain, and rub until the noodles are no longer slippery. Divide evenly between two soup bowls.

5. Reheat the stock and ladle over the noodles in each bowl. Add a spoonful of the kimchi mixture, sprinkle with the gim and scallions, and serve right away.

Kimchi Hand-Torn Noodle Soup

KIMCHI-SUJEBI 김치수제비

Serves 2 generously

One day I read an interview with Choi Jin-sil, a famous Korean actress. When she was growing up, her mom was too poor to buy rice, so they ate noodles instead, since flour was cheaper than rice. She said her favorite food was kimchi sujebi, a soup made with fermented kimchi and hand-torn wheat noodles.

I'd never heard of the dish, but when I read the interview, I had to make it. Now it's my go-to recipe for sujebi. It's very simple, but hearty and comforting. Only a few ingredients are required, as the kimchi provides everything you need. Be sure to use fermented, sour kimchi for this, not fresh. You need it for the delicious complex flavor that it contributes to the broth. You can use your own homemade kimchi that has fermented for a few days, or you can use store-bought. Taste, and if it's not sour, leave it at room temperature for a few days until it has fermented.

FOR THE DOUGH

2 cups all-purpose flour

½ teaspoon kosher salt

1 tablespoon vegetable oil

FOR THE SOUP

7 cups Anchovy-Kelp Stock (page 74) or Vegetable Stock (page 78)

8 ounces fermented kimchi, preferably Traditional Napa Cabbage Kimchi (page 112), or store-bought fermented kimchi, chopped

2 tablespoons kimchi brine

1 medium onion, sliced (about 1 cup)

2 garlic cloves, minced

1 teaspoon kosher salt

2 scallions, sliced

1 teaspoon toasted sesame oil

MAKE THE DOUGH

If using a food processor fitted with the dough blade: Pour ¾ cup water into the food processor, then add the flour, salt, and oil. Process for about 2 minutes, until the dough forms a ball on the blade. Transfer the dough to a large bowl or cutting board and knead for another minute by hand. Seal in a zipper-lock plastic bag and set aside to rest for about 10 minutes. *(You can refrigerate the dough for 2 to 3 days.)*

If making by hand: Combine the flour, salt, oil, and ¾ cup water in a large bowl. Mix with a wooden spoon until the ingredients come together into a lumpy dough. Knead the dough by hand until it forms a firm, smooth ball, 10 to 12 minutes. Seal in a zipper-lock plastic bag and set aside to rest for about 10 minutes. *(You can refrigerate the dough for 2 to 3 days.)*

MAKE THE SOUP

In a large pot, combine the stock, kimchi, brine, onion, garlic, and salt. Cover and cook for 15 minutes over medium-high heat, until the kimchi has softened slightly and the onion is translucent. If the soup begins to boil over, crack the lid. Remove from the heat.

MAKE THE NOODLES AND SERVE

1. Uncover the soup and bring back to a boil. Fill a small bowl with water and wet your hands so the dough doesn't stick to them. Hold the dough ball in one hand and, with your other hand, pinch the dough and pull out a little piece, repeating until you get a paper-thin, bite-size piece, about 2 inches wide by 1½ inches long and ⅛ inch thick. Tear it off and drop into the boiling soup. It may take two or three pulls before you can get the dough thin enough. Wet your hands again and continue to stretch and tear off noodles and drop them into the boiling soup, wetting your fingers whenever the dough begins to stick, until all the dough is used up. Make sure that your noodles are thin, and work as quickly as you can. The whole process should not take much longer than 5 minutes. It will become easier with practice.

  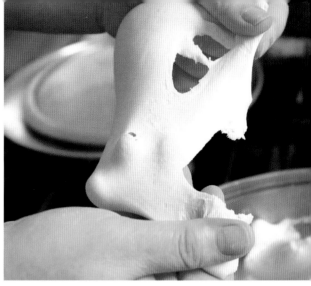

2. Stir the noodle soup with a ladle or wooden spoon. Add the scallions, cover, and boil for another 5 minutes over medium-high heat (crack the lid if necessary to prevent the soup from boiling over), until all the noodles are floating and cooked through.

3. Remove from the heat and stir in the sesame oil. Ladle the soup into individual bowls and serve right away.

Spicy Knife-Cut Noodle Soup

JANG-KALGUKSU 장칼국수

Serves 2 generously

This soup is similar to Kimchi Hand-Torn Noodle Soup (page 60), but the noodles are cut with a knife instead of being hand-torn. I add potato starch to the flour so that the noodles have a chewy texture.

Korean knife-cut noodle soup is versatile, and there are many variations. I add a generous amount of hot pepper paste to this one, and soybean paste as well for a deep, spicy flavor. I add zucchini matchsticks along with the noodles, which become smooth and sweet in the spicy broth, and at the very end, after ladling the soup with the noodles into bowls, I top each serving with baby spinach.

Although I think it's worth it to make your own noodles, you can substitute store-bought noodles. You can find many brands of premade and frozen noodles in Korean markets; be sure to buy thin ones. *The photo is on page 70.*

FOR THE NOODLES

2 cups all-purpose flour, plus more for dusting

¼ cup potato starch

½ teaspoon kosher salt

1 tablespoon vegetable oil

FOR THE SOUP

7 cups Anchovy-Kelp Stock (page 74) or Vegetable Stock (page 78)

1 teaspoon kosher salt

1 medium onion, sliced

4 garlic cloves, minced

¼ cup Korean hot pepper paste (gochujang)

1 tablespoon Korean fermented soybean paste (doenjang)

1 small zucchini, cut into matchsticks

2 teaspoons toasted sesame oil

2 cups baby spinach or arugula, cleaned

MAKE THE NOODLES

1. If using a food processor fitted with the dough blade: Pour ¾ cup water into the food processor, then add the flour, potato starch, salt, and oil. Process for about 2 minutes, until the dough forms a ball on the blade. Transfer the dough to a large bowl or cutting board. Knead for another minute by hand, seal in a zipper-lock plastic bag, and set aside to rest for about 10 minutes. *(You can refrigerate the dough for 2 to 3 days.)*

If making by hand: Combine the flour, potato starch, salt, oil, and ¾ cup water in a large bowl. Mix with a wooden spoon until the ingredients come together into a lumpy dough. Knead the dough by hand until it forms a firm, smooth ball, 10 to 12 minutes. Seal in a plastic bag and set aside to rest for about 10 minutes. *(You can refrigerate the dough for 2 to 3 days.)*

2. Remove the dough ball from the bag. Knead for 1 minute, then divide the dough into 2 equal balls. Take one to roll out and put the other back in the bag to prevent it from drying out.

3. Dust a large cutting board with flour. Roll the dough ball out into a thin rectangle, about 10 by 14 inches. Dust the dough and flip it over from time to time as you roll it out to prevent it from sticking.

4. Sprinkle the dough with flour and fold up into thirds or quarters, sprinkling the folded surface with flour each time you fold it over to prevent it from sticking together. Cut into thin noodles, about ⅛ inch wide. Push the noodles aside and repeat with the other dough ball.

5. Sprinkle more flour over all the noodles. Unfold the noodles by gently tossing them into the air and letting them fall down gently onto the cutting board. Repeat until all the noodles are unfolded and separated.

MAKE THE SOUP

1. Pour the stock into a large pot. Add the salt, onion, and garlic. Lower a fine-mesh strainer into the pot and add the hot pepper paste and soybean paste to the strainer. Push the pastes through the strainer with a spoon. Discard any residue left in the strainer.

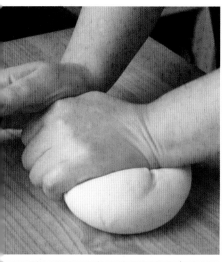

2. Cover and cook over medium-high heat for 10 to 12 minutes. The stock should be boiling vigorously. Crack the lid if it begins to boil over.

3. Add the zucchini and the noodles and stir with a wooden spoon. Cover, increase the heat to high, and boil for 5 minutes, or until the noodles are cooked through. Crack the lid if necessary to prevent the soup from boiling over. Remove from the heat.

4. Drizzle with the sesame oil and stir. Ladle the soup into large, shallow soup bowls. Top each bowl with some spinach and serve.

Spicy Knife-Cut
Noodle Soup
(page 68)

SPECIAL FOOD

ON THE TWO MAJOR KOREAN HOLIDAYS

Traditionally Koreans lived by the lunar calendar, which counts time by the cycles of the moon. Now that the Gregorian calendar is the standard around the world, most Koreans keep track of both, using the lunar to mark our cherished holidays.

For Koreans, the most important aspect of any holiday is the gathering of families, to visit with each other and enjoy food together. In contemporary Korea, this usually means that the grown-up children and grandchildren living in the city visit their parents or grandparents in the ancestral home in the countryside. Grandparents are always excited to see their grandchildren, and they prepare a lot of homemade food. They often make extra quantities of foods like kimchi, homemade fermented soybean paste, and toasted sesame oil made from their harvested sesame seeds, so their family can take some back to the city.

Breakfast is the biggest meal on these holidays. Sweet Potato Starch Noodles with Vegetables and Meat (page 323), Bulgogi with Noodles (page 157), Braised Beef Short Ribs (page 163), pancakes, soups, and Rice Cakes Dusted with Soybean Powder (page 373) feature heavily, and grandmothers are excited to have the opportunity to make Honey Cookies (page 363) for their grandchildren.

NEW YEAR'S DAY (SEOLLAL)

Held on the day of the second new moon after the winter solstice, New Year's Day falls on a different date every year, sometime in late January or early February.

The beginning of the new year is an important time. It's when we start afresh and look forward to good health and success. It's also the day when our age goes up one year, rather than on the date of our birthdays. Rice Cake Soup (page 62) is essential for breakfast on this day, and eating it in the morning is considered to be the confirmation that we are one year older.

Today most Koreans celebrate January 1 as well as the traditional Korean Seollal, and we eat rice cake soup on that day, too. But when I was growing up, we observed only Seollal and it was a big day! My mom would give us all new clothes: pants and tops, shoes, gloves, and hats. My siblings and I would immediately put them on and go outside to show off to our friends, who were also wearing their new clothes. We spent the rest of the holiday morning admiring each other's clothes and playing together.

HARVEST MOON FESTIVAL (CHUSEOK)

A three-day festival starting on the fifteenth day of the eighth month on the full moon, Chuseok falls sometime in September or October. This traditional celebration of the end of the bountiful fall harvest is similar to American Thanksgiving. Rice Cakes Steamed on Pine Needles (page 368) are unskippable on this day. Koreans who don't have time to make them will buy them, and rice cake shops are overflowing with cakes ready to be taken away. They are made with that year's freshly harvested rice and taste like the prosperity of the season. Korean pears, persimmons, and apples are at their peak at this time, so dishes featuring these fruits are also popular.

SOUPY

BUBBLING SOUPS AND STEWS

Korean soups (guk 국) and stews (jjigae 찌개) have a special place in our cuisine as the ultimate side dish with rice, and are served at breakfast, lunch, and dinner. Our personal milestones are often marked by bowls of soup. Seaweed Soup is the one that all of us eat on our birthdays.

Traditional meals include both jjigae and guk. Jjigae, brought to the table hot in a pot or traditional Korean earthenware bowl, is a shared dish, thicker and saltier than guk, with heavier, chunkier ingredients. Guk is more brothy and is served in individual bowls. They are both essential to a meal because they complement rice and drier side dishes. Slurping something soupy helps these drier foods go down. Some Koreans mix their rice right into their soup to make a one-bowl meal on the spot.

I used to serve jjigae in the traditional way, with the stew in the middle of the table and everybody dipping their spoons into it. But some people are uncomfortable with double-dipping, and over time I've come to prefer giving everyone their own small bowl and ladling out individual servings. How you serve it is up to you.

No matter what type of soup or stew you are making, you must begin with a good broth. Sometimes it's made by stir-frying beef and adding water to it, but many of the dishes in this chapter begin with Anchovy-Kelp Stock, which is the traditional base for many Korean soups and stews. I make sure to keep some on hand in the freezer. I've also included a recipe for Vegetable Stock.

The variety of soups and stews in the Korean repertoire is truly amazing: meaty or meatless; hot and spicy or mild; clear or thick with meat, vegetables, seaweed, and seafood. Many of the soups and stews in this chapter have deep personal and cultural significance, some are hearty workaday meals, and all go perfectly with rice.

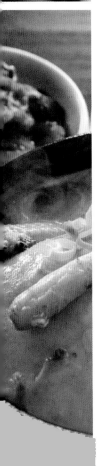

Anchovy-Kelp Stock

MYEOLCHI-DASIMA-GUKMUL 멸치다시마국물

Makes 3 quarts

I like to call this my magic potion. The flavor-rich, delicately refreshing clear stock tastes of pure umami and serves as a base for many Korean dishes.

Dried anchovies are used in many Korean soups and stews. We remove the intestines and the heads, to keep the color of the stock light and to prevent the stock from becoming bitter. You'll need large dried anchovies—about 3½ inches long—for this recipe. You can find them in the freezer or refrigerator section in Korean grocery stores. Don't substitute small dried anchovies; they don't have enough flavor for stock.

12 to 15 large dried anchovies, intestines and heads removed (see page 427)

1 pound Korean radish or daikon, peeled and sliced into ⅓-inch-thick rounds

1 ounce dried kelp (aka kombu)

1 medium onion (about 7 ounces), sliced thin

1 daepa (large green onion) or 4 to 6 scallions, cut crosswise into 2-inch-long pieces

1. In a large pot, combine 4½ quarts (18 cups) water and the anchovies, radish, kelp, onion, and daepa or scallions. Cover and cook over medium-high heat for 30 minutes. If the mixture begins to boil over, uncover, stir, and then cover with the lid slightly cracked.

2. Lower the heat to medium and boil, still covered, for 1 hour, until the radish is translucent and the broth is fragrant.

3. Reduce the heat to low and simmer, covered, for 10 minutes. Strain through a fine-mesh strainer over a large bowl (see pages 76 to 77 for ideas for reusing the radish and kelp). You will have 12 to 13 cups of clear stock.

4. Let cool and use whenever a recipe calls for stock. The stock can be stored in airtight containers in the refrigerator for up to 1 week or in the freezer for up to 3 months.

REUSING STOCK INGREDIENTS

Once you've made Anchovy-Kelp Stock or Vegetable Stock (page 78), be sure to reserve the radish and kelp; they can be stored in the refrigerator for up to 4 days. You can then make more delicious dishes.

Radish Pancakes

MU-JEON 무전

Serve with Soy-Vinegar Dipping Sauce (page 132) and rice or enjoy as a snack.

Serves 4

1 pound cooked sliced radish from Anchovy-Kelp Stock (page 74) or Vegetable Stock (page 78), each piece cut in half

1½ teaspoons kosher salt

1 cup all-purpose flour

1 cup Anchovy-Kelp Stock or Vegetable Stock

¼ to ⅓ cup vegetable oil, as needed

1. Spread the cooked radish slices out on a work surface side by side. Sprinkle ½ teaspoon of the salt evenly over the tops.

2. Combine the flour, remaining 1 teaspoon salt, and stock in a bowl to make the batter. Mix well.

3. Heat a nonstick skillet over medium-high heat. Add about 2 tablespoons vegetable oil and swirl the pan to coat evenly.

4. Dip each piece of radish into the batter by hand, making sure to coat both sides evenly, and transfer to the skillet. Get as much batter on the radish as you can. Work in batches so you don't overcrowd the skillet.

5. Cook for about 2 minutes, until the bottom is slightly crispy and lightly colored. Turn over with a spatula and cook for another 2 to 3 minutes, until the other side becomes light golden brown. Flip over and cook for another minute, then transfer to a plate and serve.

Stir-Fried Kelp

DASIMA-BOKKEUM 다시마볶음

Serve as a side dish with rice.

Serves 4

2 tablespoons vegetable oil

Cooked kelp (about 7 ounces) from Anchovy-Kelp Stock (page 74) or Vegetable Stock (page 78), cut into 1½-inch squares

1 small onion, sliced thin (about ½ cup)

1 garlic clove, minced

4 teaspoons soy sauce

2 teaspoons sugar

1. Heat the vegetable oil in a large skillet over medium-high heat. Add the kelp and stir-fry with a wooden spoon for 2 to 3 minutes, until the kelp looks a little shiny and springy.

2. Add the onion and garlic and stir-fry for 1 minute.

3. Add the soy sauce and sugar and stir-fry for another 1 to 2 minutes, until the onion becomes translucent. Remove from the heat and serve. The kelp will keep in the refrigerator for up to 3 days.

Vegetable Stock

YACHAE-GUKMUL 야채국물

Makes 2½ quarts

I developed this bright, flavorful vegetable stock as a fish-free alternative to Anchovy-Kelp Stock (page 74). Like that recipe, it can be used as a base for many dishes. It has a nice savory flavor from the dried kelp and shiitake mushrooms, and also tastes sweet because of the onion and the cabbage leaves.

   It took quite a few experiments to come up with the best mix of ingredients and the right proportions for this recipe, as even slight adjustments affected the flavor.

5 large dried shiitake mushrooms

1 ounce dried kelp (aka kombu)

1 pound Korean radish or daikon, peeled and cut crosswise into ½-inch-thick round slices or into quarters

1 large onion, sliced

1 daepa (large green onion) or 4 to 6 scallions, cut crosswise into 2-inch-long pieces

5 ounces green cabbage leaves (4 to 6 leaves), sliced (about 2 cups)

1. Combine the mushrooms, kelp, radish, onion, daepa or scallions, and cabbage leaves in a large pot. Add 4 quarts water, cover, and cook over medium-high heat for 30 minutes. If the mixture begins to boil over, uncover, stir, and then cover with the lid slightly cracked.

2. Turn down the heat to medium and boil for another 30 minutes, until the radish is translucent and the broth is fragrant.

3. Remove from the heat. Put a mesh strainer over a large bowl and strain (to reuse the radish and kelp, see pages 76 to 77; the mushrooms can be chopped and used in a stew or stir-fry). Refrigerate for up to 1 week or freeze for up to 3 months.

Beef Bone Broth

SAGOL-GUKMUL 사골국물

Makes 4 quarts

When Korean mothers have to leave their families for a few days, they often make a big cauldron of beef bone broth so their husbands and children can survive without Mom's cooking during her absence. It's become kind of a joke in families, even depicted on Korean TV comedies—a mother is cooking up a big pot of bone broth, so her children and husband are worried. "Where are you going?"

My mom used massive leg bones and cooked them in a huge pot. She boiled them for a long time throughout the day and into the night, until the broth was milky. Because she believed it had a lot of calcium in it, she made us drink it every day, thinking it would make us grow taller. Well, I'm still short, even though I had a lot of bone broth!

We consider bone broth to be very nutritious and rejuvenating. We believe that it makes you strong, so we bring it to friends and relatives who are sick or have just gotten out of the hospital. Sometimes we just make a gift of some good leg bones, which are prized and expensive.

To achieve a milky-white broth, it's important to soak the bones in cold water first, then blanch them in boiling water for 10 minutes. You'll be surprised at all the impurities and blood that emerge.

I give the timing for this recipe, but we Koreans never watch the clock when making bone broth. Instead, we let our eyes be the judge and boil until the bones are spent: soft and spongy, with all the marrow boiled out. They should be smooth, with nothing on them at all.

The resulting broth is rich, with a nutty aftertaste. I give you three ways for serving it.

4½ pounds sliced beef leg bones and/or knuckle bones

1. Rinse the bones in two or three changes of cold water. Place in a large bowl of cold water and soak for 1 hour to remove the blood. Drain and rinse well.

2. Bring a large, heavy pot of water to a boil over medium-high heat. Add the bones and cover. Boil for 10 minutes.

3. Drain the bones, rinse with cold running water, and drain well. Wash the pot thoroughly.

4. Put the bones in the clean pot. Add 6 quarts fresh water and cover. Cook over medium-low heat for 6 hours.

5. Add 2 quarts water, cover, and simmer for 4 hours. Repeat two more times; the total cooking time is 18 hours. The broth will be milky and the bones will be very smooth, with no meat attached.

6. Remove from the heat. Remove all the bones from the broth and discard. Let the broth cool to room temperature and refrigerate for at least 7 hours or preferably overnight. If the weather is cold, you can place the pot outside.

7. Remove and discard the thick layer of solid fat on the surface. Reheat the broth until liquified and serve hot. The broth can be refrigerated for 4 to 5 days or frozen for up to 1 month.

THREE WAYS TO SERVE BONE BROTH

- Serve the broth on its own, topped with chopped scallion.

- Ladle about 2½ cups hot bone broth into a bowl and serve with rice, chopped scallion, kosher salt and ground black pepper, kimchi, and other side dishes.

- Use for Rice Cake Soup with Bone Broth (page 62).

Beef Bone Broth (page 80) with various side dishes

Clear Soybean Paste Soup

MALGEUN-DOENJANGGUK 맑은 된장국

Serves 2

This soup is one of the easiest to make in this book. All you need is good fermented soybean paste and stock. The clarity and simplicity make this soup a good companion for spicier one-bowl rice dishes that have a lot of ingredients, like Bibimbap with Sliced Raw Fish (page 52) and Avocado, Mushroom, and Vegetable Bibimbap (page 54).

2½ cups Anchovy-Kelp Stock (page 74), Vegetable Stock (page 78), or unsalted chicken broth

2 tablespoons Korean fermented soybean paste (doenjang)

1 scallion, sliced

1. Pour the stock into a saucepan and set a strainer in the pot. (It can be submerged.) Spoon the soybean paste into the strainer.

2. Gently break up the paste in the strainer with a wooden spoon so that it sifts into the stock. Discard any dregs remaining in the strainer.

3. Cover the pot and bring to a boil over medium-high heat. As soon as it starts boiling—the cover of your pot will shake—remove from the heat.

4. Ladle the soup into two bowls. Sprinkle with scallion and serve.

Clockwise: Diced Radish Kimchi (page 116), Seasoned Salty Pickled Peppers
(page 258), Soybrean Sprout Soup, and Multigrain Rice (page 44)

Soybean Sprout Soup

KONGNAMULGUK 콩나물국

Serves 2 to 3

If you can make kongnamulguk well, you are considered a good Korean home cook. The mildly spicy broth tastes wonderful with the crispy-nutty soybean sprouts. I eat it with rice and also add well-fermented kimchi, mixing the rice, soup, and kimchi together in my bowl. It's a high-protein soup because of the soybean sprouts, and it's also high in vitamin C.

I learned this recipe from my aunt, who was a very good cook. Her special touch was to season her spicy broth with dried anchovies, which she wrapped in a soup pouch and removed after the soup was done.

6 large dried anchovies, cleaned (see page 427)

1 (12-ounce) package soybean sprouts, cleaned (see page 421) and drained

4 garlic cloves, minced

½ medium onion, sliced (about ½ cup)

1 tablespoon Korean hot pepper flakes (gochu-garu)

2 teaspoons fish sauce

2 teaspoons soy sauce

1 teaspoon kosher salt

2 scallions, sliced diagonally

2 teaspoons toasted sesame oil

1 tablespoon toasted sesame seeds, ground with a mortar and pestle or coffee grinder

1. Tie the anchovies in a piece of cheesecloth or a stock pouch.

2. In a medium saucepan, combine the soybean sprouts, garlic, onion, hot pepper flakes, fish sauce, soy sauce, and salt. Add the anchovy pouch and 5 cups water, cover, and cook for 20 minutes over medium-high heat. Add the scallions and stir with a wooden spoon. Reduce the heat to medium, cover, and cook for another 10 minutes. Remove from the heat. Remove the anchovy pouch and discard. Stir in the sesame oil.

3. Ladle into individual soup bowls, top each serving with sesame seed powder, and serve. The soup can be refrigerated for up to 4 days.

Soybean Paste Soup
with Cabbage

BAECHU-DOENJANGGUK 배추된장국

Serves 4

This is the soup we make most often at home: We eat it for breakfast, lunch, and dinner. I have one friend who, even after more than thirty years in New York, cannot go more than a few days without it. Whenever she travels with her husband, she seeks out a Korean restaurant so that she can get some. If they go on a cruise or someplace where there are no Korean restaurants, she brings the ingredients so that she can make it.

The broth has a deep, comforting flavor, and the cabbage adds texture and sweetness. It's light, since there is no grease in it, and after eating it I feel very healthy.

8 to 10 large dried anchovies, cleaned (see page 427)

1 pound napa cabbage leaves, white-stemmed chard, or bok choy

3 tablespoons Korean fermented soybean paste (doenjang)

4 garlic cloves, minced

2 green chili peppers, sliced diagonally

1 tablespoon all-purpose flour

2 teaspoons fish sauce

1. Tie the anchovies in a piece of cheesecloth or place them in a stock pouch.

2. Bring a large pot of water to a boil. Add the cabbage and blanch, stirring with a wooden spoon for 1 to 2 minutes, until the cabbage is just tender and a brighter shade of green. Drain and rinse in cold water to stop the cooking and remove any lingering dirt. Drain and squeeze out the excess water.

3. Chop the cabbage into small pieces and put them in the same pot. Add the soybean paste, garlic, chili peppers, flour, and fish sauce. Mix the ingredients together by hand or with a wooden spoon, then add the anchovy pouch and 6 cups water.

4. Cover and cook over medium-high heat for about 25 minutes, until the cabbage is very tender and the anchovy flavor is fully infused. Crack the lid if the soup boils over. Reduce the heat to medium and cook, covered, for another 5 minutes.

5. Remove the anchovy pouch and discard. Ladle the soup into bowls and serve.

Soybean Paste Stew
with Beef

SOGOGI DOENJANG-JJIGAE 소고기 된장찌개

Serves 4

I was recently asked by a TV producer to name Korea's national dishes. My answer? Without hesitation, kimchi, rice, and soybean paste stew, a comforting, economical dish that has been a cornerstone of Korean cuisine for centuries.

The key to any successful doenjang-jjigae, in all its variations, is in the broth, which, along with every step and ingredient in the recipe, serves to bring out and accentuate the transformative properties of doenjang, fermented soybean paste. The classic stew calls for anchovy stock, along with seafood. But this recipe uses thinly sliced brisket with a bit of fat. You can also make a vegetarian version of doenjang-jjigae using mushrooms for the broth (see the variation at right).

You can serve this stew in any type of bowl, but for the full effect, serve it in a Korean earthenware bowl, straight from the burner and still bubbling hot. Traditional Korean earthenware bowls will hold the heat right up until you finish eating.

4 ounces beef brisket, sliced thin

2 garlic cloves, minced

1 medium potato, peeled and cut into ½-inch dice (about ¾ cup)

1 medium onion, cut into ½-inch dice (about 1 cup)

1 small zucchini, cut into ½-inch dice (about 1 cup)

¼ cup Korean fermented soybean paste (doenjang)

1 teaspoon Korean hot pepper paste (gochujang; optional)

8 ounces medium-firm tofu, cut into ½-inch pieces

1 green chili pepper or jalapeño, sliced

1 scallion, cut into ½-inch pieces

1. Place a heavy 1½- to 2-quart pot or earthenware bowl over medium-high heat. When it is hot, add the beef and garlic and cook, stirring, for 2 minutes, until the beef is no longer pink. Add 2 cups water. Cover and cook for 10 minutes. If it begins to boil over, crack the lid.

2. Add the potato, onion, zucchini, fermented soybean paste, and hot pepper paste (if using). Cover, reduce the heat to medium, and cook for another 10 minutes. If the soup begins to boil over, crack the lid.

3. Stir the stew to make sure that the soybean paste is evenly incorporated. Add the tofu, green chili pepper, and scallion. Cook, uncovered, for about 3 minutes, until the tofu softens and the stew is bubbling. Serve. You can refrigerate the stew for up to 3 days. Reheat gently on top of the stove.

VARIATION

Vegetarian Soybean Paste Stew with Mushrooms
Substitute 3 dried shiitake mushrooms for the beef. Put the mushrooms in a bowl, add 2½ cups warm water, and leave to soak for 3 to 4 hours, until the mushrooms are soft and the water is fragrant and lightly colored. Set a strainer over a bowl and drain. Cut the mushrooms into small pieces and measure out 2 cups of the broth. In Step 1, stir-fry the mushrooms with the garlic for 2 minutes and add the reserved 2 cups of broth instead of water. Cover and cook over medium-high heat for 10 minutes. Continue as directed.

Seaweed Soup

MIYEOKGUK 미역국

Serves 4

Koreans have a special attachment to seaweed soup because we believe it helps moms recover quickly after childbirth. New mothers eat it with rice for a full month after having a baby. Because of this tradition, Korean moms always prepare this soup for breakfast on their children's birthdays. Even after children have grown up and no longer live at home, their moms will call to wish them a happy birthday, and the first question is always: "Did you make miyeokguk?" The children answer by saying, "Thank you for bringing me into this world, Mom!"

A few years ago, I traveled to Costa Rica with my daughter. Because I knew her birthday would be during the trip, I hid a small amount of miyeok soup ingredients in my backpack. On that morning, I surprised her by making miyeokguk in our hotel room. It made her very happy; she knew how much I loved her.

I usually add beef, as in this recipe, but you can also use fresh fish, clams, mussels, shrimp, or oysters. Or you can make a vegetarian miyeokguk, using vegetable stock instead of water

½ ounce (about 1 cup) dried miyeok (aka wakame), rinsed and soaked in cold water for 30 minutes

1 pound beef brisket or skirt steak, cut into thin strips, about 1 inch by ½ inch and ¼ inch thick

4 garlic cloves, minced

5 teaspoons fish sauce

1 teaspoon toasted sesame oil

1. Drain the miyeok and transfer to a cutting board. Cut into bite-size pieces.

2. In a large pot, combine the miyeok and 8 cups water. Cover and cook over medium-high heat for 10 minutes, until it is vigorously boiling.

3. Add the beef, cover, and cook for 30 minutes.

4. Stir in the garlic and fish sauce. Reduce the heat to medium, cover, and cook for 20 minutes, or until the broth is savory and the beef is tender.

5. Stir in the sesame oil. Ladle into bowls and serve. The soup can be refrigerated in an airtight container for up to 4 days.

Spicy Beef and Radish Soup

MAEUN-SOGOGI-MUGUK 매운소고기무국

Serves 2

This spicy soup comes from Gyeongsang province in southeast Korea. In Korean cuisine, beef and radishes are good friends. Both the sweet flavor of the radish and the meaty flavor of the steak permeate the broth for a soup that is doubly savory. Be sure to slice the radish into thin pieces.

I usually use skirt steak because its tender but chewy texture contrasts so nicely with the crispy soybean sprouts. Add a whole bowl of rice to the hot, steaming soup, and with the rice, vegetables, meat, and spice, you'll have a satisfyingly hearty and balanced meal.

2 teaspoons toasted sesame oil

8 ounces trimmed skirt steak, cut into bite-size pieces

8 ounces Korean radish or daikon, peeled and cut into bite-size pieces, about 1 inch by 1½ inches and ⅛ inch thick

1 tablespoon Korean hot pepper flakes (gochu-garu)

4 garlic cloves, minced

6 ounces soybean sprouts (about 2 cups), cleaned (see page 421) and drained

5 ounces white mushrooms or king oyster mushrooms, sliced (about 2 cups)

4 scallions, sliced diagonally into 1½-inch-long pieces

4 teaspoons fish sauce

1 teaspoon kosher salt

1. Heat the sesame oil in a large, heavy saucepan over medium-high heat. Add the beef and stir with a wooden spoon for about 2 minutes, until the beef is fragrant and no longer pink.

2. Add the radish and stir for about 2 minutes, until the radish becomes slightly translucent. Add the hot pepper flakes and stir for about 1 minute, until the radish is shiny and well coated with the hot pepper flakes.

3. Add the garlic, soybean sprouts, mushrooms, and 5 cups water. Cover and cook for 15 minutes. If the soup boils over, crack the lid.

4. Add the scallions, fish sauce, and salt. Cover, reduce the heat to medium, and cook for 20 to 25 minutes, until the radish is translucent.

5. Remove from the heat and serve.

Salty Pickled Peppers
(page 256), Oxtail
Soup, Fluffy White
Rice (page 41); *middle:*
seasoning paste

Oxtail Soup

SOKKORITANG 소꼬리탕

Serves 4

The collagen in the oxtails gives this broth substantial body without making it fatty or greasy. You can find packaged, cut oxtails in most Korean grocery stores and regular supermarkets.

When I lived in Columbia, Missouri, I used to get together with other Korean immigrant housewives on a regular basis for a potluck party. We'd often tell funny stories about our lives as expats in the U.S. We had all studied English in Korea, but sometimes simple vocabulary escaped us and we needed to improvise. One lady told the story of trying to buy oxtails at a huge American grocery store. She didn't know the word in English but asked a salesclerk for "cow" and then mooed and flapped her hand around her behind like a tail. The salesclerk laughed, but he understood!

It's best to make this a few days before you wish to serve it so that you can chill the broth overnight and remove the fat from the top. The bones need to soak for 3 hours, and then the soup cooks for 2 hours 20 minutes. There is some good meat lodged between the bones, and after the long simmer, it becomes very tender and moist. It will fall off the bone with a little prodding of your chopsticks. But if you boil the oxtail for too long, the meat will come right off the bone into the soup, which you don't want.

Oxtail soup and fermented, crispy Diced Radish Kimchi (page 116) go well together, along with rice, of course. I also serve a spicy paste on the side, plus bowls of kosher salt and ground black pepper, so everybody at the table can season their soup as they wish.

FOR THE OXTAIL BROTH

2½ pounds skinned oxtails

1½ pounds Korean radish or daikon, peeled and cut in half lengthwise

4 garlic cloves, minced

Kosher salt

FOR THE SEASONING PASTE (OPTIONAL)

1 tablespoon soy sauce

1 tablespoon toasted sesame oil

1 garlic clove, minced

2 tablespoons Korean hot pepper flakes (gochu-garu)

FOR SERVING

1 daepa (large green onion) or 6 scallions, thinly sliced

Kosher salt

Ground black pepper

MAKE THE OXTAIL BROTH

1. Trim away and discard any excess solid fat attached to the oxtail pieces. Place the oxtails in a large bowl and rinse a few times with cold water. Cover with cold water and soak for 3 hours, changing the water every hour.

2. Bring 2½ quarts water to a boil in a heavy pot over medium-high heat. Add the oxtails and boil for 12 minutes. Foam and bubbles will accumulate on the surface of the water, and the water will be brownish. Drain and rinse the bones thoroughly.

3. Wash out the pot. Add the oxtail bones, radish, garlic, 2 teaspoons salt, and 4 quarts fresh water. Cover and place over medium-high heat. It should come to a rolling boil in about 20 minutes; at that point, reduce the heat to medium-low and simmer, still covered, for about 2 hours, until the radish is fully cooked and the meat is very tender but still attached to the bones.

4. Remove the pot from the heat. Transfer the bones and radish to a bowl and let cool. Put the bones in an airtight container and refrigerate. Cut the radish into bite-size pieces, about 1½ inches by 1 inch and ½ inch thick. Put the radish in an airtight container and refrigerate.

Recipe Continues

5. Let the broth cool to room temperature. Refrigerate for several hours or overnight, until the fat floats to the top and solidifies. Remove and discard the solid fat with a spoon or a skimmer. You should have 9 to 10 cups of bone broth.

MAKE THE SEASONING PASTE (IF USING)

Combine the soy sauce, sesame oil, garlic, and hot pepper flakes in a small bowl and mix well. Cover and refrigerate.

SERVE

1. Add the oxtail bones to the pot of broth and bring to a boil over high heat.

2. For each serving, put about ¼ cup chopped daepa or scallion in a large soup bowl. Top with 6 or 7 pieces of cooked radish. Add a few pieces of oxtail bones and ladle in the hot broth. Serve with the seasoning paste (if using), and set bowls of salt and pepper on the table. Or, you can ladle the soup into earthenware bowls (see sidebar).

TO SERVE IN EARTHENWARE BOWLS

Bring the broth with the oxtail bones to a boil following the directions above in Step 1. Proceed with Step 2, but instead of serving, divide among earthenware bowls and heat directly over high heat until bubbling.

Kimchi Stew

KIMCHI-JJIGAE 김치찌개

Serves 4

We use kimchi for so much more than a side dish. When I lived in Missouri, a friend from China came to pick me up for the picnic of the English class we were taking. As I opened my fridge to get the dishes I'd prepared, she looked astonished at the sight of my huge container of kimchi.

I never had a chance to explain why I'd made so much, but when you taste this stew of simmered kimchi and juicy, fatty pork belly in a spicy, flavorful broth, you'll understand why having plenty of kimchi on hand is always a good idea.

Recently one of my followers commented that her stew wasn't flavorful enough. After some discussion, I realized she was using freshly made kimchi. That won't work at all. You have to use well-fermented kimchi for this recipe. It softens as it simmers but still retains a bit of crunchiness, and the sour taste gives the stew its distinctive flavor.

Serve with rice.

1 pound fermented Traditional Napa Cabbage Kimchi (page 112), cut into 1-inch pieces

¼ cup fermented kimchi brine (optional)

1 pound pork belly or pork shoulder, cut into bite-size pieces, about 1 inch square and ¼ inch thick

1 medium onion, sliced (about 1 cup)

1 daepa (large green onion) or 4 scallions, sliced diagonally

1 tablespoon Korean hot pepper paste (gochujang)

1 tablespoon Korean hot pepper flakes (gochu-garu)

2 teaspoons sugar

1 teaspoon kosher salt

2 teaspoons toasted sesame oil

2½ cups Anchovy-Kelp Stock (page 74) or unsalted chicken or beef broth

8 ounces medium-firm tofu, sliced ¼ inch thick

1 scallion, sliced, for garnish

1. Combine the kimchi, kimchi brine (if using), pork, onion, daepa or scallions, hot pepper paste, hot pepper flakes, sugar, salt, sesame oil, and stock in a large, shallow pot. Cover and cook over medium-high heat for 10 minutes. If the mixture begins to boil over, uncover, stir, and then cover with the lid slightly cracked.

Recipe Continues

2. Uncover and stir the stew with a large spoon. Lay the tofu over the top and reduce the heat to medium. Cover and cook for another 15 minutes, cracking the lid if the soup bubbles over, or until the pork is thoroughly cooked and the kimchi is tender.

3. Sprinkle with the scallion and serve.

VARIATION

Vegetarian Kimchi Stew

Substitute king oyster, fresh shiitake, or white mushrooms for the pork. Cut into thick slices. Use Vegetable Stock (page 78) instead of Anchovy-Kelp Stock.

TOFU STEW

Sundubu-jjigae is a spicy, seasoned stew made with a type of silky soft tofu called sundubu. Served hot at the table in its traditional earthenware bowl, it's impossible to resist.

Chodang village in Gangwon province in Korea is well known for its traditional methods of making sundubu, handed down over generations. The key is the bright, clean seawater they use from the East Sea, which has just the right amount of magnesium chloride to perfectly coagulate the tofu.

Sundubu-jjigae became popular after Hee-sook Lee opened a restaurant, BCD Tofu House, in Los Angeles in 1996. She created many kinds of sundubu-jjigae, including kimchi, pork, beef, seafood, and vegetarian versions, all with different levels of spiciness. Now there are BCD restaurants in several countries. The one in Toronto is my favorite: The stews taste the best and their earthenware bowls are the largest.

North Americans sometimes freak out because a raw egg is added just before the stew is served. But you don't have to worry, because the egg cooks in the steaming broth. Usually I finish about half the stew before I eat the egg. By this time, it is cooked, and I break it up and mix it in.

I continue the tradition Hee-sook Lee began at BCD by offering recipes for seafood, vegetarian, and meat-lover's sundubu-jjigae in this book.

HOW TO SERVE SUNDUBU-JJIGAE IN KOREAN EARTHENWARE BOWLS

Divide the stew into Korean earthenware bowls. (A 3-cup bowl is perfect for one serving.) Put the bowls directly on stovetop burners over medium-high heat. Crack an egg into the center of each bowl and heat until bubbling. Sprinkle with scallion and serve with rice, kimchi, and more side dishes.

Spicy Soft Tofu Stew with Meat

GOGI SUNDUBU-JJIGAE 고기 순두부찌개

Serves 2 generously

You need only a small amount of meat (gogi) to enrich the stock of this stew with a deep flavor. I use either skirt steak, pork tenderloin, or chicken breast—all cuts that cook quickly in the broth. I also add chewy shiitake mushrooms, which contribute even more savory depth.

You can vary the heat to your taste. I like it spicy, so I use the full ¼ cup of hot pepper flakes. But even half that amount adds plenty of flavor and spice.

¼ cup Korean hot pepper flakes (gochu-garu)

2 teaspoons toasted sesame oil

¼ teaspoon ground black pepper

1 tablespoon vegetable oil

½ medium onion, diced

2 garlic cloves, minced

4 ounces beef skirt steak, pork tenderloin, or boneless, skinless chicken breast, cut into small pieces

2 dried shiitake mushrooms, soaked in cold water for 4 to 5 hours until soft, drained, and cut into ¼-inch pieces

2 cups Anchovy-Kelp Stock (page 74) or unsalted chicken broth

2 (11-ounce) tubes soft tofu (page 34) or 22 ounces silken tofu

2 tablespoons fish sauce

2 large eggs

2 scallions, chopped

1. Combine the hot pepper flakes, sesame oil, and black pepper in a small bowl and mix well with a spoon until the hot pepper flakes absorb all the oil. Set aside.

2. Heat the vegetable oil in a large saucepan over medium-high heat. Add the onion and garlic and stir with a wooden spoon for 2 to 4 minutes, until the onion turns slightly brown and crispy.

3. Add the meat and shiitakes and stir for 2 to 3 minutes, until the meat is lightly colored.

4. Add the stock. Cover and cook for 5 to 7 minutes, until the meat is fully cooked and the stew is boiling vigorously.

5. Cut the tubes of tofu in half and squeeze them into the boiling stew. If using silken tofu, scoop or squeeze from the box into the stew. Break up the tofu in the stew with a wooden spoon, then stir in the hot pepper mixture and the fish sauce. Cover and cook for 3 to 4 minutes, until bubbling.

6. Carefully crack the eggs into the boiling stew and cook for another minute. Gently ladle the stew into two soup bowls without disturbing the eggs. Scoop up each egg and place one in each bowl. Sprinkle with the scallions and serve. Or, to serve in Korean earthenware bowls, see page 101.

Spicy Soft Tofu Stew with Seafood

HAEMUL SUNDUBU-JJIGAE 해물 순두부찌개

Serves 2

When given the choice at a sundubu restaurant (see page 101), I always choose the seafood option. In my homemade version I combine mussels, shrimp, squid, and oysters to make a hearty, savory stew. I like my sundubu-jjigae spicy, but even 1 tablespoon of hot pepper flakes will be delicious.

4 medium shrimp (about 3 ounces) in the shell

¼ cup Korean hot pepper flakes (gochu-garu)

2 teaspoons toasted sesame oil

¼ teaspoon ground black pepper

1 tablespoon vegetable oil

½ medium onion, diced

2 garlic cloves, minced

¼ leek, thinly sliced on the diagonal into 2½-inch-long pieces

2 cups Anchovy-Kelp Stock (page 74)

2 (11-ounce) tubes soft tofu (see page 34) or 22 ounces silken tofu

2 ounces squid body or tentacles, cleaned (see page 431) and cut into bite-size pieces

4 large fresh or frozen mussels, shucked and rinsed

4 medium fresh or frozen oysters, shucked and rinsed (optional)

2 tablespoons fish sauce

2 large eggs

2 scallions, chopped

1. Using scissors, cut down the back of the shrimp shell and make a shallow slit down the length of it, exposing the dark vein that runs down the center. Insert a toothpick about ¼ inch deep between the second and third segments on the back of each shrimp and gently pull up the vein and remove. Rinse and pat dry. Refrigerate until you are ready to use.

2. Combine the hot pepper flakes, sesame oil, and black pepper in a small bowl and mix well with a spoon until the hot pepper flakes absorb all the oil. Set aside.

3. Heat the vegetable oil in a large saucepan over medium-high heat. Add the onion, garlic, and leek and stir with a wooden spoon until the onion and leek are slightly brown and crispy, 2 to 4 minutes. Add the stock. Cover and cook for 5 to 6 minutes more, until boiling vigorously.

4. Cut the tubes of tofu in half and squeeze them into the boiling stew. If using silken tofu, scoop or squeeze from the box into the stew. Break up the tofu in the stew with a wooden spoon, then add the hot pepper mixture, along with the shrimp, squid, mussels, and oysters (if using). Add the fish sauce and stir a few times.

5. Cover and cook for 5 to 6 minutes, until all the seafood is fully cooked and the broth is infused with its savory flavor.

6. Carefully crack the eggs into the boiling stew and cook for another minute. Gently ladle the stew into two soup bowls without disturbing the eggs. Scoop up each egg and place one in each bowl. Sprinkle with the scallions and serve. Or, to serve in Korean earthenware bowls, see page 101.

Spicy Soft Tofu Stew with Vegetables

YACHAE SUNDUBU-JJIGAE 야채 순두부찌개

Serves 2

I created this stew especially for vegetarians. It's actually vegan, because instead of the traditional egg, I enrich the stew with ground sesame seeds, which I add just before serving. I love all the different textures in this dish—creamy tofu, crisp-tender cauliflower, and chewy mushrooms.

¼ cup Korean hot pepper flakes (gochu-garu)

2 teaspoons toasted sesame oil

¼ teaspoon ground black pepper

1 tablespoon vegetable oil

½ medium onion, diced

2 garlic cloves, minced

¼ leek, sliced thinly on the diagonal into 2½-inch-long pieces

4 ounces cauliflower florets (about 1⅓ cups)

2 dried shiitake mushrooms, soaked in cold water for 4 to 5 hours until soft, drained, and cut into ¼-inch pieces

½ teaspoon soy sauce

2 cups Vegetable Stock (page 78)

2 (11-ounce) tubes soft tofu (see page 34) or 22 ounces silken tofu

1½ teaspoons kosher salt

1 tablespoon toasted sesame seeds, ground with a mortar and pestle or coffee grinder

2 scallions, chopped

1. Combine the pepper flakes, sesame oil, and black pepper in a small bowl and mix well with a spoon until the hot pepper flakes absorb all the oil. Set aside.

2. Heat the vegetable oil in a large saucepan over medium-high heat. Add the onion, garlic, and leek and stir with a wooden spoon until the onion and leek turn slightly brown and crispy, 2 to 4 minutes. Add the cauliflower, mushrooms, and soy sauce and cook, stirring, until the mushrooms are tender, 2 to 3 minutes.

3. Add the stock. Cover and cook for 5 to 6 minutes more, until the stew is boiling vigorously.

4. Cut the tubes of tofu in half and squeeze them into the boiling stew. If using silken tofu, scoop or squeeze from the box into the stew. Break up the tofu in the stew with a wooden spoon, then stir in the hot pepper mixture and salt. Cover and cook for 3 to 4 minutes, until bubbling.

5. Ladle the stew into two soup bowls, top with the ground sesame seeds and scallions, and serve. Or, to serve in Korean earthenware bowls, see page 101.

KIMCHI

MORE IS BETTER

Koreans have been making kimchi for thousands of years as a way to preserve fresh and in-season vegetables and enhance their flavors. The techniques have been passed down from mother to daughter, mother-in-law to daughter-in-law, and family to family. During kimchi-making season in the late fall, when cabbages are at their best, communities gather together to make huge batches that will sustain them through the long winter. We also have quicker kimchis for summer and spring that are meant to be eaten over just a few days or weeks, like Cucumber Water Kimchi. I've also given you a recipe for Vegetarian Kimchi in this chapter.

All our senses are activated when we eat kimchi, by its flavor, color, aroma, texture, and even its sound. For that reason, it's a great companion to everything, and we eat it at nearly every meal. It can be fresh like a salad or fermented over days, weeks, even months. Kimchi is usually served as a side dish with rice, and it's also a main ingredient in many other Korean dishes, like Noodle Soup with Kimchi Seasoning (page 65) and Kimchi Stew (page 99). While the most popular kind is made with napa cabbage, kimchi can also be made with many other vegetables, such as mustard greens, Korean radish, bok choy, and cucumber.

Once a baby begins to eat rice, a mother's first choice for a side dish is kimchi. We wash it off to remove the spiciness, then cut or tear it into very small pieces, and put a tiny piece on top of a tiny amount of rice on a spoon. We are proud when we see our babies enjoying kimchi.

Making kimchi is easy. The bacteria that do the work are already in the vegetables, waiting for the right salty, moist conditions. These bacteria create lactic acid and carbon dioxide, which preserve the color and texture of the vegetables as they ferment. At the same time, the bacteria block other harmful bacteria from growing.

Kimchi tastes best—nicely acidic with a wonderfully satisfying crispness—when it is at its peak fermentation. After that it begins to get sour, and the vegetables get softer. Under the right conditions and made with a lot of salt, it will remain edible for years, but generally, it will become increasingly sour and soft over time.

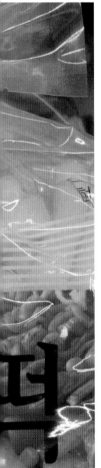

ONGGI

KOREAN EARTHENWARE

Traditional Korean earthenware crocks, jars, and bowls can be used for so many things: soybean paste, soy sauce, hot pepper paste, fermented salty fish (jeotgal 젓갈), alcoholic drinks, bubbling soup or stew (ttukbaegi 뚝배기), and, of course, kimchi. They're made from untreated clay, which when fired has many microscopic holes in the surface. These holes allow gas to pass in and out, which is perfect for fermentation: The fermenting item gets oxygen when it needs it, and the gases that are expelled during fermentation are released.

The term *onggi* includes the entire range of Korean pottery, tableware, and tools made by firing clay in this particular way. But most of the time when Koreans talk about onggi, they mean the most common kind of earthenware crocks. Many Koreans also refer to onggi by their size: danji 단지, a small jar; hangari 항아리, a medium jar; and dok 독, a very large jar. The dok are so big that a person can hide inside one, and indeed, during the Korean War many families hid their daughters in their doks to protect them from enemy soldiers.

Korean earthenware can be hard to find outside of Korea. The crocks are heavy and fragile, so not many stores will ship them. If you want one, you'll probably have to visit the kitchenware section of a Korean grocery. Look up! Though sometimes onggi are stocked on the floor, they're usually displayed high above everything else, in boxes. Ask one of the stockpeople to help you find them.

I prefer onggi to glass or plastic containers. They look better and ferment better, resulting in better kimchi. I have a collection of danji and hangari in the corner of my New York City apartment. It's my modern version of the traditional Korean jangdokdae, the place where a family would store all their onggi crocks and jars in the days when everyone fermented their own pastes, sauces, and side dishes. Not only are home-fermented dishes more delicious than store-bought, but I feel like I am part of Korean tradition and history when I make them.

CLEANING ONGGI

When you wash onggi, don't use soap, because it will get into and remain in the microscopic holes, and you'll taste it in your food. I use coffee grounds if there is something really greasy in the onggi to clean. Put some on a washcloth or sponge with some water and scrub vigorously, then rinse well. After cooking in an earthenware pot, I use a wire scrubber to clean anything that has stuck to the bottom.

After fermenting seafood such as Fermented Clams (page 259), I fill the onggi with hot water and let it sit for 24 hours. Rinse and repeat until the smell is gone.

Traditional Napa Cabbage Kimchi

TONGBAECHU-KIMCHI 통배추김치

Makes about 4 pounds

The name for this kimchi is "whole napa cabbage" because you do not cut the cabbage into small pieces when you make it, although you can cut it into smaller pieces when you serve it. This kimchi is very pretty because the stacked cabbage leaves look orderly when they are cut.

When I visited Korea a few years ago, I had a meetup potluck party with my YouTube viewers in Seoul. It was late fall, so Korean cabbage was abundant everywhere and at its peak. To make kimchi, I chose a huge, good-looking head of cabbage that weighed a little more than 8 pounds—quite a normal size for batches in Korea. But some of my readers have been requesting smaller batches for years, so I finally developed a recipe that calls for only a small head.

This is the smallest amount of tongbaechu-kimchi that I can imagine making. If you want a bigger batch, double, triple, or quadruple this recipe. And if your cabbage is larger than 3 pounds, simply remove some leaves. I use 1 cup of hot pepper flakes, but some of my readers tell me that my spicy is their deadly, so use less if you want it milder.

1 (3-pound) head napa cabbage

6 tablespoons kosher salt

2 tablespoons glutinous rice flour or all-purpose flour

1 tablespoon sugar

9 garlic cloves, peeled

1 teaspoon minced peeled ginger

¼ medium Korean pear or ½ Bosc pear, peeled, cored, and cut into chunks

½ medium onion, cut into chunks

¼ cup fish sauce

1 tablespoon salty fermented shrimp (sauejeot)

1 cup Korean hot pepper flakes (gochu-garu) or to taste

6 ounces Korean radish or daikon, peeled and cut into matchsticks

1 small carrot, cut into matchsticks (about ⅓ cup)

3 ounces Asian chives or 6 scallions, chopped (about 1 cup)

3 scallions, sliced diagonally

Toasted sesame seeds (for fresh kimchi)

1. Cut a 3-inch slit through the core of the cabbage. Using both hands, split the cabbage in half by pulling the cabbage apart at the slit. Cut a 2-inch slit just through the core of each half so that the leaves are loosened but still attached to the core and the cabbage half is intact.

2. Fill a large bowl with water and dunk the cabbage in the water. Drain the water and put the cabbage back in the bowl.

3. Sprinkle the salt between the leaves, more on the thick white ribs than on the thinner green leaves. Let stand for 2 hours, turning the cabbage over every 30 minutes to distribute the salt evenly.

4. Meanwhile, combine the flour and 1 cup water in a small saucepan and place over medium-high heat. Stir until the mixture begins to bubble, 2 to 3 minutes. Add the sugar and stir until the mixture is slightly translucent and has the consistency of a runny porridge, 2 to 3 minutes. Remove from the heat and let cool thoroughly.

5. Drain the cabbage, place the bowl in the kitchen sink, and fill it with cold water. Split the cabbage halves in half again and rinse under cold running water. Swish the cabbage around in the water to remove any dirt between the leaves. Change the water a few times and repeat until very clean. Put the clean cabbage in a colander to drain well. Dry the bowl.

Recipe Continues

KEEPING KIMCHI

Kimchi can last for a long time if it's made with enough salt and kept at low (but not freezing) temperatures. It's light and crispy at the beginning, deepens in flavor as it reaches peak fermentation, and then sours and softens as it ages further. You can enjoy it at any of these stages. I like the crispy texture and spicy, heavy, savory flavor when it's freshly made, but I also like its pungent and sour flavors when it's at its peak. After the peak, it's perfect to use in Kimchi Stew (page 99), Noodle Soup with Kimchi Seasoning (page 65), and Stir-Fried Kimchi with Tuna Dosirak (page 282). When I see that my kimchi is running low, I make more.

In the summer, my grandmother made small quantities of kimchi often, storing them in her small onggi jar, which she placed in a basin next to her well. A couple of times a day, she carefully poured cold water from the well into the basin so it kept the onggi cool. In the winter, she made a large batch and kept it in crocks buried in the ground just up to the lids to keep the temperature regulated and prevent them from freezing.

These days some people still store kimchi in onggi, but most people keep their kimchi in plastic or glass containers in the refrigerator (even those who use onggi refrigerate the crocks). We open the containers every day to take out some kimchi, so the gases are always being released. But if you do not eat kimchi often and you're keeping it in a sealed container, open occasionally to let out the gases from fermentation; otherwise it may explode from the pressure!

To keep the inside of my fridge smelling fresh, I used to double-wrap my kimchi container in plastic bags, but I've discovered that placing a bowl of fresh coffee grounds in the refrigerator and changing it daily filters the air perfectly. Some of my readers use baking soda or even activated charcoal (the kind used in fish tanks).

6. Put the garlic, ginger, pear, and onion in a food processor and process to a puree. Transfer to the bowl.

7. Add the cooled flour mixture to the bowl, along with the garlic puree, fish sauce, fermented shrimp, and hot pepper flakes. Mix well with a wooden spoon. Add the radish, carrot, chives, and scallions and mix well.

8. Cut away as much of the cabbage cores as you can, taking care to leave each quarter intact. If the cabbage is still wet, squeeze gently to remove excess water.

9. Spread some garlic paste from the bowl over each leaf by hand (wear disposable gloves if you like), then put the quarters in one or more glass jars or airtight containers. Press down on the kimchi so it's well packed and no air can get inside, then put the lid on the container.

10. You can serve the kimchi right away, sprinkled with toasted sesame seeds. (We don't serve fermented kimchi with sesame seeds.) Or you can let the kimchi ferment. It takes about 2 weeks to ferment in the refrigerator; for faster fermenting, leave it at room temperature for 1 to 2 days, depending on the warmth of your kitchen, until the kimchi smells and tastes sour. Before serving, put the kimchi on a cutting board, cut into bite-size pieces, and transfer to a plate or a small shallow bowl. Store in the refrigerator and use as needed, until the kimchi runs out. The kimchi will continue to ferment in the refrigerator and become more sour. You can enjoy it at every stage. Whenever you remove kimchi from the jar, be sure to press down on the remaining kimchi with a spoon to prevent it from being exposed to air.

Diced Radish Kimchi

KKAKDUGI 깍두기

Makes about 5 pounds

Kimchi made with large Korean radishes is the second most popular kimchi, after Traditional Napa Cabbage Kimchi (page 112). It's great both freshly made and fermented, so you can eat some of it right after you make it and put the rest aside. Well-fermented kkakdugi is always served with rice and goes well with just about any Korean soup or stew, especially Soybean Sprout Soup (page 87) and Oxtail Soup (page 97).

5 pounds Korean radish or daikon, peeled and cut into ¾-inch dice	1 cup Korean hot pepper flakes (gochu-garu) or to taste
3 tablespoons kosher salt	⅓ cup fish sauce or ½ cup store-bought soup soy sauce
3 tablespoons sugar	
10 scallions, chopped	2 tablespoons salty fermented shrimp (sauejeot), chopped
7 garlic cloves, minced	
2 teaspoons minced peeled ginger	

1. In a large bowl, combine the radish, salt, and sugar and mix by hand. Let stand for 1 hour, tossing every 20 minutes to distribute the salt evenly.

2. Place a strainer over another bowl and drain the radishes. Reserve ½ cup of the brine and discard the rest.

3. Put the radishes back in the bowl and add the scallions, garlic, ginger, hot pepper flakes, fish sauce, fermented shrimp, and reserved brine. Mix together by hand until well incorporated. (Wear disposable gloves if you like.) Transfer to one or more glass jars or airtight containers. Press down on the kimchi so it's well packed and no air can get inside, then put the lid on the container.

4. You can serve the kimchi right away or let it ferment. To ferment the kimchi, store it at cool room temperature for 1 or 2 days, until it smells and tastes sour. After a day, there will be quite a bit of liquid in the jar or container. When you open the jar, the mixture may be bubbling. Press down on the kimchi so that it's submerged in brine, cover, and refrigerate. The kimchi will continue to ferment in the refrigerator and become more sour. You can enjoy it at every stage. Whenever you remove kimchi from the jar, be sure to press down on the remaining kimchi with a spoon to prevent it from being exposed to air.

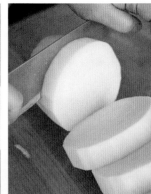

Vegetarian Kimchi

CHAESIK KIMCHI 채식 김치

Makes about 4 pounds

When my vegetarian and vegan readers around the world attempt to make vegan versions of my kimchi recipes, the number one question is what to use instead of fish sauce and fermented shrimp. In the past, I suggested soy sauce, but I was never completely satisfied with that recommendation because it alters the bright color of the kimchi and makes it a little brownish. After some experimentation, I came up with this recipe, which uses a mix of vegetable stock and salt. I'm pleased with the results!

I'm grateful to my vegetarian readers and viewers for requesting this. Now I can make it when my vegetarian friends come over, or when I'm looking for a bit of a change.

1 (3-pound) head napa cabbage

9 tablespoons kosher salt

2 tablespoons glutinous rice flour or all-purpose flour

1⅓ cups Vegetable Stock (page 78)

1 tablespoon plus 1 teaspoon sugar

9 garlic cloves, peeled

1 teaspoon minced peeled ginger

1 medium onion, cut into chunks (about ¾ cup)

1 cup Korean hot pepper flakes (gochu-garu) or to taste

6 ounces Korean radish or daikon, peeled and cut into matchsticks

3 ounces Asian chives or 6 scallions, cut into ½-inch-long pieces (about 1 cup)

1 small carrot, peeled and cut into matchsticks (about ⅓ cup)

6 scallions, sliced diagonally

Toasted sesame seeds (for fresh kimchi)

1. Cut the cabbage lengthwise into quarters. Cut away the core of each quarter. Cut the leaves crosswise into 1- to 1½-inch-long pieces and transfer to a large bowl. Toss with 6 tablespoons of the salt and 1 cup water. Let stand for 2 hours, tossing the cabbage every 30 minutes to salt evenly.

2. Meanwhile, combine the flour and 1 cup of the vegetable stock in a small saucepan and place over medium-high heat. Stir until the mixture begins to bubble, 2 to 3 minutes. Add 1 tablespoon of the sugar and stir until the mixture is slightly translucent and has the consistency of a runny porridge, 2 to 3 minutes. Remove from the heat and allow to cool thoroughly.

3. Drain the cabbage and rinse several times with cold running water, until very clean. Drain well. Dry the bowl.

4. Put the cooled flour mixture, the remaining ⅓ cup vegetable stock, remaining 3 tablespoons salt, remaining 1 teaspoon sugar, garlic, ginger, and onion in a food processor and process to a puree. Transfer the puree to the bowl.

5. Add the hot pepper flakes and stir well with a wooden spoon. Stir in the radish, chives, carrot, and scallions. Mix well with a wooden spoon.

6. Add the cabbage and gently toss and mix together by hand (wear disposable gloves if you like). Transfer to one or more glass jars or airtight containers. Press down on the kimchi so it's well packed and no air can get inside, then put the lid on the container.

7. You can serve the kimchi right away, sprinkled with toasted sesame seeds. Or you can let the kimchi ferment. It takes about 2 weeks to ferment in the refrigerator; for faster fermenting, leave it at room temperature for 1 to 2 days, depending on the warmth of your kitchen, until the kimchi smells and tastes sour. Once the kimchi is fermented, store in the refrigerator until the kimchi runs out. The kimchi will continue to ferment in the refrigerator and become more sour. You can enjoy it at every stage. Whenever you remove kimchi from the jar, be sure to press down on the remaining kimchi with a spoon to prevent it from being exposed to air.

Bite-Size Napa Cabbage Kimchi

MAK-KIMCHI 막김치

Makes about 4 pounds

Mak means "easy" in Korean. This kimchi is easier to make and eat than Traditional Napa Cabbage Kimchi (page 112) because the cut-up cabbage is easier to handle than the cabbage quarters.

My mom often added freshly shucked oysters when she made mak-kimchi. I've made the oysters optional here, but I wanted to introduce you to my family's own recipe. When I was young, I was always excited when my mom made kimchi because I knew I'd have a wonderful meal that day. She always served her freshly made kimchi with rice and soup. A large plate of spicy kimchi with chopped fresh oysters, generously sprinkled with toasted sesame seeds, was so refreshing.

1 (3-pound) head napa cabbage

6 tablespoons kosher salt

2 tablespoons glutinous rice flour or all-purpose flour

1 tablespoon sugar

⅓ cup fish sauce

9 garlic cloves, peeled

1 teaspoon minced peeled ginger

1 small onion, cut into chunks (about ¾ cup)

1 cup Korean hot pepper flakes (gochu-garu) or to taste

6 ounces Korean radish or daikon, peeled and cut into matchsticks

3 ounces Asian chives or 6 scallions, cut into ½-inch-long pieces (1 cup)

6 scallions, sliced diagonally

12 small, sweet oysters, shucked, rinsed, drained, and chopped (optional)

Toasted sesame seeds (for fresh kimchi)

1. Cut the cabbage lengthwise into quarters. Cut away the core of each quarter. Cut the white ribs of each quarter in half lengthwise. Then cut crosswise into 1- to 1½-inch-long pieces and transfer to a large bowl. Toss with the salt and 1 cup water. Let stand for 2 hours, tossing the cabbage every 30 minutes to salt evenly.

2. Meanwhile, combine the flour and 1 cup water in a small saucepan and place over medium-high heat. Stir until the mixture begins to bubble, 2 to 3 minutes. Add the sugar and stir until the mixture is slightly translucent and has the consistency of a runny porridge, 2 to 3 minutes. Remove from the heat and allow to cool thoroughly.

3. Drain the cabbage and rinse several times with cold running water, until very clean. Drain well. Dry the bowl.

4. Put the cooled flour mixture, fish sauce, garlic, ginger, and onion in a food processor and process to a puree. Transfer the puree to the bowl.

5. Add the hot pepper flakes and stir well with a wooden spoon. Stir in the radish, chives, scallions, and oysters (if using). Mix well with a wooden spoon.

6. Add the cabbage and gently toss and mix together by hand (wear disposable gloves if you like). Transfer to one or more glass jars or airtight containers. Press down on the kimchi so it's well packed and no air can get inside, then put the lid on the container.

7. You can serve the kimchi right away, sprinkled with toasted sesame seeds. Or you can let the kimchi ferment. It will take about 2 weeks to ferment in the refrigerator; for faster fermenting, leave it at room temperature for 1 to 2 days, depending on the warmth of your kitchen, until the kimchi smells and tastes sour. Once the kimchi is fermented, store in the refrigerator. The kimchi will continue to ferment in the refrigerator and become more sour. You can enjoy it at every stage. Whenever you remove kimchi from the container, be sure to press down on the remaining kimchi with a spoon to prevent it from being exposed to air.

Mustard Greens Kimchi

GAT-KIMCHI 갓김치

Makes about 2 pounds

Yeosu, the southern port city in South Korea where I grew up, is well known for its gat-kimchi because the neighboring island, Dolsan, grows very high-quality mustard greens. Their stems are thick, crisp, and succulent, the leaves soft and tender. The locals say the soil and the ocean breeze on their island create the perfect growing conditions for the greens, and all across Korea, Dolsan mustard greens kimchi is well known as the best. I have a friend in New York whose mom, who lives in Yeosu, makes this kimchi and sends it all the way to her in New York. By the time it lands in the U.S., it's well fermented and ready to eat.

I have found mustard greens that are similar to the mustard greens from Dolsan in New York's Chinatown, and sometimes in Korean grocery stores. You can serve the kimchi right after it's made, but it's tastier when it's fermented. Use either green or red mustard greens with long, plump stems.

2 pounds mustard greens, with stems, cut into 2- to 2½-inch pieces

3 tablespoons kosher salt

1 tablespoon glutinous rice flour or all-purpose flour

1 tablespoon sugar

4 garlic cloves, minced

1 teaspoon minced peeled ginger

¼ medium onion, thinly sliced

¼ cup fish sauce

¼ cup Korean hot pepper flakes (gochu-garu)

1. Rinse the mustard greens in cold water, drain, and put them in a large bowl. Sprinkle with the salt and gently mix and rub in with both hands. Let stand for 2 hours, turning every 30 minutes to salt evenly.

2. Meanwhile, combine the flour and ½ cup water in a small saucepan and place over medium-high heat. Stir until the mixture begins to bubble, about 2 minutes. Add the sugar and stir for another minute, until the mixture is slightly translucent and has the consistency of a runny porridge. Remove from the heat, scrape into a large bowl, and let cool thoroughly.

3. To make the kimchi paste, add the garlic, ginger, onion, fish sauce, and hot pepper flakes to the flour mixture and mix well with a wooden spoon.

4. Wash the mustard greens in several changes of cold water. Drain and transfer to the bowl with the kimchi paste. Gently toss and mix together by hand (wear disposable gloves if you like). Transfer to one or more glass jars or airtight containers. Press down on the kimchi so it's well packed and no air can get inside, then put the lid on the container.

5. You can serve the kimchi right away or let it ferment. It takes about 2 weeks to ferment in the refrigerator; for faster fermenting, leave it at room temperature for 1 to 2 days, depending on the warmth of your kitchen, until the kimchi tastes and smells sour. Once the kimchi is fermented, store in the refrigerator. The kimchi will will continue to ferment in the refrigerator and become more sour. You can enjoy it at every stage. Whenever you remove kimchi from the jar, be sure to press down on the remaining kimchi with a spoon to prevent it from being exposed to air.

Spicy Stuffed Bok Choy Kimchi

CHEONGGYEONGCHAE-SOBAGI 청경채소박이

Makes about 3 pounds

This pretty kimchi makes a great substitute for Traditional Napa Cabbage Kimchi (page 112). Be sure to choose large, leafy bok choy with wide ribs, which is easier to stuff than baby bok choy.

I learned the recipe from a friend from Canada who had owned a large Korean restaurant in Hong Kong.

Serve with rice.

2 pounds large (7 to 8 inches long) bok choy

5 tablespoons kosher salt

1 tablespoon glutinous rice flour or all-purpose flour

1 teaspoon sugar

½ cup Korean hot pepper flakes (gochu-garu)

3 tablespoons fish sauce

7 garlic cloves, minced

1 teaspoon minced peeled ginger

8 ounces Korean radish or daikon, peeled and cut into 2-inch matchsticks

1 small carrot, cut into 2-inch matchsticks

1 small or ½ medium onion, thinly sliced

7 scallions, trimmed, cut into 3-inch-long threads

Toasted sesame seeds (for fresh kimchi)

1. Rinse the bok choy well with cold water and drain. Sprinkle the salt between the leaves, with more on the thick white ribs than the green leafy parts. Put the salted bok choy in a large bowl. Let sit for 1 hour, flipping and mixing every 20 minutes to salt evenly.

2. Meanwhile, combine the flour and ½ cup water in a small saucepan and place over medium-high heat. Stir until the mixture begins to bubble, about 2 minutes. Add the sugar and stir for another minute, until the mixture is slightly translucent and has the consistency of a runny porridge. Remove from the heat, scrape into a large bowl, and let cool thoroughly.

3. To make the kimchi paste, add the hot pepper flakes, fish sauce, garlic, and ginger to the flour mixture and mix well with a wooden spoon.

4. Wash the bok choy in cold water several times. Drain well.

5. In a large bowl, combine the radish, carrot, onion, and scallions. Add the kimchi paste and mix together well by hand (wear disposable gloves if you like) for a few minutes, until the vegetables and the kimchi paste are incorporated nicely.

6. Place a bok choy in the bowl with the vegetables and kimchi paste, and stuff the mixture between the leaves, pushing it down between the ribs and pressing the leaves together tightly. Transfer the stuffed bok choy to an airtight container. Repeat with the rest of bok choy and kimchi paste mixture. Press down on the kimchi so it's well packed and no air can get inside, then put the lid on the container.

7. You can serve the kimchi right away, sprinkled with toasted sesame seeds. Or let it ferment. It takes about 2 weeks to ferment in the refrigerator; for faster fermenting, leave it at room temperature for 1 to 2 days, depending on the warmth of your kitchen, until the kimchi tastes and smells sour. Once the kimchi is fermented, store in the refrigerator. The kimchi will continue to ferment in the refrigerator and become more sour. You can enjoy it at any stage. Whenever you remove kimchi from the jar, be sure to press down on the remaining kimchi with a spoon to prevent it from being exposed to air.

8. It's best to serve bok choy kimchi in a way that makes it look elegant and easy to eat. Lay the bok choy on your cutting board. Cut off the top at the ends where the leaves come together, without disturbing the shape of the bok choy. Then cut crosswise into slices, about 2 inches long, so you have layered stacks of large bite-size pieces topped with kimchi filling. Gently transfer the whole vegetable to a plate so as not to disturb its shape, without mixing it up like a salad. Pour on some brine from the container.

Cucumber Water Kimchi

OI MULKIMCHI 오이 물김치

Makes 3½ quarts

This kimchi is thirst quenching and wonderful served chilled on a hot summer day. I use less hot pepper this kimchi because I want to enjoy the clear brine. It's also good as a soup, with rice, and I sometimes add ice cubes. Subtle sweetness from pear and apple tempers the broth's saltiness.

    Unlike other kimchis, this should be eaten within a week after this ferments, so the cucumbers and radishes stay crisp. The kimchi makes a great accompaniment for Spicy Grilled Chicken (page 146).

2½ pounds seedless cucumbers

¼ cup plus 1 tablespoon kosher salt

1 large apple, peeled, cored, and grated

½ medium Korean pear or 1 Bosc or Anjou pear, peeled, cored, and grated

1 tablespoon all-purpose flour mixed with 1 tablespoon water

5 ounces Korean radish or daikon, peeled and cut into matchsticks

2 ounces Asian chives or 2 to 3 scallions, cut into 1½-inch pieces (about ⅔ cup)

1 green chili pepper, cut crosswise into thin slices

1 small red chili pepper, cut crosswise into thin slices

1 tablespoon fish sauce

6 garlic cloves, minced

2 teaspoons minced peeled ginger

1 tablespoon Korean hot pepper flakes (gochu-garu)

1. Cut the cucumbers into 2- to 2½-inch-long pieces. Cut each piece lengthwise in half. Cut each half lengthwise into 2 or 3 equal pieces. Put the cucumber sticks in a 4-quart jar or airtight container. Sprinkle with 1 tablespoon of the salt and toss well.

2. In a large saucepan, combine the grated apple and pear, remaining ¼ cup kosher salt, flour mixture, and 2 quarts water. Stir well with a wooden spoon and place over medium-high heat. Bring to a rolling boil, cover, and reduce the heat to medium. Boil, stirring occasionally, for 5 to 6 minutes, until the fruit pulp and water are nicely combined. If the mixture begins to boil over, uncover, stir, and then cover with the lid slightly cracked.

3. Place a fine-mesh strainer over the container with the cucumbers. Strain the hot brine over the cucumbers, stirring and pressing as much fruit pulp as you can through the strainer with the wooden spoon. Discard any pulp in the strainer and stir the brine and cucumbers. Cool thoroughly.

4. Add the radish matchsticks, chives, green and red chili peppers, and fish sauce to the cucumbers. Stir well.

5. Tie the garlic, ginger, and hot pepper flakes in a piece of cheesecloth. Immerse the cheesecloth pouch in the brine and squeeze the pouch until the brine turns pink and the garlic and ginger are infused into the brine. Discard the pouch or let it soak in the brine for a couple of hours and remove it later.

6. You can serve this right away, but this kimchi tastes better when it's fermented and cold. To ferment it, cover the kimchi container and let sit at room temperature for 24 hours. If the kimchi tastes a little sour, transfer to the refrigerator. If not, wait a little longer. Refrigerate until cold. The fermentation time depends on your room temperature—the warmer your kitchen, the faster it will ferment.

7. To serve, ladle some kimchi and brine into bowls. Store in the refrigerator and use within a week.

VARIATION

Quick Cold Noodles with Cucumber Water Kimchi
The cucumber water kimchi broth tastes wonderful with thin wheat-flour noodles (somyeon). Cook the noodles following the directions in Noodle Soup with Kimchi Seasoning (page 65), rinse in cold water, drain, and place in a large bowl. Pour over enough of the cucumber water kimchi brine to submerge the noodles, then add some cucumbers and a few ice cubes.

SAUCES AND GARNISHES

FOR SEASONING, DIPPING, AND EMBELLISHING

Korean sauces can transform something as simple as rice and vegetables into a feast. They range from simple to complex. On the easy end of the spectrum is Soy-Scallion Seasoning Sauce, a quickly assembled sauce that is used in many side dishes but is also strong enough to stand by itself with rice as a simple bibimbap. At the other end is the complex Vinegared Soy–Hot Pepper Paste Seasoning Sauce, whose flavors— sweet, hot, spicy, vinegary, salty—will make your bibimbap come alive.

Some sauces go hand in hand with certain dishes. We always accompany raw fish with Sweet, Sour, and Spicy Dipping Sauce, and Leaf Wraps and Rice (page 48) and all types of Korean barbecue require Soybean Paste Dipping Sauce.

Quintessential Korean garnishes are also part of what makes a dish look and taste uniquely Korean. Some, like Yellow Egg Paper Strips, may not add a lot of flavor, but they make any dish pop with their bright color. And I can't imagine any Korean-style barbecue without curly Seasoned Scallions.

Soy-Scallion Seasoning Sauce

GANJANG-YANGNYEOMJANG 간장양념장

Makes about ½ cup

The ease of making this basic seasoning sauce conceals the complexity of its flavor. It is wonderful spread over grilled or pan-fried fish or simply mixed with rice. I usually make it right before using it so that the freshly chopped scallion and sesame seeds remain crispy and tasty.

¼ cup soy sauce

2 teaspoons toasted sesame oil

2 teaspoons Korean hot pepper flakes (gochu-garu)

1½ teaspoons sugar

1 garlic clove, minced

3 scallions, chopped

1 teaspoon toasted sesame seeds

Combine all the ingredients in a bowl. Mix well with a spoon until the sugar has dissolved, then serve. The sauce will keep in an airtight container in the refrigerator for up to 3 days.

Vinegared Soy-Hot Pepper Paste Seasoning Sauce

CHOGOCHUJANG YANGNYEOMJANG 초고추장 양념장

Makes about ½ cup

There are so many flavors working together in this sauce—hot pepper paste, soy sauce, vinegar, sugar, pungent garlic and ginger—that I often use it to make the simplest kind of quick bibimbap. I toss it with crispy lettuce, cucumber slices, a little sliced onion, carrot matchsticks, and warm rice, plus a lot of toasted sesame oil. It's a fast, satisfying, delicious, and nutritious meal. I also use it for Bibimbap with Sliced Raw Fish (page 52) and Avocado, Mushroom, and Vegetable Bibimbap (page 54).

¼ cup Korean hot pepper paste (gochujang)

2 tablespoons white vinegar

1 tablespoon soy sauce

1 tablespoon sugar

3 garlic cloves, minced

1 teaspoon minced peeled ginger

1 scallion, chopped

Combine all the ingredients in a bowl and mix well with a spoon until the sugar has dissolved, then serve. Store in an airtight container in the refrigerator for up to 1 week.

Soy-Vinegar Dipping Sauce

CHO GANJANG 초간장

Makes about 2 tablespoons

This sauce adds just a little salty and sour flavor to boost dishes. It goes well with Korean pan-fried dishes like Zucchini Pancake (page 226), Squash Blossoms Stuffed with Tofu-Sesame Filling (page 208), Pan-Fried Cod Fillets with Sesame Oil (page 172), and Seafood Scallion Pancake (page 302). It also makes a perfect sauce for Steamed Dumplings (page 305).

I make it in small quantities to be used up in one sitting, but you can double or triple the recipe. If you have any left over, store in an airtight container in the refrigerator for up to 3 days; after that the scallions will lose their crunch and refreshing flavor.

1 tablespoon soy sauce

1 teaspoon white vinegar

¼ teaspoon Korean hot pepper flakes (gochugaru)

1 teaspoon toasted sesame seeds

1 tablespoon chopped scallion

Combine the soy sauce, vinegar, and hot pepper flakes in a small bowl. Add the sesame seeds and scallion and serve.

Sweet, Sour, and Spicy Dipping Sauce

CHOGOCHUJANG 초고추장

Makes about ⅓ cup

¼ cup Korean hot pepper paste (gochujang)

5 teaspoons white vinegar

1 tablespoon rice syrup or 2 teaspoons sugar

Pinch of toasted sesame seeds

Combine the hot pepper paste, vinegar, and rice syrup in a small bowl. Mix well, sprinkle with the sesame seeds, and serve. Store in an airtight container in the refrigerator for up to 2 weeks.

Living in a harbor city where my dad's business was related to seafood, we used to say: "Is there anything to dip today?" meaning, do we have any raw fish for dipping today?

This red sauce goes well with any kind of fish, as well as with sea squirts, freshly shucked oysters, sea cucumber, blanched seafood such as octopus and squid, and vegetables and mushrooms.

Soybean Paste Dipping Sauce

SSAMJANG 쌈장

Makes about ½ cup

You can find ssamjang in any Korean grocery store, almost always in a green tub, but making your own is very easy and will make a huge difference in taste, because you will be using fresher, more varied ingredients.

Use this zingy dipping sauce for Leaf Wraps and Rice (page 48), Lettuce-Wrapped Bulgogi Rice Dosirak (page 276), Soy Butter Pan-Grilled Chicken (page 143), Spicy Grilled Chicken (page 146), Grilled Beef Short Ribs (page 159), and any kind of Korean barbecue. I like to have it around just for dipping cucumber and carrot sticks, a perfect way to enjoy those vegetables. It makes a great dip for green chili peppers as well, either whole or cut crosswise into thick slices.

½ cup Korean fermented soybean paste (doenjang)

1 teaspoon Korean hot pepper paste (gochujang)

1 garlic clove, minced

1 scallion, chopped

2 teaspoons sugar

1 tablespoon toasted sesame oil

1 teaspoon toasted sesame seeds

Combine the soybean paste, hot pepper paste, garlic, scallion, sugar, and sesame oil in a bowl and mix together well with a spoon until the sugar has dissolved. Sprinkle with the sesame seeds and serve. It's best to serve this fresh, but it will keep in an airtight container in the refrigerator for up to 2 weeks.

Seasoned Scallions

PAJEORI 파절이

Serves 4

In Korea we serve this classic with Korean barbecue, such as Grilled Beef Short Ribs (page 159) and Soy Butter Pan-Grilled Chicken (page 143). We eat a few strips of it with every bite of meat. We also wrap it up with meat in a lettuce leaf ssam style (see page 48). Whatever the delivery method, pajeori greatly enhances the taste of any barbecue.

¼ cup soy sauce

2 tablespoons Korean hot pepper flakes (gochu-garu)

1 tablespoon sugar

1 tablespoon toasted sesame oil

1 tablespoon toasted sesame seeds

14 scallions, trimmed, cut into 3-inch threads, soaked in cold water for 5 minutes, and drained (see page 420)

1. Combine the soy sauce, hot pepper flakes, sugar, sesame oil, and sesame seeds in a bowl. Mix well until the sugar has dissolved and the mixture is slightly creamy.

2. If serving right away, divide the scallions evenly among four small plates. Spoon the sauce over the scallions. Everybody should mix the scallions and sauce together with chopsticks.

3. If not serving right away, put the scallion threads in a zipper-lock plastic bag and the sauce in an airtight container and store them in the refrigerator for up to 3 days. When you are ready to serve, take them out of the refrigerator and serve as described above.

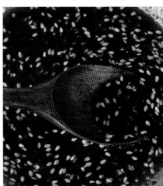

Yellow Egg Paper Strips

GYERAN-NOREUNJA-JIDANCHAE
계란노른자지단채

Makes enough to garnish 2 to 8 portions, depending on the dish

These bright yellow strips of cooked egg yolk make a simple garnish that we use in many dishes, such as Rice Cake Soup (page 62) and Sweet Potato Starch Noodles with Vegetables and Meat (page 323). You can also make white egg paper strips using the whites, but the yellow egg paper strips are easier, and so beautiful!

2 large egg yolks

Pinch of kosher salt

1 teaspoon vegetable oil

1. Beat the egg yolks with a pinch of salt. Strain into another small bowl and discard any stringy bits remaining in the strainer.

2. Heat a large nonstick skillet over medium-high heat. Add the vegetable oil and swirl to coat. Wipe off the excess oil with a paper towel so only a thin layer remains in the skillet.

3. Reduce the heat to low and pour the egg mixture into the skillet. Spread it to about a 4-inch diameter. Turn off the heat and cook in the hot skillet until set. Turn the egg paper over and allow it to set for another minute.

4. Transfer to a cutting board, slice the egg paper into thin strips, and serve. Store in an airtight container or zipper-lock plastic bag in the refrigerator for up to 3 days.

MEATY

CHICKEN, DUCK, BEEF, AND PORK

Some Americans think Korean food is all about beef and pork barbecue. I can understand this, because our barbecue is delicious and so much fun to share and eat. If you've never made it before, you'll be hooked after you make Grilled Beef Short Ribs. It's easy to marinate and grill the meat, and such a pleasure to eat it Korean style—wrapping it in a lettuce leaf, with garlic, Soybean Paste Dipping Sauce (page 134) and other condiments, and rice. It's a communal meal, with everybody around a big table taking pieces of meat from the tabletop grill with chopsticks and sharing the side dishes.

But there's much more to the Korean meat repertoire. My regular readers and viewers love all the chicken and pork dishes and meaty soups I've shown them as much as they love Korean barbecue. They go crazy for the juicy Spicy Stir-Fried Pork; they can't believe how simple it is, and how quickly they can make such a delicious dish. They also find the Korean-Chinese take on sweet-and-sour chicken addicting—my Sweet, Crunchy Fried Chicken started a craze around the world! Make any of these dishes once and I guarantee you'll make them again and again and serve them at all your parties.

Meat has long been thought of as precious in Korean cuisine, and we know how to get every ounce of deliciousness out of it. Some of these dishes are dear to me because moms serve them for special occasions. For example, I associate Braised Beef Short Ribs with birthdays, anniversaries, New Year's Day, and the Korean harvest festival, Chuseok.

You'll find dishes in this chapter that are legendary for their restorative powers. Duck Soup is well known for being packed with essential nutrients, proteins, and vitamins, and we eat Chicken Ginseng Soup on the hottest days of summer to restore our energy, revitalize our appetites, and even cool down.

Meaty dishes in Korean cuisine are all about balance. They're usually seasoned and spiced just enough to bring out their best qualities and flavors and served with plenty of vegetables.

Chicken Ginseng Soup

SAMGYETANG 삼계탕

Serves 2 generously

On hot summer days in Korea, you will find long lines of people waiting to get into samgyetang restaurants to eat this comforting, energizing chicken and rice soup. Each earthenware bowl arrives sizzling hot, with a whole small chicken (I use Cornish game hens) stuffed with rice, jujube, ginseng, and garlic in a delicate, garlicky broth. The earthenware bowl keeps everything hot while you eat.

Eating this soup takes time. Slowly you pick up bites of chicken, so tender after the long simmer that they're falling off the bone, and dip them into a sauce—sesame salt dipping sauce, or sweet and sour soy dipping sauce, or both. Along with the chicken, you eat the rice filling with the soft, sweet jujube. I use only one jujube per chicken, not because I'm stingy but because more than one would make the broth brown; it should be light and milky. The ginseng root, which I simmer on top of the chicken rather than inside of it (as is done traditionally), adds a shot of earthy bitterness that contrasts nicely with the herbal broth and chicken. Cucumbers with Soybean Paste Dipping Sauce (page 134) and kimchi are served alongside.

The tradition of eating samgyetang to beat the heat is rooted in ancient Korean medicine, which tells us that the chicken, ginseng, garlic, and jujube fortify your body, and that the bubbling broth makes you sweat, which cools you off and brings your body back into equilibrium with your environment.

Before you begin cooking this soup, leave time to soak the rice for 1 hour. You can serve the soup with either or both of the dipping sauces.

FOR THE SOUP

½ cup short-grain white rice or white glutinous rice

2 (1½-pound) Cornish game hens

2 large dried jujubes, washed

14 garlic cloves, peeled, root ends trimmed away

2 small whole fresh ginseng roots, rinsed, knob ends trimmed away

1 teaspoon kosher salt

FOR THE SESAME SALT DIPPING SAUCE

2 teaspoons toasted sesame seeds

1 teaspoon kosher salt

¼ teaspoon ground black pepper

2 tablespoons toasted sesame oil

FOR THE SWEET AND SOUR SOY DIPPING SAUCE

3 tablespoons soy sauce

2 tablespoons white vinegar

1 teaspoon honey or sugar

½ medium onion, coarsely chopped

1 green chili pepper, coarsely chopped

FOR SERVING

Ground black pepper

2 to 3 scallions, thinly sliced

Kosher salt

Traditional Napa Cabbage Kimchi (page 112) or Diced Radish Kimchi (page 116)

1 to 2 small green or red chili peppers, sliced

Cucumber spears or sticks

Soybean Paste Dipping Sauce (page 134)

MAKE THE SOUP

1. Rinse the rice in two changes of water and soak in cold water for 1 hour. Drain.

2. Remove any giblets from the Cornish hens (refrigerate for another purpose). Rinse the hens thoroughly with cold water. Trim away any excess fat and the wing tips, if desired.

3. Stuff each hen with 1 jujube, 2 tablespoons rice, and 3 or 4 garlic cloves. Put the hens in a large, heavy pot and put a ginseng root on top of each one. Put the remaining rice and garlic in the pot and add 2 quarts water.

Recipe Continues

4. Cover and place over medium-high heat for 15 minutes, or until it reaches a rolling boil; you will see steam escaping from underneath the lid. Lower the heat to medium and cook for another 15 minutes.

5. Uncover the pot and stir the soup gently with a wooden spoon. Cover, turn the heat down to medium-low, and simmer for 40 minutes. The broth should be milky and the chicken should be tender enough so that you can easily pull it away from the bone with chopsticks. Stir in the salt and remove from the heat.

MEANWHILE, MAKE THE DIPPING SAUCES

1. Combine all the ingredients for the sesame salt dipping sauce in a bowl and mix together well. Cover and set aside.

2. Combine all the ingredients for the sweet and sour soy dipping sauce in another bowl. Cover and set aside.

SERVE

Transfer the hens and ginseng roots to two large soup bowls or earthenware bowls (if using earthenware, add 2 tablespoons water first and heat over medium heat until hot). Ladle in the broth with some rice and garlic cloves, then sprinkle freshly ground black pepper and sliced scallions over the hens. Set a bowl of salt on the table for seasoning the broth. Place plates on the side of each bowl. Using chopsticks, a spoon, or a fork, lift off bites of chicken and dip into the sauce of your choice. Transfer the stuffing and ginseng to a plate and enjoy that with the chicken and broth. Be careful when you eat the jujube—it has a pit in the middle. Serve the soup with kimchi, sliced peppers, and cucumber sticks dipped in the soybean paste dipping sauce.

IT'S HOT OUT THERE!

Koreans call the three hottest days of the summer sambok (3 bok 삼복). The dates are on the lunar calendar and vary from year to year, but they usually fall in July and August. The first day is called chobok (first hot day 초복); 10 days later is jungbok (middle hot day 중복); and 20 days after that is malbok (last hot day 말복). I always made samgyetang for my family on bok days. Although it is traditionally made with a small young chicken for two generous servings, I used to buy a large chicken so the soup would feed my whole family. We'd always have cold watermelon for dessert.

Soy Butter Pan-Grilled Chicken

GANJANG-BEOTEO DAKGUI 간장버터 닭구이

Serves 2

In case you didn't know, soy sauce and butter is an awesome combination! Soy sauce is salty and savory, butter nutty and rich. When the two are combined with grilled chicken, the resulting dish is juicy, savory, and rich tasting. For maximum flavor, I recommend you use thighs and drumsticks. I buy whole chicken legs and bone them myself.

Serve with rice, kimchi, Soybean Paste Dipping Sauce (page 134), and lettuce. Cut the chicken into bite-size pieces with scissors at the table. Enjoy as is or make ssam (see page 48) by wrapping a piece of meat and some scallion threads (see page 420) in a lettuce leaf with some sauce, and rice if you wish.

2 garlic cloves, minced

1 scallion, chopped

2 tablespoons soy sauce

2 tablespoons rice syrup or 1 tablespoon sugar

¼ teaspoon ground black pepper

1 pound chicken thighs and drumsticks, boned and scored (see page 434)

1 tablespoon unsalted butter

Seasoned Scallions (page 135), for serving

1. Combine the garlic, scallion, soy sauce, rice syrup, and black pepper in a bowl and mix well with a spoon to combine.

2. Add the chicken and mix well by hand to marinate. Cover and refrigerate for at least 30 minutes and up to several hours.

3. Prepare a medium-high outdoor grill or heat a cast-iron skillet or grill pan over medium-high heat. Using tongs, remove the chicken from the marinade and place it on the grill or in the pan, spreading it out so it cooks in an even layer. Cook for about 2 minutes, until the sauce sizzles and the bottom is nicely colored. Flip the chicken and cook for another 1 or 2 minutes. Scrape the marinade in the bowl onto the chicken.

Recipe Continues

4. Lower the heat to medium (or move the chicken to a cooler part of the grill) and cook for 5 to 6 minutes, flipping the meat from time to time and moving it around so that it doesn't burn or overcook. To check to see if the chicken is fully cooked, insert a skewer or fork into it; if the juice runs clear, it's fully cooked.

5. Using tongs or a fork, rub half of the butter all over the chicken and cook for another 30 seconds. Turn the chicken over, rub the remaining butter over the other side, and cook for another 30 seconds. Transfer to a plate and serve with the seasoned scallions.

A DISH FOR A
BLIND DATE

Cooking with dairy products is a relatively recent phenomenon in Korea. I can vividly remember the first time I tried margarine, which was more widely available at first than butter. When I was in middle school, I'd go to my friend Younghee's house every morning, and if she was still eating breakfast, she'd call me in while she finished. Sometimes she'd be eating a quick bibimbap made with margarine, soy sauce, and white rice, and she'd share it with me. The flavor of the soy sauce mixed with the rich, fatty margarine and hot rice was novel.

Years later, when I was a college freshman, my maternal grandmother came up with the idea of grilling chicken with soy sauce and margarine when she made a picnic lunchbox for me. In those days, most Koreans started dating during their first year of college, and I had been set up on a blind-date

picnic. As was the custom at that time, a number of other blind-date couples from my class would be there, too. My mom and my grandma worked together to make a lunchbox that could be shared and that would impress everyone.

Normally my grandmother's cooking was traditional, but she wanted me to impress my friends and my date, and since margarine was new and hip at the time, she used it in her chicken dish. She put it in three large stacking containers, for the rice, chicken, and side dishes, and it took up all the room in my backpack. Everyone loved it.

Once butter became more widely available in Korea, I started using it instead of margarine for my pan-grilled chicken. I don't remember my date's face from that day, but I've never forgotten this technique.

Spicy Grilled Chicken

MAEUN-DAKGUI 매운닭구이

Serves 2

This is a spicy version of my savory Soy Butter Pan-Grilled Chicken (page 143). It's succulent, garlicky, and satisfyingly hot and sweet.

Expect some fumes when you cook this. Do it on an outdoor grill if you can. A couple of years ago, I rented a house in California's Mojave Desert to celebrate my mom's eightieth birthday with my whole family. The house had a big grill and we grilled all kinds of meat, some spicy and some not. This was the most popular dish among my family. They kept asking for more, even though it was 110 degrees outside!

To serve, cut the chicken into bite-size pieces with scissors at the table, and roll it up in lettuce leaves with rice and Soybean Paste Dipping Sauce (page 134). Cucumber Water Kimchi (page 126) goes well with it.

2 garlic cloves, minced

1 scallion, chopped

½ teaspoon minced peeled ginger

¼ cup Korean hot pepper paste (gochujang)

1 tablespoon Korean hot pepper flakes (gochu-garu)

¼ teaspoon ground black pepper

2 to 3 tablespoons rice syrup or 2 tablespoons sugar, to taste

1 tablespoon toasted sesame oil

1 pound chicken thighs and drumsticks, boned and scored (see page 434)

1. Combine the garlic, scallion, ginger, hot pepper paste, hot pepper flakes, ground black pepper, rice syrup, and sesame oil in a bowl and mix well with a spoon to combine.

2. Add the chicken and mix well by hand to marinate. Cover and refrigerate for at least 30 minutes and up to several hours.

3. Prepare a medium-high outdoor grill or heat a cast-iron skillet or grill pan over medium-high heat. Using tongs, remove the chicken from the marinade and place it on the grill or in the pan, spreading it out so it cooks in an even layer. Cook for about 2 minutes, until the sauce sizzles and the bottom is nicely colored. Flip the chicken and cook for another 1 or 2 minutes. Scrape the marinade in the bowl onto the chicken.

4. Lower the heat to medium (or move the chicken to a cooler part of the grill) and cook for 5 to 6 minutes, flipping the meat from time to time and moving it around so that it doesn't burn or overcook. To check to see if the chicken is fully cooked, insert a bamboo skewer or fork into it; if the juice runs clear, it's fully cooked.

5. Transfer to a plate and serve.

CLEAN YOUR GRILL

I soak my grill pan in warm soapy water for a few hours. Then I put on my rubber gloves and scrub it with a wire scrubber. All of the residue quickly disappears and the pan is nice and clean.

Sweet and Sour Chicken

DAK-TANGSUYUK 닭탕수육

Serves 4

Tangsuyuk, which was created by Chinese immigrants living in Korea, is a classic dish of crispy meat in a fruity sweet and sour sauce. It's one of the most popular Chinese-Korean dishes. Traditionally this dish was made with pork, but restaurants usually offer beef, too. Some of my readers have told me that they've made it at home with chicken breast instead of pork or beef. I tried it, and it turned out so well that the chicken version is the one I've chosen for this book.

The key to good tangsuyuk is a crispy coating. The batter for the coating is made with soaked potato starch. Double-frying is essential.

Sometimes I like to serve the sweet and sour sauce on the side, for dipping, but usually I pour it over the crispy chicken just before serving. Either way, offer soy-vinegar dipping sauce on the side.

NOTE
You will need to begin this at least 1½ hours ahead to give the starch time to soak and settle.

1 cup plus 3 tablespoons potato starch

1 pound boneless, skinless chicken breast, cut into strips, about 3 inches long by ½ inch wide and ⅓ inch thick

1½ teaspoons kosher salt

¼ teaspoon ground black pepper

Vegetable oil

1 large egg white

3 to 4 dried wood ear mushrooms, soaked in cold water for 30 minutes, drained, roots trimmed off, and caps cut into bite-size pieces

½ small onion, sliced (½ cup)

4 canned pineapple rings, cut into ½-inch pieces, plus 1 cup juice from the can (if there is less than 1 cup in the can, add water)

3 tablespoons white vinegar

1 tablespoon soy sauce

¼ cup brown or white sugar

1 cup diced red-fleshed nectarines, plums, or apple (½-inch dice)

¼ English cucumber, cut into ½-inch cubes

½ teaspoon toasted sesame oil

Soy-Vinegar Dipping Sauce (page 132)

PREPARE AND FRY THE CHICKEN

1. Combine 1 cup of the potato starch and 3 cups water in a bowl. Stir well, then let sit until the starch settles at the bottom of the bowl, about 1½ hours.

2. Combine the chicken, ½ teaspoon of the salt, and the black pepper in a bowl. Mix well with a spoon. Cover and refrigerate while you prepare the other ingredients.

3. When ready to cook, heat 2 inches vegetable oil in a large, deep pan over medium-high heat until the temperature reaches 340 degrees F, 8 to 10 minutes.

4. Meanwhile, remove the chicken from the refrigerator, sprinkle with 1 tablespoon of the potato starch, and mix well by hand to coat evenly.

5. Pour off the water from the starch mixture, so you are left with the solidified starch at the bottom of the bowl. Add the egg white to the soaked starch and stir together with a spoon until smooth. Add the soaked starch mixture to the chicken and mix by hand until the chicken is well coated.

6. Working in batches, gently drop the chicken pieces into the oil. They will puff up and float to the surface. Cook, stirring occasionally, until light brown and a little crunchy, 3 to 4 minutes. Use a slotted spoon or tongs to transfer the fried chicken to a strainer set over a bowl to drain. Reserve the oil.

MAKE THE SAUCE

1. Combine the remaining 2 tablespoons potato starch and 2 tablespoons water in a small bowl and mix well. Set aside.

2. Heat 1 tablespoon vegetable oil in a large skillet over medium-high heat. Add the mushrooms and onion and stir-fry for about 2 minutes, until the onion is slightly translucent and fragrant.

3. Reduce the heat to medium and add 1 cup water, the pineapple juice, vinegar, soy sauce, sugar, and remaining 1 teaspoon salt. Bring to a boil.

4. Stir the starch slurry with a spoon and gradually stir it into the boiling sauce. Cook until the sauce is thick and shiny, 2 to 3 minutes. Remove from the heat.

FRY THE CHICKEN AGAIN

1. Reheat the vegetable oil over medium-high heat until the temperature reaches 340 degrees F.

2. If the chicken pieces have stuck together, gently separate them with your hands. Add all the chicken to the hot oil and fry, stirring with tongs, until all the pieces are golden brown and very crunchy, 8 to 10 minutes. Transfer to a strainer set over a bowl to drain the excess oil. Arrange on a large platter.

SERVE

Reheat the sauce over high heat until bubbling. Add the nectarine, pineapple, and cucumber and stir for 2 to 3 minutes, until the sauce comes back to a boil. Stir in the sesame oil. Either transfer the sweet and sour sauce to a ceramic bowl and serve with a spoon or pour the sauce over the fried chicken. Serve with the dipping sauce alongside.

Sweet, Crunchy Fried Chicken

DAKGANGJEONG 닭강정

Serves 4

Of the hundreds of recipes that I've posted on my website and YouTube, this is the most popular. Over the years I've received many touching, funny, and happy stories from people trying, loving, and sharing my recipe with others. My best friend in New York said, after trying it: "I think you must have added some drug to this because I'm so addicted!"

Fried chicken has been incredibly popular in Korea since the 1970s, and there are many fried chicken shops around the country. There are also countless styles and variations. This version is crunchier than any fried chicken you've probably ever eaten. It's quite sweet, a little tangy, with just a whisper of heat (the dried red chili peppers are more fragrant than spicy), and a bit sticky. The yellow mustard in the recipe is not a traditional Korean ingredient: Just as Korean chicken shop owners do, I like to add my own twist.

If you can't find wingettes or drumettes, use a cleaver to cut regular drumsticks into two pieces each, 2 to 2½ inches long.

The fried chicken will stay crispy for hours. Covered and refrigerated, it will even stay audibly crispy until the next day.

FOR THE CHICKEN

2½ pounds chicken wingettes or drumettes or small pieces of chicken (see headnote)

¼ teaspoon kosher salt

¼ teaspoon ground black pepper

½ cup potato starch

Vegetable oil

⅓ cup toasted peanuts (optional)

FOR THE SAUCE AND GARNISH

½ cup rice syrup or honey

3 tablespoons soy sauce

2 tablespoons brown or white sugar

2 teaspoons white vinegar

2 teaspoons yellow mustard

2 tablespoons vegetable oil

3 garlic cloves, minced

1 teaspoon minced peeled ginger

8 small dried red chili peppers

2 teaspoons toasted sesame seeds

2 to 3 teaspoons crushed red pepper flakes (optional)

MAKE THE CHICKEN

1. Mix the chicken pieces, salt, and black pepper in a large bowl. Transfer to a large zipper-lock bag, add the potato starch, close the bag, and mix well by flipping the bag over and back again until the chicken is well coated.

2. Place a large mesh strainer over a bowl.

3. Heat 2 inches vegetable oil in a large, deep pan or wok over medium-high heat until it reaches about 340 degrees F, 8 to 10 minutes. If you don't have a thermometer, test it by dipping a tip of a chicken piece into the oil. If it bubbles, it's ready. Carefully add the chicken to the oil one piece at a time, working in batches to avoid overcrowding.

Recipe Continues

4. Deep-fry, turning the chicken with tongs, until all sides are light golden brown and crunchy, 10 to 12 minutes. As each piece is done, transfer it to the strainer. Once the chicken has drained, transfer it to a large bowl. Repeat with the rest of the chicken, making sure to bring the oil back up to 340 degrees F between batches.

5. Return the oil to 340 degrees F over high heat and carefully add all the chicken—there's no need to work in batches this time. The chicken will look a little soggy at first. Deep-fry, turning occasionally, until all the chicken pieces are dark golden brown and very crunchy, another 10 to 13 minutes. Transfer the chicken pieces to the strainer or a rack to drain, then place in a large bowl.

6. If using the peanuts, place them in a slotted spoon or a small mesh strainer, carefully dip them into the hot oil, and fry for 15 to 30 seconds, just until light golden brown. Transfer to a small bowl.

MAKE THE SAUCE AND SERVE

1. Mix the rice syrup, soy sauce, sugar, vinegar, and mustard in a small bowl.

2. Heat a large pan or wok over medium-high heat. Add the oil, garlic, ginger, and chili peppers and stir for 30 seconds to 1 minute, until the garlic is a little crispy and fragrant. Add the soy sauce mixture and stir. Let it bubble for 2 to 3 minutes, until the mixture is shiny and a little sticky. Remove from the heat if not using right away and reheat until bubbling when ready to finish the chicken.

3. Add the chicken and peanuts (if using) to the bubbling sauce and toss with a wooden spoon to coat nicely. Sprinkle with the toasted sesame seeds and a few teaspoons crushed red pepper flakes (if using). Transfer to a large plate or platter and serve. The chicken will remain crunchy for several hours if left at room temperature, or you can cover and refrigerate it for up to 3 days.

Duck Soup

ORI-TANG 오리탕

Serves 6 to 8

Koreans know ori-tang as a dish that fortifies your body with good nutrients—protein, vitamins, minerals, calcium, and fiber. Duck fat is high in good unsaturated fat, so this is a healthy meal.

Restaurants in the city of Gwangju, in the South Jeolla province of Korea where I used to live, are famous for this soup, and many tourists come to the town just to eat it. The South Jeolla style of ori-tang calls for a generous amount of perilla seed powder, mixed with water, strained, and added to the soup. Restaurants serve the rich, nutty, creamy soup bubbling hot, in earthenware bowls.

Every mom in the Jeolla countryside also has her own special ori-tang recipe. When she hears that her children will be visiting from the city, the first thing she does is soak the fernbrake and taro stems she dried in the spring. She usually cooks two or three ducks in a large cast-iron cauldron for lunch and dinner, and even the next day.

Duck meat is delicious, but it's a little tough and has a gamy quality, so it needs to be prepared with special ingredients and care. If you don't have a heavy cleaver, it's best to let the butcher cut it into 2-inch chunks, as directed in the recipe. If you can find only frozen duck, ask your butcher to cut it up for you and thaw it in the refrigerator overnight. You'll need to shop in a Korean grocery store or online for the perilla seed powder and the dried taro stems and fernbrake, though I've suggested a substitute for the taro stems. Make sure to start a day ahead if you are using stems.

FOR THE SEASONING PASTE

¼ cup Korean hot pepper flakes (gochu-garu)

¼ cup soy sauce

¼ cup Korean fermented soybean paste (doenjang)

2 tablespoons fish sauce

12 large garlic cloves, minced

2 tablespoons minced peeled ginger

2 teaspoons ground black pepper

½ teaspoon kosher salt

FOR THE SOUP

1 (3½- to 4-pound) duck, cut into 2-inch chunks, rinsed, and drained

1 pound soaked fernbrake (see page 422; about 1½ ounces dried), drained and cut into 3-inch pieces

1 pound soaked and prepared taro stems (see page 424; about 1½ ounces dried), drained and cut into 3½-inch pieces, or 4 celery stalks, halved lengthwise and cut crosswise into 3½-inch pieces

12 scallions, cut into 3½-inch pieces

1 leek, halved lengthwise and cut into 3½-inch pieces, or 8 to 10 additional scallions, cut into 3½-inch pieces

1½ cups perilla seed powder

MAKE THE SEASONING PASTE

Combine all the ingredients for the seasoning paste in a bowl and mix well.

MAKE THE SOUP

1. Bring a large pot of water to a boil over medium-high heat. Add the duck, cover, and cook for 10 minutes. Drain and rinse under cold running water to remove the brownish foam and any surface oil. Drain again.

2. Wash the pot thoroughly and return it to the stove. Return the clean duck to the pot. Add the seasoning paste and 3 quarts water.

3. Cover the pot and cook for 40 minutes over medium-high heat. It will probably take 15 to 20 minutes for the mixture to reach a boil, but the entire cooking time is 40 minutes from the time you place the pot on the heat. Crack the lid if it begins to boil over.

4. Add the softened fernbrake and taro stems or celery and the scallions and leek. Reduce the heat to medium. Cover and cook for another 40 minutes, or until the vegetables and duck are tender.

5. Combine the perilla seed powder and 1 cup water in a bowl. Mix well and add to the soup, stirring with a spoon. Cover and cook for 5 minutes over medium-high heat.

6. Remove the pot from the heat and stir. Ladle the soup into individual bowls and serve. The soup can be refrigerated for up to 3 days.

Bulgogi
with Noodles

BULGOGI-WA DANGMYEON 불고기와 당면

Serves 4 to 6

Bulgogi, one of the most famous and popular Korean dishes, is cooked meat, usually beef, marinated in a sweet, flavorful mix that both seasons and tenderizes the meat. It is often cooked at the table, though it can also be prepared on the stove, then served with rice, side dishes, and soup. There are various ways to cook bulgogi: The meat can be pan-seared, grilled, broiled, or cooked in a pan with the marinade and vegetables, as here. You can also make bulgogi stew by adding a little water, salt, and more vegetables, and cooking it in a shallow pot.

I am always fine-tuning my bulgogi recipe, and this is my favorite version so far. The marinade is a puree of onion and pear mixed with soy sauce, sugar, sesame oil, pepper, and garlic; and I introduce sweet potato starch noodles (or glass noodles) and lots of scallions into the stew. The chewy texture and translucent appearance of the noodles go beautifully with the bulgogi.

Serve with rice, kimchi, soup, and more side dishes.

FOR THE BEEF AND MARINADE

2 pounds top sirloin or tenderloin (available sliced in Korean groceries)

1 large Korean pear or 2 ripe Bosc pears (about 1 pound), peeled, cored, and cut into chunks

1 medium onion, coarsely chopped

8 garlic cloves

¼ cup soy sauce

¼ cup sugar

2 tablespoons toasted sesame oil

1 teaspoon ground black pepper

FOR THE NOODLES

4 ounces sweet potato starch noodles or glass noodles

1 teaspoon soy sauce

1 teaspoon toasted sesame oil

FOR THE VEGETABLES

6 scallions, trimmed, cut into 3-inch threads, soaked in cold water for 5 minutes, and drained (see page 420)

1 small carrot, peeled and cut into 3-by-¼-inch matchsticks

1 cup (2 ounces) trimmed enoki mushrooms (roots cut off and discarded, mushrooms separated)

MARINATE THE BEEF

1. If slicing the beef yourself, wrap it in plastic wrap and put it in the freezer for 1 hour. Unwrap and, holding your knife at an angle, slice across the grain into ⅛-inch-thick slices.

2. Combine the pear, onion, and garlic in a food processor and puree until smooth, about 1 minute. Transfer to a large bowl or baking dish.

3. Add the sliced beef to the pear puree and toss, using a spoon to coat well. Marinate for 10 minutes.

4. Add the soy sauce, sugar, sesame oil, and pepper and toss together. Cover and refrigerate for at least 30 minutes and up to 4 hours (no longer or the meat may fall apart, especially tender meat).

MAKE THE NOODLES

1. Bring a pot of water to a boil. Add the noodles and boil for 5 to 6 minutes, until tender but still chewy. Drain and rinse with cold water.

2. Cut the noodles a few times with a kitchen knife and toss with the soy sauce and sesame oil. Cover and set aside.

COOK THE MEAT AND VEGETABLES AND SERVE

1. Transfer the marinated beef, along with all of the marinade in the dish, to a deep, wide skillet. Put the noodles in one corner. Spread the scallions, carrot, and mushrooms on top of the meat. For stovetop cooking, place the skillet over high heat. Or, for tabletop cooking, place a butane gas burner in the center of your dinner table and place the skillet on the burner. Set the burner on high heat.

Recipe Continues

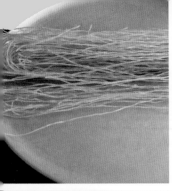

2. When the meat starts bubbling, turn and stir the meat, vegetables, and noodles with tongs. Cook until the beef is no longer pink and the noodles look translucent, about 7 minutes, stirring and turning often with tongs. Transfer some cooked bulgogi, noodles, and vegetables to each plate and serve.

VARIATION

Omit the noodles and cook the meat with the vegetables as directed.

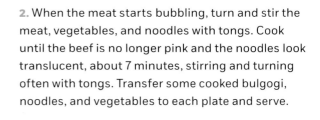

Grilled Beef Short Ribs

SOGALBI-GUI 소갈비구이

Serves 4

If you are a fan of Korean barbecue, this traditional galbi is for you. I make it for special guests. The short ribs are cut into strips that remain attached to the bone, then the meat is rubbed on both sides with a sweet and savory marinade, rolled up, and refrigerated. Galbi are usually cooked at the table on a tabletop grill. The meal works best when one person takes charge of preparing and cooking the meat. In my house, that's me.

Choose larger short ribs with thick chunks of meat attached to the bone so that you will be able to easily cut the meat into thin strips with a sharp knife. You won't be able to do this if the meat on the ribs is too thin.

Be sure to serve with a lot of lettuce and vegetables, in the traditional Korean style.

1 ripe Bosc pear or ½ large Korean pear, peeled, cored, and cut into chunks

½ medium onion, cut into chunks

8 garlic cloves, peeled, plus more to grill (optional)

2 teaspoons minced peeled ginger

¼ cup mirim (aka mirin) or water

¼ cup soy sauce

¼ cup rice syrup or 3 tablespoons sugar (in addition to the one that follows) or honey

1 tablespoon sugar

1 teaspoon ground black pepper

2 scallions, chopped

2 tablespoons toasted sesame oil

2 pounds beef short ribs

Optional: Fluffy White Rice (page 41), lettuce leaves, perilla leaves, Soybean Paste Dipping Sauce (page 134), Seasoned Scallions (page 135), and sliced garlic cloves, for serving

1. In a food processor, combine the pear, onion, garlic, ginger, and mirim. Process for 1 to 2 minutes, until creamy. Transfer to a large bowl. Add the soy sauce, rice syrup, sugar, black pepper, scallions, and sesame oil and stir well with a wooden spoon. Set aside.

2. Rinse the ribs in cold water to remove any blood and remaining bone fragments. Drain and pat dry with paper towels.

3. Place a rib on the cutting board with the bone side down and the thick layer of meat facing up. Holding your knife with the blade parallel to the cutting board, cut horizontally into the meat just above the bone. Slice through the meat just to the edge, taking care not to cut all the way through—you want to leave a "hinge" at the edge. Also, avoid cutting through the layer of fat, which tends to break apart when you open up the flap. Open the piece of meat out from the hinge like a book.

4. Press down on the meat, turn it over, and again cut the thick piece of meat from the side closest to the bone, making sure to leave a hinge rather than cut through the other edge. Open it up like a book, turn the meat over again, flatten, and repeat. Each time you turn the meat over, you will have a longer strip on the cutting board, attached to the bone at one end. Repeat until you have one long, evenly thin strip of meat attached to the bone.

5. Gently score both sides of the meat on the diagonal. Score the sides and surface of the bones as well.

6. Repeat with all the ribs and lay them on your cutting board side by side.

7. Spread a layer of marinade over the top of the ribs and gently pat into the meat. Turn the meat over and repeat. Beginning with the bone end, roll up the strips of meat. Transfer to a large, shallow bowl, pour in any remaining marinade, cover with plastic, and refrigerate for at least 1 hour and up to 3 hours.

Recipe Continues

8. Place a grill pan, preferably nonstick, over a butane gas burner on your table and heat over medium-high heat. Place a few rolled ribs in the pan and use tongs to unroll the ribs onto the rest of the grill pan so they lie flat. Cook for 2 to 3 minutes, then flip over and continue to cook for another 2 to 3 minutes, until both sides of the meat are no longer pink. Add any remaining marinade to the pan while cooking. The meat is very thin, so it shouldn't take long. Using scissors, cut the cooked meat into bite-size pieces while still in the pan and transfer to individual plates. Repeat until all the short ribs are cooked.

9. If you wish, grill some additional garlic cloves along with the meat.

10. Serve with your choice of rice, lettuce and/or perilla leaves, soybean paste dipping sauce, seasoned scallions, and garlic. Eat as ssam by wrapping a piece of meat in a lettuce and/or perilla leaf, with raw or grilled garlic, seasoned scallions, sauce, and rice, if you wish.

CLEANING TIP

The marinade will leave a crust in the pan once the meat is cooked. Soak in hot soapy water until the crust loosens, and scrub the pan with a wire scrubber if it's a cast-iron pan, or a stiff brush if it's nonstick.

Braised Beef Short Ribs

GALBIJJIM 갈비찜

Serves 4 to 6

My family is always thrilled when they see galbijjim on the table. In Korea this richly flavored dish is usually made for special occasions like New Year's Day, the Korean harvest festival of Chuseok, a family member's birthday, or another special day or party, like an anniversary.

The beefy ribs are braised in a sweet and savory soy sauce broth until the meat can be easily pierced with a skewer and is just about falling off the bone. It stays intact, though, maintaining a tender, juicy texture. And the mirim makes the dish smell so good.

But what makes this dish extra special are the colorful ingredients braised along with the beef and ginkgo nuts, with pine nuts added as a garnish. Fresh, good-quality chestnuts are available only in the fall, but Korean grocery stores stock frozen and canned chestnuts year-round. I use canned chestnuts all the time for galbijjim; they taste better than frozen and work better in the dish.

FOR THE SEASONING SAUCE AND VEGETABLES

4 dried shiitake mushrooms, washed and soaked in 2½ cups cold water for 3 to 4 hours, until soft

½ cup mirim (aka mirin) or water

⅓ cup soy sauce

¼ cup dark brown or white sugar

½ teaspoon ground black pepper

8 garlic cloves, minced

1 teaspoon minced peeled ginger

8 ounces Korean radish or daikon, peeled

1 or 2 large, thick carrots (about 8 ounces), peeled

FOR THE BEEF SHORT RIBS

2 pounds beef short ribs, rinsed and soaked in cold water for 30 minutes

12 canned chestnuts, drained, or 12 fresh chestnuts, shelled and skinned (see page 418)

8 large dried jujubes, pitted (see page 423)

2 tablespoons rice syrup or 5 teaspoons sugar or honey

12 pine nuts, tips removed (see page 421)

12 ginkgo nuts, shelled and cooked (see page 419)

MAKE THE SEASONING SAUCE AND VEGETABLES

1. After soaking the mushrooms, place a strainer over a bowl and drain.

2. Measure out 2 cups of the soaking water and transfer to a medium bowl; discard the remainder. Add the mirim, soy sauce, sugar, pepper, garlic, and ginger and mix well with a spoon. Set the seasoning sauce aside.

3. Remove the stem from each mushroom and discard or reserve for future use in Vegetarian Soybean Paste Stew with Mushrooms (page 90) or another dish. Cut each mushroom cap into quarters and transfer to a bowl.

4. Cut the radish into 1½-inch cubes and round the edges of each cube with a paring knife to make (approximately) 1-inch balls. Add to the bowl with the mushrooms.

5. Cut the carrots into 1½-inch cubes and round the edges of each cube with a paring knife to make (approximately) 1-inch balls. Add to the mushrooms and radish balls.

COOK THE BEEF SHORT RIBS

1. Fill a large, heavy pot halfway with water and bring to a boil over medium-high heat. Drain the ribs, rinse again, and add to the boiling water. Blanch for 5 minutes, stirring a few times. Drain and rinse thoroughly with cold water. Return the ribs to the pot and add the seasoning sauce. Cover and cook over medium-high heat for 20 minutes.

2. Stir in the mushrooms, radishes, and carrots. If using fresh chestnuts, stir them in now. Cover, reduce the heat to low, and cook for 1 hour, stirring occasionally.

Recipe Continues

3. Stir in the jujubes, canned chestnuts (if using), and rice syrup. Cover and simmer for another 10 minutes, or until the meat is just about falling off the bone. Thicker short ribs will take longer. To check, poke the meat with a wooden skewer. If the meat is tender enough to serve, the skewer should go through easily. If it does not, cook a little longer, anywhere from 15 to 30 minutes, depending on the thickness of the short ribs.

4. Increase the heat to high and spoon any remaining broth from the bottom of the pot over the meat and vegetables for a few minutes, until most of the sauce has reduced and the meat and vegetables are nicely glazed. Transfer to a large platter, sprinkle with the pine nuts and ginkgo nuts, and serve.

Spicy Stir-Fried Pork

DWAEJIGOGI-BOKKEUM 돼지고기볶음

Serves 2 to 3

I learned to make this spicy, sweet, juicy stir-fried pork dish from a cousin who lives in the Korean countryside. It's incredibly easy to make. You add all the ingredients to the pan, turn on the heat, and in 15 minutes, boom! A gorgeous, red, glistening pork dish is ready.

To get the juiciest results, be sure to choose pork belly with a little fat. If you use something leaner, like tenderloin, you'll need to add a little bit of vegetable oil so it will fry without burning and turn out nice and shiny.

1 pound pork belly, cut into ⅛-inch-thick pieces (see headnote)

1 small onion, sliced

4 scallions, cut into 2-inch pieces

5 garlic cloves, minced

1 teaspoon minced peeled ginger

¼ cup Korean hot pepper paste (gochujang)

2 tablespoons Korean hot pepper flakes (gochu-garu)

1 tablespoon soy sauce

1 tablespoon toasted sesame oil

1 tablespoon sugar

¼ teaspoon ground black pepper

½ teaspoon toasted sesame seeds

Combine all the ingredients except for the sesame seeds in a large, heavy skillet and mix well with a wooden spoon. Place the pan over medium-high heat and cook for 12 to 13 minutes, stirring with the wooden spoon, until the pork is fully cooked, juicy, and a little bit crispy on the edges. Transfer to a large plate, sprinkle with the sesame seeds, and serve.

Glazed Meatballs

WANJA-JORIM 완자조림

Serves 2

These glazed meatballs are very versatile. They can be served simply with rice, but they also make great party food because they hold well. Even if you serve them a few hours after you make them, as I did when I hosted a meetup for my readers in New York City and served them as appetizers on skewers, they will still be juicy and delicious. Everybody loves them! It's no wonder they were my children's favorite lunchbox dish.

8 ounces lean ground beef

1 garlic clove, minced

3 teaspoons soy sauce

5 teaspoons rice syrup or 4 teaspoons sugar

1 teaspoon toasted sesame oil

Pinch of ground black pepper

1 tablespoon glutinous rice flour or or all-purpose flour

1 tablespoon vegetable oil

1. Combine the ground beef, garlic, 1 teaspoon of the soy sauce, 2 teaspoons of the rice syrup or 1 teaspoon of the sugar, the sesame oil, and the pepper in a bowl and mix well with a spoon or by hand.

2. Spoon the flour onto a large baking sheet. Divide the meat mixture into 10 equal pieces in the bowl. Roll each piece into a ball between your palms and put them on the baking sheet one by one. Gently roll in the flour to coat evenly.

3. Heat a large skillet over medium-high heat. Add the vegetable oil and swirl to coat evenly. Add the meatballs and cook for about 2 minutes, turning them with a spatula.

4. Reduce the heat to medium and continue cooking and turning until the meatballs are fully cooked, 2 to 3 minutes.

5. Carefully wipe the excess oil from the skillet with paper towels; you can avoid burning your fingers by pushing the paper towel along the pan with the bottom of a spoon. Stir in the remaining 3 teaspoons rice syrup or sugar and 2 teaspoons soy sauce. Turn and roll the balls in the pan for about 1 minute to evenly coat.

6. Remove from the heat and serve, or store in an airtight container in the refrigerator for up to 3 days and reheat in the microwave.

Korean Pork Barbecue

DWAEJI-GOGI-GUI 돼지고기구이

Serves 4

This recipe is Korean barbecue at its most elemental. It re-creates an experience you may be familiar with if you've ever been to a Korean barbecue restaurant: a blazing tabletop butane burner, sizzling pork on a slightly domed Korean grill pan, Korean side dishes on the table, a stew for diners to share, and maybe a bottle or two of beer or soju.

Although Korean barbecue is traditionally cooked and eaten at the table, if you don't have the setup to eat it that way (see page 35), you can cook the meat in the kitchen and then bring it to the table. I can guarantee that whether prepared at the stove or at the table, this will be better and cheaper than what you'll find in any restaurant. The best part of Korean barbecue is sitting around the table cooking, talking, drinking, and telling stories. You don't need a restaurant for that!

FOR THE TABLE

Soybean Paste Dipping Sauce (page 134)

Seasoned Scallions (page 135)

4 tablespoons toasted sesame oil, plus more for the pan

4 pinches of kosher salt

4 pinches of ground black pepper

FOR THE RICE AND SIDE DISHES (OPTIONAL)

Fluffy White Rice (page 41) or Multigrain Rice (page 44)

Garlicky Cooked Soybean Sprouts (page 193)

Blanched Seasoned Spinach (page 194)

Soybean Paste Stew with Beef (page 90)

Sautéed Zucchini with Perilla Seeds (page 338)

Traditional Napa Cabbage Kimchi (page 112)

FOR THE PORK AND VEGETABLES

2 pounds pork shoulder, cut into 4-inch-square slices, about ½ inch thick

Kosher salt

½ teaspoon coarse sea salt

1 to 2 bunches green or red lettuce, washed and spun dry

1 bunch perilla leaves (20 to 24 leaves), washed and drained (optional)

3 to 4 green chili peppers, cut crosswise into ½-inch slices

8 peeled garlic cloves, sliced thin

1 large carrot, cut into 3-by-½-inch sticks

1 English cucumber, cut into 3-by-½-inch sticks

Toasted sesame oil

1 large onion, peeled and sliced crosswise into ½-inch-thick rings

PREPARE THE TABLE

1. Place the gas burner and grill pan (if using) on the table. Put out a bowl of soybean paste dipping sauce.

2. Divide the seasoned scallions evenly among four small plates. Place one plate at each place setting.

3. Get out four small bowls, one for each diner. Prepare a simple sesame oil dipping sauce by combining 1 tablespoon sesame oil, a pinch of kosher salt, and a pinch of pepper in each bowl. No need to mix.

4. If serving rice and side dishes, arrange them in bowls on the table.

5. Place the pork on a large platter and sprinkle evenly with the coarse sea salt.

6. Arrange the lettuce and perilla leaves, sliced chili peppers, sliced garlic, carrot sticks, and cucumber sticks on a plate and place on the table.

Recipe Continues

COOK THE MEAT

1. Turn on the gas burner and heat the grill pan, or heat a grill pan or heavy skillet on the stove over medium-high heat. When the pan is hot, drizzle in a small amount of sesame oil and add the pork and onion.

2. Turn down the heat to medium and let the pork cook for about 2 minutes, until the bottom is lightly browned and a little crusty. Using tongs, turn the meat over and cook for 3 to 4 minutes, until the other side is lightly browned.

3. Using kitchen scissors, cut the pork into bite-size pieces while still on the heat, flipping the pieces over as you cut them. Cook 1 or 2 minutes more, until the pork is fully cooked. If you want your garlic cooked, you can add it to the grill and cook until lightly browned. Transfer the cooked pork, onion, and garlic to a large plate and serve.

Stack a lettuce leaf and perilla leaf (if using). Dip a piece of pork into the sesame oil dipping sauce, then place it on the leaf stack. Add a slice of onion, some seasoned scallion, soybean paste dipping sauce, sliced green chili pepper, and a slice of raw or cooked garlic. Fold the lettuce leaf over to wrap the barbecue. The wrap should be small enough to eat in one bite. Take bites of rice, side dishes, and carrot and cucumber sticks dipped in soybean paste dipping sauce between wraps.

GOOD STUFF FROM THE OCEAN

ESSENTIAL KOREAN SEAFOOD DISHES

Korea is a peninsula, and I grew up in the port city of Yeosu, on the very southern edge of it. I was surrounded by fish and seafood day and night—literally. My father owned and ran a fish auction house, where we also lived for a time. We had a room in the back of the auction house, and out in front there were huge mounds of the latest catch coming in and out every day. I came to recognize all the fish and sea creatures of Korea and tasted them at their best, fresh and in season. All my friends in Yeosu knew to come to me with any seafood-related question.

I like all kinds of seafood, raw and cooked, fresh and fermented and dried. In the course of sharing the recipes in this chapter, I'll show you how to handle and clean some of the most common seafood in Korean cuisine, such as butterfish, mackerel, Spanish mackerel, octopus, and squid.

The fish and shellfish called for in this book are mostly varieties that I can get in grocery stores and fish markets in the United States and Canada. But for recipes calling for sea squirts, you'll need to go to a Korean market, where you'll find them sold in the frozen seafood section.

Seafood is so important to me and so central to Korean cuisine that it appears in recipes in many of the other chapters throughout this book. Some of my favorite dishes, such as Stir-Fried Dried Shrimp (page 242) and Steamed Dumplings (page 305), are all about seafood. What can I say? Koreans love seafood!

Pan-Fried Cod Fillets
with Sesame Oil

DAEGU-JEON 대구전

Serves 4

I have made this classic, popular dish countless times for my family. I decided to experiment with the traditional recipe by adding a little toasted sesame oil to the fish before pan-frying it. Just a few drops made a surprising difference; the nutty oil gives it so much flavor.

Although it's best to make and serve the dish right away, Koreans usually make it in large quantities the day before big get-togethers or special occasions, such as New Year's Day and Chuseok (see page 71).

The key is not to brown the fillets. They should be bright yellow from the egg coating; the color is beautiful and will stimulate your appetite. To achieve this, you must cook them over heat that is no higher than medium. The finished fish will be delicate and moist, with a soft, flaky texture.

I call for cod, but any mild, white-fleshed fish can be used: Halibut, pollock, flounder, and snapper all work.

8 ounces cod fillets

½ teaspoon plus a pinch of kosher salt

Pinch of ground white pepper

2 teaspoons toasted sesame oil

3 tablespoons all-purpose flour

1 large egg plus 1 large egg yolk

2 tablespoons vegetable oil

FOR SERVING (OPTIONAL)

½ scallion, green part only, sliced

½ small red chili pepper, sliced

Soy-Vinegar Dipping Sauce (page 132)

1. Before cutting the fish, freeze it for an hour or so to firm it up. Hold your knife at a 45-degree angle and cut the fish into 3-by-1-inch pieces, about ⅛ inch thick. You should get 16 to 18 pieces. Spread out the slices on the cutting board.

2. Sprinkle the fillets evenly with ½ teaspoon salt and a pinch of ground white pepper. Drizzle the toasted sesame oil over the top and quickly massage with both hands to spread the seasonings evenly. Season only the top of the fish; no need to flip the fillets over.

3. Sprinkle the flour over the tops of the fish slices. Shake them gently to coat the slices evenly.

4. Whisk the egg and egg yolk together in a shallow bowl. Fish out the egg threads with a fork. Whisk in the pinch of salt.

5. Heat a large nonstick skillet over medium heat. Add 1 tablespoon of the vegetable oil and swirl to coat the skillet.

6. One by one, carefully dip 8 or 9 fish pieces into the beaten eggs and place in the skillet. Cook for 2 to 3 minutes, just until light golden brown, then turn over and cook for another 2 to 3 minutes. Transfer to a plate one by one.

7. Wipe out the skillet with a paper towel, add the remaining 1 tablespoon vegetable oil, and repeat with the remaining fish pieces and beaten eggs.

8. If desired, top each piece with some sliced scallion and red chili pepper and serve with the dipping sauce. You can wrap the cooked fish and store it in the refrigerator for up to 3 days or in the freezer for up to 1 month; pan-fry briefly to reheat before serving.

Pan-Fried Mackerel

GODEUNGEO-GUI 고등어구이

Serves 4

When mackerel is pan-fried, the thin part of the belly tastes like crunchy potato chips, and the thick part of the fish is firm, salty, and juicy. You can use either very fresh mackerel or flash-frozen mackerel for this recipe. If they are very fresh, their backs will be clean and blue, their bellies firm and white, their gills firm and red, and their eyes clear. When I find fresh ones like this, I can't resist buying them for this recipe. I buy several at once, butterfly them, flour them, and freeze what I don't want to cook right away. Since I always have kimchi and rice on hand, I take out an individually wrapped mackerel from my freezer, pan-fry it (no need to thaw), and set a delicious table for my family in about 15 minutes.

I know many people like to fillet mackerel before cooking it, but without the bones, it doesn't look delicious to me. I simply lift out the backbone from the cooked fish all in one piece, like a comb. Any small rib bones left can easily be picked out by hand, and most are small and soft enough to chew anyhow. But, if you prefer, you can ask your fishmonger to fillet the fish for you when you buy it. My fishmongers know that I always want the whole fish, so I don't have to say "Don't clean, please" anymore.

1 (1- to 1½-pound) fresh or flash-frozen whole mackerel, head on if possible

2 to 2½ teaspoons kosher salt

2 tablespoons all-purpose flour

Vegetable oil

1. If using frozen mackerel, thaw for several hours or overnight in the refrigerator.

2. If the mackerel has not been cleaned, place it on a cutting board. Using a sharp knife, slit the fish from right below the head along the belly to the tail so that you can remove and discard the intestines. Cut all along the belly so you can open the fish, but take care not to cut through to the other side.

3. Turn the fish around. Cut into the head so you can split it open (butterfly it); do not cut off the head. Using both hands, open up the fish and wash it thoroughly under cold running water. Drain and transfer the fish to a clean cutting board. Sprinkle the butterflied fish evenly with the salt inside and out. Transfer to a plate, cover, and refrigerate for 2 hours.

4. Remove the fish from the refrigerator and briefly rinse with cold water to remove the excess salt. Drain and pat dry with paper towels on a cutting board. Cut the fish in half crosswise so you have 2 butterflied pieces. Sprinkle both sides of the fish with flour to coat evenly.

5. Heat about 2 tablespoons vegetable oil in a large skillet over medium-high heat. Depending on the size of your skillet, you may need to work in batches, adding more oil as needed. When the oil is hot, add the fish, skin side down, and cook for about 2 minutes, until lightly browned on the bottom. Turn and cook for another 6 to 10 minutes, depending on the thickness, flipping occasionally with your spatula until both sides are crispy and golden brown.

6. Transfer to a plate and serve.

NOTE

If you have more than one fish but don't want to cook them all, clean them as directed. After flouring them in Step 4, wrap each piece in plastic wrap, put them in a plastic bag, and freeze for up to 3 months. Whenever you want pan-fried mackerel, take out a piece and proceed with the recipe; there's no need to thaw.

Pan-Fried Seasoned Spanish Mackerel

SAMCHI-YANGNYEOM-GUI 삼치양념구이

Serves 4 to 6

Spanish mackerel is a less oily variety of mackerel, with fewer bones. My goal was to develop a recipe for people who don't like to fillet their own fish at the table without sacrificing any of the flavor. I experimented with many different ingredients and made the dish over and over again until I got it right. I started with soy sauce and added some mirim for sweetness. Then I added some garlic, but it was too strong. The fish still needed something, and that turned out to be ginger. Boom!

If mirim is not available, substitute water plus 1 or 2 teaspoons sugar or honey, to your taste. I describe how to fillet the fish on page 426, but you can also just ask your fishmonger to fillet it for you if you prefer.

Timing note: You will need to marinate the fish for 2 hours before cooking.

¼ cup soy sauce

¼ cup mirim (aka mirin; see headnote)

2 teaspoons minced peeled ginger

1½ to 2 pounds Spanish mackerel fillets (for how to clean and fillet, see page 426)

½ cup all-purpose flour

3 tablespoons vegetable oil

½ teaspoon toasted sesame seeds

A few threads of shredded dried red pepper (silgochu; optional)

1. Combine the soy sauce, mirim, and ginger in a large, shallow bowl and mix well.

2. Cut the fillets crosswise into 3- to 3½-inch pieces and add them to the marinade. Mix well by hand to season evenly. Cover and refrigerate for 2 hours.

3. Put the flour on a large baking sheet or cutting board. Remove the fish from the marinade and coat each piece evenly with flour.

4. Heat a large skillet over medium heat and add the vegetable oil. When it is hot, add a few pieces of fish, skin side down, and cook for 2 to 3 minutes, until crispy and light brown on the bottom. Turn the fillets over with a spatula and cook until light brown on the other side, another 3 to 4 minutes.

5. Reduce the heat to low and cook, turning once or twice, for 2 to 3 minutes more, until both sides are fully cooked and golden brown. Remove from the heat, sprinkle with the sesame seeds and shredded dried red pepper, if using, and serve.

NOTE

If you don't want to cook all the fish at the same time, flour the marinated fish as described in Step 3. Wrap what you don't need in plastic wrap, place in a plastic bag, and freeze for up to 1 month. You can cook the frozen fillets as directed without thawing.

Braised Butterfish
with Radish

BYEONGEO-MUJORIM 병어무조림

Serves 4

Also known as silver pomfret, byeongeo is one of the most popular fish in Korean cuisine. Its flesh is buttery soft, smooth, and slightly oily. We prepare it many ways—broiled, pan-fried, stewed, or braised. When the fish is very fresh, its skin looks like shiny silver!

In this recipe, the fish is braised with Korean radish, onion, and fresh chili, and seasoned with lots of garlic, hot pepper flakes, ginger, and soy sauce. The fish and radish absorb the flavors of the seasonings, and the juicy radish lends sweetness to the fish while the fish adds a savory dimension to the radish.

If you can't find butterfish, you can use mackerel, cutting it crosswise into 1½-inch pieces rather than braising the whole fish.

FOR THE SEASONING PASTE

3 tablespoons soy sauce

1 to 2 tablespoons Korean hot pepper flakes (gochu-garu)

1 teaspoon sugar

6 garlic cloves, minced

1 teaspoon minced peeled ginger

FOR THE BRAISE

1 (1 to 1½-pound) butterfish (silver pomfret) or pompano, scaled, head removed, cleaned, rinsed, and patted dry

8 ounces Korean radish or daikon, peeled and cut into 1½-by-1-inch pieces, about ¼ inch thick

½ medium onion, sliced

3 scallions, cut into 1-inch pieces

1 green chili pepper or jalapeño, sliced diagonally

1 red chili pepper, sliced diagonally (optional)

1. Combine all the seasoning paste ingredients in a bowl and mix well with a spoon.

2. Score both sides of the fish diagonally three or four times. This will help the fish absorb the seasonings.

3. In a sauté pan large enough to accommodate the fish, arrange the radish and onion in an even layer. Place the fish on top in the center of the pan and spread the seasoning paste over the fish.

4. Add 2½ cups water and cover. Place over medium-high heat and cook for 15 to 20 minutes, until the radish is a little translucent. If the water begins to boil over after 7 or 8 minutes, crack the lid.

5. Push the fish and radish to the side. Using a large spoon, scoop up several spoonfuls of broth and spoon it over the fish and radish. Reduce the heat to medium. Cover and simmer for another 10 to 15 minutes, spooning more broth over the fish and radish from time to time.

6. Reduce the heat to low and add the scallions, green chili pepper, and red chili pepper (if using). Cover and simmer for 4 to 5 minutes. You can serve from the pan at the table or transfer the fish and radish to a plate or platter. Set out a bowl for fish bones.

Deep-Fried Fish Fillets

SAENGSEON-KKASEU BANCHAN 생선까스 반찬

Serves 4

These white fish fillets are crispy on the outside and flaky on the inside. They're coated with Korean bread crumbs called ppang garu. Like panko, which can be substituted, these bread crumbs are very dry, airy, and chunky. They don't become soggy when fried, and the crunchiness lasts a long time. I marinate the fish fillets in soy sauce before I fry them so they're extra flavorful. They go well with rice and don't need a dipping sauce or other seasonings.

If I use frozen fillets, I thaw them overnight in the refrigerator, drain them, and pat them dry with paper towels, since the thawed fillets release a lot of water, and they need to dry properly before being coated with the crumbs.

8 ounces pollock or cod fillets, cut into 1-by-2-inch pieces, about ½ inch thick

1 tablespoon soy sauce

1 teaspoon toasted sesame oil

¼ teaspoon ground black pepper

1 large egg

Pinch of kosher salt

¼ cup all-purpose flour

1 cup Korean bread crumbs or panko

Vegetable oil

1. Put the fish pieces on one half of a large baking sheet or baking dish and add the soy sauce, sesame oil, and pepper. Mix with your hands to season the fish evenly. Leave for 10 minutes, flipping the pieces occasionally to make sure all sides are well marinated.

2. In a wide, shallow bowl, beat the egg with the salt. Put the flour and bread crumbs in separate piles on the other half of the baking sheet or dish, next to the seasoned fish.

3. Lightly coat the seasoned fish pieces with the flour. One by one, dip each floured piece into the beaten egg. Place the piece on the pile of bread crumbs and use a fork to coat with bread crumbs as thoroughly and evenly as you can. When all the fish pieces have been dipped and coated, there will still be some bread crumbs left. Coat each piece of fish with the remaining bread crumbs, pressing down with your fingers so that the fish is tightly coated. Use all the bread crumbs.

4. Heat 1½ inches vegetable oil in a large skillet over medium-high heat. Depending on the size of your skillet, you may need to work in batches. When the oil reaches 340 degrees F, carefully add the fish, one piece at a time, and fry until crisp and light golden brown on the bottom, 2 to 3 minutes. Turn the pieces over with tongs and fry for about 2 more minutes. Turn them over again and fry until they are crunchy and golden brown on all sides, about 1 more minute.

5. Transfer the cooked fish one by one to a mesh strainer set over a bowl. Gently shake the fried fillets in the strainer to remove the excess oil. Serve.

Steamed Fish Cake

JJIN-EOMUK 찐어묵

Makes one 1-pound fish cake; serves 8 to 12 as a snack or side dish

Unlike store-bought Korean fish cakes, which have more starch than fish, my homemade version contains equal portions of squid, shrimp, and white-fleshed fish, blended with just enough potato starch and flour to bind everything together. My fish cake is different from store-bought in other ways, too: It is rolled into a cylinder with the help of a gimbap mat, rather than pressed out flat like the ones you find in the freezer at Korean markets, and it is steamed rather than deep-fried, so it is much healthier.

This recipe makes a generous amount of fish cake, which can be used in a variety of ways. You can use it in Fish Cake Soup (page 394) or Stir-Fried Fish Cake (page 248), add it to Seaweed Rice Rolls (page 267), or serve it as a snack or side dish as I do here, with drinks. When serving as a snack, simply cut the steamed fish cake into squares, or slice it and pan-fry in a little bit of vegetable oil until slightly crisp on the surface and serve with Soy-Vinegar Dipping Sauce (page 132).

You will need parchment paper and a bamboo gimbap mat, as well as a steamer that is wide enough to accommodate the roll.

4 ounces white fish fillets (snapper, haddock, cod, or pollock), patted dry with paper towels

4 ounces skinned squid body, cleaned (see page 431) and patted dry

5 ounces shrimp, peeled and deveined (see page 427)

⅓ cup coarsely chopped onion

1 garlic clove, peeled

1 large egg white

¼ cup potato starch

3 tablespoons all-purpose flour

½ teaspoon sugar

½ teaspoon kosher salt

¼ teaspoon ground white pepper

1. Combine all the ingredients in a food processor and process until thick, doughy, and smooth, 1 to 2 minutes.

2. Place a bamboo gimbap mat (approximately 9 inches square) on a cutting board. Cut parchment paper to fit the mat and place on top. (The parchment paper will prevent the mixture from oozing into and sticking to the mat.) Spoon the fish cake mixture onto the bottom edge of the parchment and spread it gently over the bottom two-thirds of the parchment with a spoon or rubber spatula. Lift the bottom edge of the mat with both hands and bring it up to the top edge of the mixture. Very gently squeeze to shape the mix into a cylinder, taking care that you don't squeeze it out the sides. Continue to roll up the mat.

3. Set up a steamer that is wide enough to accommodate the roll (at least 9½ inches). Bring 2 inches water to a boil in the bottom of the steamer. Line the steamer basket with a cotton cloth and place the roll on top. Cover and steam for 30 minutes over medium-high heat.

4. Remove from the heat. Open and let cool for 5 minutes.

5. Transfer the roll to a cutting board. Carefully unroll the fish cake and remove the parchment paper. Don't worry if it sticks to the roll; it will pull off easily. Cut the roll into bite-size pieces and serve. Or, if using for other recipes, follow those directions for cutting. Cover well and refrigerate for up to 1 week or double-wrap and freeze for up to 3 months. Thaw in the refrigerator; if you are serving it steamed as a snack or side dish, steam for 5 to 10 minutes before serving.

Spicy Fish Stew

MAEUNTANG 매운탕

Serves 4

Maeuntang is a spicy, savory fish stew that is well known and loved by all Koreans. Made with fresh fish, it's usually served with rice. The whole fish, bones and head included, infuse the stew with flavor. Homemade stock contributes even more depth, but you will also have delicious results if you use water.

When I traveled to the Pacific coast of Mexico, I stayed at a hotel in the small town of Puerto Escondido that was full of Americans and Canadians who spent their winters there. Most of the rooms had kitchens. On the beach nearby, in the early morning, fishermen would bring in their catches and I could buy fresh fish right off the boat. I brought some back to my room and made maeuntang for lunch, which I shared with the people who were staying next door.

One of my guests was so interested in what I made that she asked me to explain everything in detail. After I got back home, she sent me a photo of her own Korean-style fish party she had with her friends. She's been cooking and making Korean food ever since. *The photo is on page 186.*

FOR THE SEASONING PASTE

6 garlic cloves, minced

1 teaspoon minced peeled ginger

1 tablespoon soy sauce

1 tablespoon fish sauce or 1½ teaspoons salt

1 tablespoon Korean hot pepper paste (gochujang)

2 tablespoons Korean hot pepper flakes (gochu-garu)

FOR THE STEW

1 (1½- to 2-pound) whole flounder or snapper

4½ cups Anchovy-Kelp Stock (page 74) or water

6 ounces Korean radish or daikon, sliced ⅛ inch thick and cut into 1-inch squares (about 1 cup)

½ large onion, sliced (about 1 cup)

1 medium zucchini, cut diagonally into ⅛-inch slices (about ¾ cup)

1 daepa (large green onion) or 4 scallions, sliced diagonally

1 green chili pepper, sliced diagonally

1 small bunch enoki mushrooms, trimmed and washed (about 1 cup)

2 to 3 ounces chrysanthemum greens, trimmed and washed (about 1 cup), or tender fresh flat-leaf parsley leaves and stems or fresh basil leaves

1 red chili pepper, sliced diagonally

1 to 2 teaspoons Korean hot pepper flakes (gochu-garu; optional)

Fluffy White Rice (page 41), for serving

1. Mix all the seasoning paste ingredients in a small bowl. Set aside.

2. Prepare the fish. Remove the scales with a scale scraper or a knife. Cut off the fins with kitchen shears and slit open the stomach with a sharp knife. Remove the intestines. If there's roe, save it and add it to the stew when you add the fish.

3. Cut the fish crosswise into 1½- to 2-inch pieces. Rinse under cold running water until no longer slippery, removing any mud in the gills with a kitchen brush under cold running water. Drain and refrigerate until you are ready to cook.

4. In a large, shallow pot, combine the stock and radish. Cover, place over medium-high heat, and cook for 15 minutes, until the radish is translucent.

5. Add the onion, fish, and the seasoning paste. Stir well to dissolve the paste. Cover and cook for 20 minutes, until the fish is fully cooked.

6. Add the zucchini, daepa or scallions, and green chili pepper. Cover and cook for 5 minutes, until the zucchini is just tender but still has a bright green color and some texture.

7. Add the mushrooms, chrysanthemum greens or parsley and basil, and red chili pepper. Sprinkle with the hot pepper flakes (if using). Cover and cook for 1 minute.

8. Set out individual serving bowls and a bowl for fish bones. Ladle some fish, broth, and vegetables into each bowl. Serve a small bowl of rice to each person. To eat the stew, fillet the fish with a spoon, transfer the bones to the bone bowl, and eat the fish, vegetables, and broth together with some rice.

Spicy Fish Stew, page 184

Octopus Slices
with Sesame Dipping Sauce

MUNEO-SUKHOE-WA CHAMGIREUMJANG
문어숙회와 참기름장

Serves 2 to 4

Octopus slices dipped in toasted sesame oil are one of my favorite snacks to serve with drinks. Packaged cooked octopus is sold in the fish section at Korean and Japanese markets.

8 ounces cooked octopus

½ to 1 teaspoon kosher salt

2 to 4 tablespoons toasted sesame oil

1 to 2 teaspoons toasted sesame seeds (optional)

Ground black pepper (optional)

1. Cut the octopus into thin slices and place on a platter or individual plates.

2. For each person, put ¼ teaspoon salt in a small dipping sauce bowl and add 1 tablespoon toasted sesame oil. Add ½ teaspoon sesame seeds and a pinch of ground black pepper, if desired.

3. Dip the octopus slices in the sauce and enjoy.

Pan-Fried Oysters

GUL-JEON 굴전

Serves 2 to 4

When freshly shucked oysters are coated in a light batter and pan-fried in just a little bit of vegetable oil, they become firm and sweet, full of ocean aroma. If freshly shucked oysters are not available, flash-frozen oysters are good enough for this dish. They make a great snack with beer or soju, as well as a side dish with rice.

FOR THE BATTER

2 tablespoons potato starch

2 tablespoons all-purpose flour

Pinch of kosher salt

1 large egg

FOR THE OYSTERS

8 ounces shucked fresh or frozen oysters (12 to 16), thawed if frozen

½ teaspoon kosher salt

1 tablespoon potato starch

1 tablespoon vegetable oil

Soy-Vinegar Dipping Sauce (page 132), for serving

1. Combine the potato starch, flour, salt, egg, and 1 tablespoon water in a bowl and mix the batter well with a fork or whisk.

2. Rinse the oysters in several changes of cold water and drain. Put the oysters in a small bowl, add the salt, and mix with a spoon. Let the oysters sit for 10 minutes; this will firm them up while seasoning them. Place a strainer over another bowl and drain the oysters. Discard the liquid.

3. Pat the oysters dry with paper towels and transfer to a bowl. Add the potato starch and gently mix by hand to coat. Add the oysters to the bowl of batter and gently mix with a spoon.

4. Heat a large nonstick skillet over medium heat. Add the vegetable oil and swirl to coat. Using a spoon, scoop up 1 or 2 oysters, along with some batter, and add to the skillet. Cook for 1 minute on each side, or until crispy and light golden brown on both sides. Transfer the cooked oysters to a plate. Repeat with the rest of oysters and the batter. Serve with the dipping sauce.

VEGETABLES

FOR EVERY TIME OF YEAR

Much of Korea is mountainous and covered in forests, and Koreans have always used the countryside as foraging grounds for wild vegetables, roots, tubers, and mushrooms. Partly because of this, our cuisine has a long and heartfelt tradition of vegetable and plant-based dishes. It's one reason why everyday Korean food is so well balanced. Even meat dishes like Korean barbecue include lots of vegetable sides.

Korean vegetable dishes inspire some of the most passionate devotion among my readers and viewers, who are also masters at veganizing my most meat-centric recipes. The dishes are varied and use a wide array of preparation methods. Some are uncooked, like Sweet, Sour, and Spicy Lettuce Salad, which is just mixed together by hand. Others are steamed and then seasoned, like Garlicky Cooked Soybean

Sprouts, or marinated and shallow-fried, like Pan-Fried Marinated Eggplant.

You will also find some of my most delicious tofu recipes in this chapter. Broccoli with Tofu and Pan-Fried Tofu with Soy-Scallion Seasoning Sauce have always been favorites of my dinner guests.

Koreans have also developed numerous techniques for preserving ingredients at peak times so that we can use them until the season comes around again. We make kimchi, of course, but we also blanch and dry many plants, such as taro stems, fernbrake, and mushrooms. Later, we rejuvenate and cook them. These methods were handed down, family to family, over generations, and are part of everyday Korean cooking. Now I share them with you.

Garlicky Cooked Soybean Sprouts

KONGNAMUL-MUCHIM 콩나물무침

Serves 4 as a side dish

This is a must-have at any gathering—I can't imagine a Korean barbecue, potluck, or party without these slightly crunchy soybean sprouts. No matter what else is on the table, kongnamul-muchim is always one of the first things to disappear. It goes with everything—meat, fish, chicken, rice, and vegetables—which is one of the reasons why it's so popular.

Whenever I make this dish, I already know what I'm going to do with the leftovers: I make a simple bibimbap by stir-frying the bean sprouts with rice and gochujang until really hot, then I add some toasted sesame oil and serve.

1 teaspoon kosher salt

1 pound soybean sprouts, cleaned (see page 421) and drained

2 garlic cloves, minced

1 scallion, chopped

2 teaspoons fish sauce or 1 tablespoon soup soy sauce

2 teaspoons toasted sesame oil

2 teaspoons toasted sesame seeds

1. In a large pot, bring 3 cups water to a boil over medium-high heat. Add the salt and stir. Add the bean sprouts and cover. Cook for about 5 minutes, until crisp-tender and fragrant, then drain.

2. Transfer the sprouts to a large bowl. When they're cool enough to handle, add the garlic, scallion, fish sauce, toasted sesame oil, and sesame seeds. Toss gently with your hands until the soybean sprouts are evenly seasoned. Serve warm or cold. The sprouts can be covered and refrigerated for 2 to 3 days. If making ahead, do not reheat; serve cold.

TIP

Always keep the lid on when cooking soybean sprouts! My mother and grandmother would never cook soybean sprouts uncovered in their kitchens, because the final dish always ended up with a fishy smell. Don't even open it for a peek!

Blanched Seasoned Spinach

SIGEUMCHI-NAMUL 시금치나물

Serves 4

Like Garlicky Cooked Soybean Sprouts (page 193), this spinach recipe is one of Korea's signature vegetable dishes. The spinach, with stems attached, retains some texture and has a wonderful garlicky flavor.

Be sure to use mature bunch spinach, not packaged baby spinach. If you can find spinach with red stem bases, that is best for this dish.

1 pound bunch spinach, preferably with red stems

4 teaspoons soy sauce

1 tablespoon toasted sesame oil

2 garlic cloves, minced

1 scallion, chopped

1 teaspoon Korean hot pepper flakes (gochu-garu; optional)

1 teaspoon toasted sesame seeds

1. Bring a large pot of water to a boil over medium-high heat. Meanwhile, clean the spinach. Trim away the brownish roots from the base of the bunch. If the bunch is large, cut it at the base into halves or quarters.

2. Add the spinach to the boiling water and stir for about 2 minutes. Drain and rinse in a few changes of cold running water to remove any remaining dirt and stop the cooking. Drain, squeeze out the excess water, and transfer to a cutting board. Cut into bite-size pieces and place in a large bowl.

3. Add the soy sauce, sesame oil, garlic, scallion, and hot pepper flakes (if using). Mix well by hand. Transfer to a serving plate and sprinkle with the sesame seeds. Serve.

HOMETOWN SPINACH

My late father's hometown, on the island of Namhae off the southern tip of Korea, produces very high-quality spinach that is harvested in late fall and shipped all over Korea. The spinach is grown in the fields in the open air near the ocean, never in a greenhouse. The firm, sweet, red-stemmed spinach from Namhae is considered the best in the country.

When I visited Korea a few years ago, I went to Namhae and stayed at a small oceanfront cottage. The owner was a local farmer who had heard about my father from other villagers. Everyone knew that I was visiting, and while I was staying there, the farmer often brought me produce that he grew.

His first gift was a basket filled with freshly picked spinach. The spinach had just been pulled from the earth and it was very sturdy. The leaves were incredibly green, without a bruise or a blemish, and the bottoms of the stems were bright red. Of course, I immediately made sigeumchi-namul, and it tasted absolutely delicious!

Sweet, Sour, and Spicy Lettuce Salad

SANGCHU-GEOTJEORI 상추겉절이

Serves 4

When I need a quick, refreshing side dish to serve with rice or Barley Rice (page 46), I make this salad. It has a wonderful crisp texture that's great for summer. I make no more of this than I can finish in one sitting, because it doesn't keep well.

2 garlic cloves, minced

2 scallions, chopped

½ small onion, thinly sliced

3 tablespoons soy sauce

1 tablespoon white vinegar

1 tablespoon toasted sesame oil

1 tablespoon Korean hot pepper flakes (gochu-garu)

2 teaspoons sugar

8 ounces green or red leaf lettuce or arugula, washed, drained, and torn into bite-size pieces

1 tablespoon toasted sesame seeds

1. Combine the garlic, scallions, onion, soy sauce, vinegar, toasted sesame oil, hot pepper flakes, and sugar in a large bowl. Mix well with a wooden spoon.

2. Add the lettuce and mix by hand to ensure that the seasonings are incorporated. Sprinkle with the sesame seeds and serve right away.

Watercress Seasoned with Soybean Paste

MULNAENGI-DOENJANG-MUCHIM 물냉이된장무침

Serves 2 to 3

All we Koreans have to do is smell this pungent seasoning mixture, and our appetites come alive. We use it to season many types of blanched green vegetables. Here, watercress is blanched until just tender, then tossed with the sauce. You can substitute bok choy or napa cabbage for the watercress.

8 ounces watercress

1 garlic clove, minced

1 scallion, chopped

1 tablespoon Korean fermented soybean paste (doenjang)

1 teaspoon Korean hot pepper paste (gochujang)

2 teaspoons toasted sesame oil

1 teaspoon toasted sesame seeds

1. Bring a large pot of water to a boil. Blanch the watercress for about 3 minutes, turning with a wooden spoon or tongs, until the leaves are wilted and tender.

2. Drain and rinse the watercress in cold water a couple of times. Squeeze out the excess water and transfer to a cutting board. Cut into pieces about 2 inches long.

3. Combine the garlic, scallion, soybean paste, hot pepper paste, and toasted sesame oil in a bowl and mix well with a wooden spoon. Add the watercress and sesame seeds and mix well by hand. Transfer to a serving bowl or plate. The watercress can be refrigerated for up to 3 days.

Cold Seaweed-Cucumber Soup

MIYEOK-OI-NAENGGUK 미역오이냉국

Serves 2 to 3

This sweet, sour, and salty green soup garnished with cherry tomatoes is an invigorating choice for a hot summer day. It's easy to make. The seaweed gives the broth a mild sea taste that goes well with the cucumber flavor. Make sure to serve it ice cold.

¼ ounce dried miyeok (aka wakame)

1 tablespoon sugar

2 teaspoons kosher salt

2 teaspoons white vinegar

2 tablespoons chopped green chili pepper

2 tablespoons thinly sliced onion

1 garlic clove, minced

½ scallion, chopped

1 cup seedless cucumber matchsticks (about 3 ounces)

3 cherry tomatoes, cut in half

1 tablespoon toasted sesame seeds, ground with a mortar and pestle

1. Put the dried miyeok in a bowl, cover with water, and soak for 30 minutes, until softened and expanded.

2. Toward the end of the soaking time bring a small saucepan of water to a boil over high heat. Drain the seaweed and blanch, stirring with a wooden spoon, for 1 minute, or until all the seaweed turns green. Remove from the heat, drain, and rinse in cold running water until cool enough to handle. Drain and squeeze out the excess water with your hands. Cut the seaweed into bite-size pieces.

3. In a large glass or ceramic bowl, combine the sugar, salt, white vinegar, chili pepper, onion, garlic, scallion, and 1 cup cold water. Stir well with a spoon until the salt and sugar have dissolved.

4. Add 6 ice cubes and stir until the brine is very cold. Add the seaweed and cucumber and gently mix everything together with a spoon. Top with the halved cherry tomatoes, sprinkle with the sesame seeds, and serve.

Sautéed Cucumber

OI-BOKKEUM 오이볶음

Serves 4

When I want a quick bibimbap or I need something green in a lunchbox, I make this fresh-tasting dish. The beautiful green color of the sliced and salted cucumbers doesn't change for hours when they are very briefly sautéed, and their texture remains crisp.

1 large English cucumber (13 to 14 ounces), thinly sliced

1½ teaspoons kosher salt

2 teaspoons vegetable oil

1 garlic clove, minced

Pinch of ground black pepper

1 teaspoon toasted sesame oil

1 teaspoon toasted sesame seeds

A few threads of shredded dried red pepper (silgochu; optional)

Fluffy White Rice (page 41), for serving

1. Combine the cucumber slices and 1 teaspoon of the salt in a bowl and toss well to salt evenly. Let sit for 10 minutes. Transfer the wet cucumber slices to a few folded layers of cheesecloth and squeeze tightly to extract as much liquid as possible.

2. Heat the vegetable oil in a skillet over medium-high heat and add the garlic, cucumber, remaining ½ teaspoon salt, and black pepper. Stir-fry with a wooden spoon for 1 minute, until the color brightens and the cucumbers are shiny.

3. Remove from the heat and stir in the sesame oil and sesame seeds. Transfer to a shallow bowl or a plate and garnish with the shredded red pepper (if using). Serve right away with rice. Or you can refrigerate the cucumber for up to 2 days and serve cold.

Spicy, Crisp Korean Radish Salad

MU-SAENGCHAE 무생채

Serves 4 to 6

This radish salad is perfect when you need a quick meal: Just mix it with rice and hot pepper paste (gochujang) to make a fast bibimbap.

The best time to make the salad is late fall, when Korean radishes are at their sweetest and juiciest. Good radishes should be firm, with smooth, shiny skin and more green color than white. The more green there is, the sweeter the radish will be.

You can use a knife or a mandoline to prepare the radish. It's best to serve the salad right away, before it becomes watery.

1 pound Korean radish or daikon, peeled and cut into thin matchsticks

1 to 2 tablespoons Korean hot pepper flakes (gochu-garu)

2 garlic cloves, minced

1 scallion, chopped

2 tablespoons plus 1 teaspoon fish sauce

2 tablespoons toasted sesame oil

1 teaspoon toasted sesame seeds

1. In a large bowl, combine the radish matchsticks, hot pepper flakes, garlic, scallion, fish sauce, sesame oil, and sesame seeds and mix well by hand until the radishes and seasonings are well incorporated and the radishes look shiny.

2. Transfer to a large plate or a shallow bowl and serve.

Pan-Fried Marinated Eggplant

GAJI-YANGNYEOM-GUI 가지양념구이

Serves 4 as a side dish

I like to think of this sweet and salty dish as a sort of vegetarian bulgogi. Marinating and pan-frying eggplant keeps it firm, flavorful, and chewy—almost meaty. The marinade glazes it as it cooks, so it glistens. Prepared this way, the eggplant looks very special, even though the recipe is easy. It's a versatile dish that makes a great side for rice and many other preparations. The eggplant tastes wonderful right off the stove, but it's even better after a few hours, when all the flavors have had time to mingle and deepen.

I usually use Korean eggplant, sold in Korean markets. They are thinner than ordinary eggplants and the skin is more tender. But regular eggplants work, too.

FOR THE MARINADE

3 garlic cloves, minced

1 scallion, chopped

¼ medium onion, chopped (about ⅓ cup)

¼ cup rice syrup or 2 tablespoons sugar

1 tablespoon soy sauce

1 teaspoon toasted sesame oil

2 teaspoons Korean hot pepper flakes (gochu-garu)

½ teaspoon kosher salt

FOR THE EGGPLANT

1 pound eggplants

1 tablespoon kosher salt

1 tablespoon vegetable oil

1 teaspoon toasted sesame seeds

1. Combine all the marinade ingredients in a large bowl and mix together well. Set aside.

2. Cut the eggplants crosswise at 3- to 4-inch intervals, then slice the pieces ½ wide by ¼ inch thick.

3. Put the eggplant strips in a large bowl and add the salt. Toss well by hand until all the eggplant is salted. Let sit for 20 minutes, tossing every 5 minutes.

4. Drain the eggplant and discard the liquid. Take up handfuls of eggplant and squeeze tightly to remove the excess liquid. Add the marinade to the bowl with the eggplant and mix together well. Cover and refrigerate for 30 minutes.

5. Heat the vegetable oil in a large, heavy skillet over medium-high heat and swirl to coat the pan evenly. Add the marinated eggplant and spread it out evenly in the skillet. Leave to sear for a few minutes, until the bottom is lightly colored. Turn over with a spatula or tongs and cook for another 2 to 3 minutes, until the other side is lightly browned. Reduce the heat to medium and continue to cook, pressing the eggplant into the pan and flipping it over from time to time, until the eggplant is cooked through and glazed and any excess marinade has evaporated, 5 to 6 minutes.

6. Transfer the eggplant to a plate. Sprinkle with the sesame seeds. Serve hot or cold. The eggplant will keep in the refrigerator for up to 3 days.

Glazed Pan-Fried Leek, Mushroom, and Pepper Skewers

BEOSEOT-GOCHU-SANJEOK 버섯고추산적

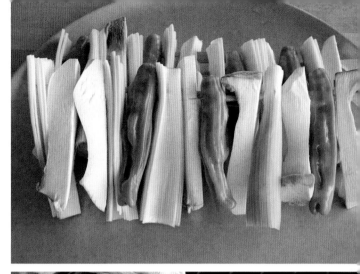

Makes 4 or 5 skewers; serves 2 to 4

Mushrooms, shishito peppers, and leeks glazed with a sweet, salty sauce look pretty, and their flavors complement each other. I think mushrooms are more delicious than meat, but you can use beef here, and you can substitute 4 scallions for the leeks (cut them into 4-inch lengths).

You'll need five 6-inch skewers.

FOR THE SAUCE

2 tablespoons soy sauce

1 tablespoon honey

2 teaspoons toasted sesame oil

1 garlic clove, minced

1 scallion, chopped

⅛ teaspoon ground black pepper

FOR THE SKEWERS

1 large or 2 small leeks (white part only)

3 or 4 king oyster mushrooms, sliced lengthwise into ½-by-3-inch-long pieces

8 large (3 to 4 inches long) shishito peppers or mild green chili peppers

2 tablespoons vegetable oil

1 teaspoon toasted sesame seeds

MAKE THE SAUCE

Combine all the ingredients in a bowl and set aside.

MAKE THE SKEWERS

1. Cut the white part of the leek in half lengthwise. Wash well, then cut into 4-inch-long pieces. Separate the pieces into sections with 3 or 4 layers of leek.

2. Skewer the mushroom pieces, peppers, and leek pieces about ¾ inch in from their ends so that they stick out from the skewers like a flag (see photo). You will have more mushrooms than leeks or peppers.

3. Heat the vegetable oil in a large skillet over medium-high heat and swirl to coat the pan evenly. Place the skewers in the skillet. Cook for 1 minute, turn the skewers over, and cook for another minute, until both sides of the vegetables are lightly colored.

4. Spoon half the sauce onto the vegetables and cook for about 2 minutes. Turn, add the remaining sauce, and cook for another 2 minutes. Let the sauce sizzle and reduce for 1 or 2 minutes, until the mushrooms, peppers, and leeks are tender and glazed. Remove from the heat and sprinkle with the sesame seeds.

5. Transfer to a plate and serve.

Broccoli
with Tofu

BROKOLI-DUBUMUCHIM 브로콜리두부무침

Serves 4

If you're looking for a healthy, nutritious, and tasty Korean dish, this is it.

I first tried it at a restaurant in Korea a few years ago. Now I make it whenever I have vegetarians over, and they rave about it. The trick is to season the tofu well with salt, a generous amount of toasted sesame oil, and sesame seeds to give it a nutty flavor.

You can substitute any green, tender vegetables, such as spinach or chrysanthemum greens, for the broccoli, but the broccoli and tofu make a particularly nice combination. The white crumbled tofu on top of the green broccoli reminds me of snow on a green pine tree in the winter.

14 ounces broccoli	1 scallion, chopped
3 teaspoons kosher salt	1 tablespoon toasted sesame oil
8 ounces medium-firm tofu	2 teaspoons toasted sesame seeds
1 garlic clove, minced	

1. Rinse the broccoli and cut away the bottom 2 inches of the stems. Cut the stems away from the crowns. Peel the stems with a paring knife and discard the skin. Slice the stems lengthwise, then cut into bite-size pieces. Cut the crowns lengthwise into individual florets. If the florets are large, slice them lengthwise into bite-size pieces.

2. Bring a medium saucepan of water to a boil over medium-high heat. Stir in 1 teaspoon of the salt. Add the tofu and cook for about 3 minutes, until soft. Using a slotted spoon, carefully remove the tofu from the water and set aside to cool. Add the broccoli to the boiling water and blanch for 4 to 5 minutes, occasionally stirring with tongs, until tender but still bright green. Drain and rinse under cold running water to stop the cooking and set the color. Drain well.

3. Put the broccoli in a large bowl, add the tofu, and crumble the tofu by hand. Add the remaining 2 teaspoons salt, the garlic, scallion, and sesame oil and mix everything together by hand. Sprinkle with the sesame seeds and serve.

Pan-Fried Tofu
with Soy-Scallion Seasoning Sauce

DUBUBUCHIM-YANGNYEOMJANG 두부부침양념장

Serves 4

This easy tofu dish is common in Korean home cooking. The tofu is pan-fried until nicely browned and crisp, and just before serving, it's topped with the seasoning sauce. You can fry the tofu ahead of time, but try to make the sauce just before serving so that the scallions and sesame seeds remain nutty and crisp.

When I first moved to New York City, I had a potluck meetup in Bryant Park, and one of my readers, Kristi, brought this dish spread out on a large platter with the seasoning sauce in a separate container. She theatrically drizzled the sauce over the tofu, which got everyone's attention; they all had to try it.

3 tablespoons vegetable oil

14 ounces medium-firm tofu, drained and cut into ⅓-inch-thick slices

½ recipe Soy-Scallion Seasoning Sauce (page 130)

1. Heat the vegetable oil over medium-high heat in a large nonstick skillet and add the tofu pieces in one layer. Cook until browned and crisp on one side, 5 to 7 minutes. Turn over and cook on the other side until nicely browned and crisp, 3 to 4 minutes. Transfer to a plate, overlapping the pieces.

2. Spoon the sauce over the tofu and serve right away.

Squash Blossoms
Stuffed with Tofu-Sesame Filling

HOBAK-KKOT-JEON 호박꽃전

Serves 4

I can never resist buying squash blossoms when I see them at the market in the summer. You can put them in salads and cook them in many ways. We Koreans especially love to fry or pan-fry them.

I adapted this dish from Buddhist cuisine. In Korea we call them squash blossom pancakes. They are slightly crispy on the surface and soft, with a light tofu filling and a nutty sesame fragrance.

Stuffing the blossoms with tofu is delicate work, but it makes all the difference in terms of making them moist and tender. The white tofu brightens them from within and accentuates the beauty of the green and yellow blossoms. They make great appetizers.

FOR THE FILLING

1 teaspoon toasted sesame seeds

3 ounces medium-firm tofu

¼ teaspoon kosher salt

1 teaspoon toasted sesame oil

FOR THE BLOSSOMS

10 large squash blossoms

2 tablespoons potato starch

FOR THE BATTER

¼ cup potato starch

2 tablespoons all-purpose flour

Pinch of kosher salt

Vegetable oil

FOR SERVING

Soy-Vinegar Dipping Sauce (page 132)

MAKE THE FILLING

Grind the sesame seeds with a mortar and pestle or crush them with a rolling pin. Put them in a medium bowl and add the tofu, salt, and sesame oil. Using a pestle or a wooden spoon, crush the tofu until the mixture is well incorporated.

STUFF THE BLOSSOMS

1. Bring a medium pot of water to a boil over high heat. Working in batches, blanch the squash blossoms for 5 seconds, stirring gently with a wooden spoon. Drain and rinse under cold running water. Squeeze gently to remove the excess water.

2. Put the blossoms side by side on a large baking sheet.. Carefully open one side of each flower and spread out the blossom petals. Sprinkle the potato starch onto all the petals.

3. Scoop up a small amount of the filling and place it around the pistil (the stalk in the center of the blossom) right above the stem. Wrap the petals gently around the filling and twist them at the ends to seal. It will look like a paintbrush-shaped packet. Repeat with the remaining flowers and filling.

MAKE THE BATTER AND FRY THE BLOSSOMS

1. Combine the potato starch, flour, salt, and ¼ cup water in a small bowl. Mix together well.

2. Heat 2 tablespoons vegetable oil in a large skillet over medium heat and swirl to evenly coat the pan. Carefully dip a squash blossom packet into the batter, making sure to coat the whole blossom, and place it in the skillet. Repeat with a few more blossoms. Work in batches so you don't overcrowd the skillet. Cook until lightly crisped, about 2 minutes. Flip, add more oil if necessary, and cook for another 1 or 2 minutes, until the other side is lightly crisp. Flip and cook for another minute or two, until both sides are crisp but not brown; lower the heat to medium-low if necessary. Transfer to a plate and serve with the dipping sauce.

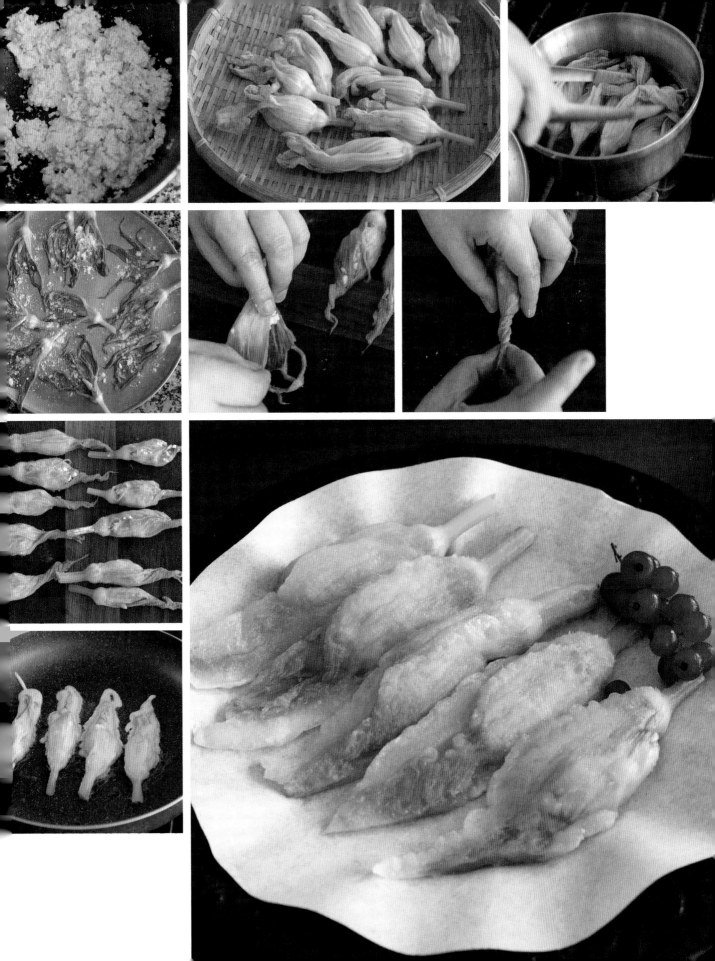

Braised Taro Roots

with Perilla Seed Powder

TORAN-DEULKKAE-JORIM 토란들깨조림

Serves 4

Every time I make this dish for guests, they fall in love with its rich and flavorful broth and the way the taro melts in the mouth. In texture, cooked taro root is similar to potato but softer, creamier, and slightly slippery. The perilla seed powder acts as a thickener for the sauce, and it is key to the distinctive nutty, herbal flavor. However, if perilla seed powder isn't available, you can use finely ground toasted sesame seeds. I add a little bit of beef to make the dish more savory, but you can skip it if you want.

Raw taro roots are toxic, so they must always be blanched and peeled as a first step to any preparation.

1 pound small (2-inch-long) taro roots

1 tablespoon vegetable oil

4 ounces beef flank, round, or brisket, cut into thin bite-size pieces (optional)

¼ medium onion, sliced

1 small carrot, sliced (about ⅓ cup)

1 garlic clove, minced

2 teaspoons kosher salt

¼ cup perilla seed powder

1. Bring a medium saucepan of water to a boil over medium-high heat. Add the taro roots and stir. Cover and cook for 10 minutes. Drain and rinse a few times with cold water. Peel the skins with a paring knife or a potato peeler. Cut the taro roots into bite-size pieces.

2. Heat the vegetable oil in a large skillet over medium-high heat. Add the beef (if using) and stir with a wooden spoon for 1 minute. Add the taro, onion, carrot, and garlic and stir for 2 to 4 minutes, until the onion is translucent.

3. Add 2½ cups water and the salt and cover. Cook for about 15 minutes, until the taro is fully cooked. Add the perilla seed powder. Stir gently with the wooden spoon and simmer for 1 minute. Remove from the heat, transfer to a shallow bowl, and serve.

Braised Taro Stems

with Perilla Seed Powder

TORAN-JULGI BOKKEUM 토란줄기볶음

Serves 4

Did you know that in addition to the root of taro, you can eat the stems? They are one of the necessary ingredients for the famous Korean Duck Soup (page 154), and they make a delicious dish on their own. You can find them in Korean grocery stores in the dried vegetable section, usually next to dried fernbrake and bellflower roots.

The recipe itself is very easy, but you do need to take the extra steps of boiling and soaking the strips of tough stems a day ahead of time to rid them of the bitter calcium oxalate they contain, which can irritate your mouth and throat.

You'll be surprised when you taste the finished dish. The texture of taro stems is soft but a little crispy. They taste and feel almost meaty! The perilla seed powder adds a rich, nutty flavor and a creamy texture.

1½ ounces dried taro stems (a little more than ½ package), soaked and prepared for cooking (see page 424), then cut into 2-inch-long pieces

2 scallions, chopped

2 garlic cloves, minced

2 teaspoons toasted sesame oil

1 teaspoon soy sauce

⅓ cup perilla seed powder

2 tablespoons vegetable oil

½ medium onion, chopped

2 tablespoons fish sauce

1. Combine the softened taro stems, scallions, garlic, sesame oil, and soy sauce in a bowl. Mix well by hand.

2. Combine the perilla seed powder and 2 cups water in another bowl and mix well.

3. Heat the vegetable oil in a large, heavy skillet over medium-high heat. Add the onion and cook, stirring with a wooden spoon, for 1 minute, or until the onion has begun to soften and is a little translucent. Add the taro stem mixture and stir for about 5 minutes, until the stems begin to wilt. Add the fish sauce and the perilla seed mixture. Stir a few times.

4. Cover, reduce the heat to medium-low, and simmer for 25 minutes, until the stems are very tender. Uncover the pot and stir. Taste. The stems should be tender; if they are still a little tough, add a little more water and continue to simmer for another 5 to 10 minutes, until tender. Serve. The taro stems will keep in the refrigerator for up to 4 days.

BANCHAN AND MITBANCHAN

SIDE DISHES TO ALWAYS HAVE ON HAND

Banchan **translates as** "side dishes," but on the Korean table, they are far from sidelined. They make our meals varied and complete. Along with mitbanchan, which are side dishes that have been preserved by salting, drying, or pickling and can keep in the refrigerator for weeks or even months depending on the recipe, banchan are at the heart of Korean cuisine.

Banchan and mitbanchan complement and harmonize with the other dishes on the table. Some are spicy, some not; some take time, some are quick. There are regional and seasonal differences in recipes—and family differences, too. The same side dish can taste totally different from one kitchen to another, depending on who made it, and when, and where.

Chefs and home cooks are always creating new side dishes. For the recipes in this chapter, I aim to be authentic instead of inventive because I want you to know what traditional banchan and mitbanchan taste like. Once you've mastered them, you can modify them to your taste and invent new ones.

Again and again, my readers and viewers have requested more of these useful recipes, which is one reason why this chapter is packed with such a wide variety of them. And since any dish served with rice, including kimchi, soup, or stew, is considered a side dish in the vocabulary of Korean cuisine, you will find other banchan and mitbanchan throughout this book.

Traditional Toasted Gim

JEONTONG GIM-GUI 전통 김구이

Serves 8 to 10

These days you can get packages of toasted gim (nori in Japanese) at just about every grocery store. But when I lived in Korea, rubbing or brushing sheets of gim with toasted sesame oil or toasted perilla seed oil, then sprinkling them with salt and toasting them at home was a common routine. Most families made and froze 50 or 100 sheets at once. It was a lot of work, but well worth the effort. The sheets are stacked in twos and only one side of each sheet is toasted. That way you retain the gim's ocean flavor and nutrients.

Some people eat toasted gim by itself as a snack, but for Koreans, it's one of our all-time classic side dishes for rice. We eat gim at every meal and pack the toasted sheets into lunchboxes.

The biggest challenge is keeping the sheets crispy until you eat them. They will start losing their crunchiness if they are exposed to air for a few hours. That's why I recommend freezing the gim right after you season and toast it.

1 tablespoon vegetable oil

1 tablespoon toasted sesame oil or toasted perilla seed oil

½ teaspoon kosher salt

10 sheets seaweed paper (gim; aka nori)

1. Combine the vegetable oil and sesame oil in a small bowl and mix well. Put the salt in another small bowl.

2. Stack the sheets of gim with the shiny side up on a large cutting board or baking sheet. Using a pastry brush or your hands, coat the gim evenly with oil. Sprinkle a pinch of salt over the gim. Slide the oiled, salted sheet under the stack. Repeat until all 10 sheets of gim are oiled and salted and the first seasoned gim is back on top.

3. Wrap the gim stack in a large sheet of parchment paper. Press down the top with your hands so the sheets soak up a bit more oil. Set aside for 10 to 30 minutes.

4. Heat a large skillet over medium heat. Place 2 sheets of gim, one on top of the other with the shiny sides up, in the skillet. Press the gim with a spatula for 20 to 30 seconds, until the bottom turns green and crisp, moving the gim around in the skillet with the spatula so that it toasts evenly. Turn the stack over and press down with the spatula to toast for another 20 to 30 seconds. Only one side of each gim will be toasted. Transfer the toasted gim to the cutting board and repeat with the rest of sheets, stacked in pairs.

5. Using scissors or a kitchen knife, cut the toasted gim in half, then cut each half into thirds so you have 6 equal pieces. Serve. Keep the gim in a small plastic bag or airtight container and serve it over the next few days. If you toast a large quantity, wrap it airtight and keep in the freezer for up to 1 month. Remove from the freezer as needed and be sure to rewrap the rest each time.

Braised Soybeans and Walnuts

KONG-HODU-JORIM 콩호두조림

Makes 1¼ pounds (about 3 cups)

After a long soak, soybeans are simmered in their soaking water, along with a generous amount of soy sauce, rice syrup, and sugar, just long enough to be cooked through. They remain a bit chewy, with a slight crunch that is enhanced by the walnuts that are added after the soybeans have simmered. Then the pot is uncovered and the heat increased a little bit so that the liquid can cook down. The result is a sweet, salty, and nutty syrup that glazes the soybeans and walnuts. They make a delicious snack or side dish, go well with beer, and are great in a lunchbox if you have any left over.

8 ounces dried soybeans (about 1¼ cups)

⅓ cup soy sauce

⅓ cup rice syrup or ¼ cup sugar

2 tablespoons sugar

1 tablespoon vegetable oil

3 garlic cloves, minced

3 ounces walnuts (about 1 cup)

1 teaspoon toasted sesame oil

1 tablespoon toasted sesame seeds

1. Pick out and discard any brownish or broken beans and put the rest in a strainer. Rinse with cold running water. Transfer the beans to a heavy saucepan, add 3 cups water, cover, and soak for at least 7 hours or overnight.

2. Pick out and discard any bean skins floating on the surface. Cover and cook over medium-high heat for 10 minutes, cracking the lid if the beans begin to boil over.

3. Reduce the heat to low and add the soy sauce, rice syrup, sugar, vegetable oil, and garlic. Stir a few times with a wooden spoon. Cover and cook for 30 minutes.

4. Meanwhile, heat a medium skillet over medium heat, add the walnuts, and stir until they become crunchy and light golden, 4 to 5 minutes. Immediately remove from the heat, transfer the nuts to a bowl, and set aside.

5. When the beans are ready, remove any floating bean skins and add the walnuts.

6. Turn up the heat to medium-high and stir for 7 to 10 minutes, until most of the liquid has evaporated and the beans are glazed and slightly wrinkly. Stir in the sesame oil and sesame seeds and remove from the heat. Allow the beans to cool, and serve. The beans can be refrigerated in an airtight container for up to 1 month.

Stir-Fried Kimchi
with Tuna

KIMCHI-CHAMCHI-BOKKEUM 김치참치볶음

Serves 4

With kimchi and seasonings, a can of tuna can make a complete meal with rice—no need for any other side dishes. I prefer well-fermented Traditional Napa Cabbage Kimchi (page 112) for this dish because I love the crisp-tender texture of the cabbage and the delightful sour, fermented flavor. The dish is one more reason to have kimchi (and tuna) on hand for quick, satisfying meals.

When the kimchi and tuna are stir-fried together, any liquid in the pan evaporates, so the dish remains dry, making it perfect to pack in a lunchbox.

2 tablespoons vegetable oil

1 pound fermented sour kimchi (see headnote), cut into 1-inch pieces

1 medium onion, sliced (about 1 cup)

1 (5-ounce) can tuna, preferably Korean oil-packed tuna, drained

2 tablespoons Korean hot pepper paste (gochujang)

2 scallions, sliced diagonally into ½-inch-long pieces

1 teaspoon sugar

1. Heat the vegetable oil in a large skillet over medium-high heat. Add the kimchi and stir-fry with a wooden spoon until the kimchi has wilted and softened slightly, 1 to 2 minutes.

2. Add the onion and stir-fry until the onion is translucent, 4 to 5 minutes.

3. Add the tuna, hot pepper paste, scallions, and sugar and cook, gently stirring and mixing but taking care not to break up the tuna too much, 2 to 3 minutes, until the kimchi is tender and looks a little translucent. The flakes of tuna should still be discernible.

4. Remove from the heat and serve hot or at room temperature. The stir-fry can be refrigerated for up to 3 days. Reheat before serving.

Mung Bean Jelly
with Soy-Scallion Seasoning Sauce

CHEONGPOMUK-MUCHIM 청포묵무침

Serves 4 to 6

You have probably seen seasoned mung bean jelly served as a side dish at a Korean restaurant, a few shimmering pieces placed just so on a plate with a bit of dark sauce and scallions. It's almost always served with Korean barbecue. The springy jelly has a neutral flavor, and you may wonder what the big deal is, until you taste it with soy-scallion seasoning sauce. It's an irresistible contrast of flavor and texture. The jelly is easy to make; the most important thing to watch is the ratio of starch to water.

½ cup mung bean starch

½ teaspoon kosher salt

1 sheet seaweed paper (gim; aka nori)

Soy-Scallion Seasoning Sauce (page 130)

Shredded dried red pepper (silgochu; optional)

1. Combine the mung bean starch, salt, and 3½ cups water in a medium saucepan and stir well with a wooden spoon.

2. Place the pan over medium-high heat and heat, stirring, until it begins to bubble, about 5 minutes. Turn down the heat to low and stir for another 1 to 2 minutes, until the paste becomes translucent.

3. Pour the hot paste into a 4-cup glass measuring cup or other container and smooth the top with the wooden spoon. Leave at room temperature until completely cool, about 2 hours. (*You can refrigerate unseasoned jelly for up to 1 week. When you're ready to serve, you will see that the color is opaque. You can make it look translucent again by blanching it in boiling water. Bring a pot of water to a boil, add the jelly, and cook until translucent and soft, 2 to 3 minutes. Then remove from the water and cool.*)

4. Meanwhile, toast both sides of the gim until very crispy (see page 425). Place in a plastic bag and crumble into small pieces with your hands.

5. When the jelly has cooled, insert a rubber scraper or spatula between the edge of the jelly and the container to separate them, then move the scraper all along the edges of the jelly to help it come out easily. If it's properly cooled and ready, the jelly will jiggle but will maintain its shape while you do this. Turn the container upside down over a cutting board and let the jelly fall out in one jiggling piece.

6. Slice the jelly into bite-size pieces (use a crinkle cutter for more attractive shapes). Transfer to a plate and spoon on some sauce. Sprinkle with the crushed gim and the shredded dried red pepper (if using).

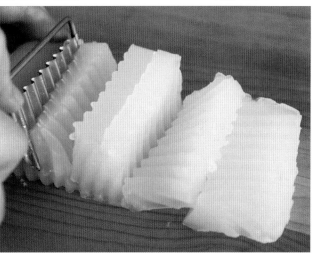

Chive Pancake

BUCHUJEON 부추전

Serves 2

When I need a simple, gorgeous, delicious side dish that can be made in a short time with just a few ingredients, I make this chive pancake. It's a classic of Korean home cooking. I use fish sauce to season the buchujeon and give it a deeper flavor, but if you want a vegetarian version, you can use salt instead.

Asian chives dry out and spoil quickly, so the first thing I do with them when I bring them home from the market is wrap them in a paper towel, seal them in a plastic bag, and put them in the fridge. The bunch keeps for a week in the fridge if wrapped this way. To make the pancake, I grab one handful, just what I can grasp between my thumb and index finger.

¾ cup all-purpose flour

2 teaspoons fish sauce or 1½ teaspoons kosher salt

4 ounces Asian chives, chopped (about 1½ cups)

¼ cup onion, chopped

2 tablespoons vegetable oil

1. Combine the flour, ¾ cup water, and fish sauce in a medium bowl and mix well. Stir in the chives and onion.

2. Heat a large nonstick skillet over medium-high heat. (If your skillet is small, divide the batter in half and cook 2 pancakes, one at a time.) Add 1 tablespoon of the oil to the hot skillet and swirl to coat the skillet.

3. Scrape all the chive batter into a mound in the center of the pan and spread it evenly so that it forms a thin round, about 11 inches in diameter. Cook until lightly browned and crispy on the bottom, 3 to 5 minutes. Shake the skillet to check its crispness. (You can hear the sound when the bottom is crisp.) Turn the pancake over with a spatula. Press the pancake down into the pan to spread and cook evenly.

4. Drizzle the remaining 1 tablespoon oil around the edge of the skillet so that it runs under the pancake. Using a spatula, lift the edges of the pancake and tilt and shake the skillet so that the oil evenly coats the bottom. Cook for 2 to 3 minutes, pressing the pancake down occasionally with the spatula, until the other side is crisp. Turn the pancake again and cook for another 2 to 3 minutes, until crisp on both sides.

5. Turn one more time and slide out onto a plate. Serve right away. Or, to serve in a lunchbox, cool for 5 minutes and cut into bite-size pieces.

Zucchini Pancake

AEHOBAKJEON 애호박전

Serves 2

This thin, savory pancake is the kind of comfort food that Koreans like to make for their families on gloomy rainy days. I first tasted it when I was in high school, at my best friend Hyegyung's house. For years I made aehobakjeon for my family using vegetable oil and adding a little toasted sesame oil for flavor.

After my first cookbook, Hyegyung contacted me, and I told her that I still remembered how delicious her mom's pancakes were and that I made them all the time. She told me that her mother had used perilla oil, not sesame oil, as a final addition to crisp and flavor the pancakes. The result is indeed tastier. If you can't find perilla oil, use toasted sesame oil.

I use all the batter at once to make one thin 10- to 11-inch pancake, but you can also make small pancakes, as long as you spread the batter as thinly as you can in the pan. They are best served right away so the edges remain crisp.

⅓ cup all-purpose flour

½ teaspoon kosher salt

1 small zucchini, cut into thin matchsticks

2 tablespoons vegetable oil

2 teaspoons perilla seed oil or toasted sesame oil

Soy-Vinegar Dipping Sauce (page 132)

1. In a medium bowl, combine the flour, salt, and ½ cup plus 2 tablespoons water and mix well. Stir in the zucchini.

2. Heat a large nonstick skillet over medium-high heat. (If your skillet is small, divide the batter in half and cook 2 pancakes, one at a time.) Add the vegetable oil to the hot skillet and swirl to coat the skillet.

3. Scrape all the zucchini batter into a mound in the center of the skillet and spread it evenly so that it forms a thin round, 10 to 11 inches in diameter. Cook until lightly browned and crispy on the bottom, 3 to 5 minutes. Shake the skillet to check its crispness. (You can hear the sound when the bottom is crisp.) Flip the pancake with a spatula and press the pancake down into the skillet. Cook on the second side until lightly browned and slightly crispy, 3 to 4 minutes.

4. Drizzle the perilla seed or sesame seed oil around the edge of the pan so that it runs under the pancake. Using a spatula, lift the edges of the pancake and tilt and shake the pan so that the oil evenly coats the bottom. Cook for 1 to 2 minutes, until the bottom is crispy. Flip the pancake over again and press the top of the pancake with the spatula. Cook for another 2 to 3 minutes, until crisp on both sides.

5. Flip over one more time and slide out onto a large plate. Serve right away with the dipping sauce.

EATING PANCAKES KOREAN STYLE

Although you can eat Korean pancakes with a fork and knife, the Korean way is to eat them with chopsticks, tearing off bite-size pieces and dipping them in the dipping sauce. We share the pancakes, and if it is difficult to get enough leverage to tear off pieces, one person holds the pancake down with his or her chopsticks so that the other can tear off a piece more easily. This is part of what makes Korean meals so congenial.

Tuna Pancakes

CHAMCHIJEON 참치전

Serves 2

It's hard for people to believe that such a delicious Korean side dish can be made from just one can of tuna. "What? You made this with just a can of tuna?"

I use the Korean canned tuna sold at Korean grocery stores because it's less watery and a little meatier than other tuna, but any unsalted water-packed or oil-packed tuna will work. If you use any other canned tuna besides Korean, add up to 1 more tablespoon flour to get the right consistency.

Many of my followers have told me that canned salmon also works nicely.

1 (5-ounce) can water-packed or oil-packed tuna, preferably Korean

¼ cup chopped onion

1 garlic clove, minced

½ teaspoon kosher salt

¼ teaspoon ground black pepper

1 large egg, beaten

1 teaspoon toasted sesame oil

1 tablespoon all-purpose flour (or up to 2 tablespoons if using non-Korean tuna)

2 tablespoons vegetable oil

1. Drain the tuna from the can into a strainer. Lightly press down on the tuna with the back of a spoon to press out more liquid (without pressing the tuna through), then transfer it to a bowl. Add the onion, garlic, salt, pepper, egg, sesame oil, and flour. Mix well with a spoon until well incorporated. Divide the mixture into 6 equal portions in the bowl with the spoon.

2. Heat the vegetable oil in a nonstick skillet over medium-high heat and swirl to coat the skillet. Scoop up 1 portion of the tuna mixture with a spoon, place it in the skillet, and flatten and round the edges to make a 2-inch disk. Repeat with the rest of the tuna mixture. Cook for 1 to 2 minutes, until the bottom turns golden brown and a little crispy. Turn and cook for another minute, until both sides are golden brown.

3. Remove from the heat and transfer the tuna pancakes to a plate. Serve right away.

KOREAN CANNED TUNA

Korean canned tuna is more chunky, meaty, and flavorful than other kinds. It's usually sold in yellow pull-top cans and comes in a variety of flavors, which are not always translated well into English. Some of the flavors are very specifically Korean, like kimchi stew–flavored tuna, or tuna flavored with jjajang sauce (black bean paste). Although some of the flavors may sound weird, like "mayo tuna" or "vegetable tuna" or "DHA tuna" (an omega-3 fatty acid that supposedly aids in brain function), they are worth trying, as many combinations taste better than they sound.

Boxed sets of tuna are common gifts to family, friends, and coworkers at Chuseok (Korean Thanksgiving). At this time of year, people often exchange nicely packaged food gifts, such as cases of pears or persimmons, yellow corvina, abalone, beef, and even Spam and tuna combo boxes.

Stir-Fried Potato and Ham

GAMJA-HAEM-BOKKEUM 감자햄볶음

Serves 4

This stir-fry is like a Korean-style chunky hash. The flavors and textures complement each other well—soft potatoes and salty, chewy ham, enhanced with onion and garlic and seasoned with soy sauce, sugar, and sesame oil. The dish is easy, comforting, and filling. My children loved it, so I often included some in their lunchboxes.

2 tablespoons vegetable oil

1 pound Yukon Gold potatoes, peeled and cut into ½- to ⅔-inch cubes (about 3 cups)

2 garlic cloves, minced

½ medium onion, cut into ⅓-inch cubes (about ½ cup)

3 ounces cooked ham, cut into ½-inch cubes (about ½ cup)

½ small carrot, peeled and cut into ⅓-inch cubes (about ¼ cup)

3 tablespoons soy sauce

1 tablespoon sugar

1 teaspoon toasted sesame oil

1. Heat the oil in a large skillet over medium-high heat. Add the potato and garlic and stir with a wooden spoon until the potato begins to cook through, about 3 minutes.

2. Add the onion, ham, and carrot and cook, stirring, until the onion begins to soften and become translucent, about 3 minutes.

3. Add the soy sauce, sugar, and ½ cup water. Cover, reduce the heat to low, and cook for another 3 minutes, until the potato and carrot are crisp-tender.

4. Uncover the skillet and increase the heat to medium-high. Cook, stirring, until the potato is fully cooked but still intact and all the ingredients are well incorporated and glazed, 7 to 8 minutes. The potato should not be at all mushy. Stir in the sesame oil and serve. This can be stored in an airtight container in the refrigerator for up to 3 days.

Rolled Omelet

GYERAN-MARI 계란말이

Serves 2 to 3

When I was a university student, I used to go to a snack bar run by an elderly woman. It was always packed with customers. All the vendor sold was gyeran-mari (rolled omelets) and rice. Her omelets were very moist because she used a lot of onion, and I have been doing the same ever since.

This omelet, modeled on hers, is simple and colorful, with savory bits of crispy vegetables inside. The recipe has many variations, and every Korean mom has her own version. Some use a lot of colorful vegetables, while others use little or no vegetables at all.

3 large eggs

½ teaspoon kosher salt

Pinch of ground white pepper

⅓ cup chopped onion

1 tablespoon chopped green chili pepper or green bell pepper

1 tablespoon chopped red chili pepper or red bell pepper

1 tablespoon vegetable oil

1. Crack the eggs into a bowl and add the salt and white pepper. Beat with chopsticks or a fork. Stir in the onion, green pepper, and red pepper. Put the vegetable oil in a small bowl and have a basting brush ready.

2. Heat a large nonstick skillet over medium-high heat. Dip the brush into the oil and brush the skillet. Reduce the heat to medium and spoon about one-third of the egg mixture into the skillet. Make sure that the onion and peppers are evenly distributed in the mix. Spread the egg mixture evenly with the spoon into a thin, rectangular pancake. Cook for 1 to 2 minutes, until the bottom is set but the top is still a little runny.

3. Lift up the right edge of the rectangle with your spatula and roll it up from right to left. Brush some oil on the cleared part of the skillet and move the rolled egg back to the right side of the oiled part of the skillet.

4. Spoon half of the remaining egg mixture into the skillet, just to the left of the omelet roll so that the eggs run into the bottom edge and extend the omelet you already cooked, shaping it into a rectangle. Let this new layer cook for 1 to 2 minutes, until set on the bottom but still a little bit runny on top.

5. Using a spatula, turn the rolled omelet over onto the new flat egg pancake and roll up the omelet from right to left. You will now have a roll on the left side. Brush the skillet with the remaining oil and push the omelet roll back over to the far right side.

6. Repeat Step 4 with the remaining egg mixture. When the last layer has set, roll up the omelet again from right to left into a long, even, rectangular shape. Reduce the heat to low and cook, turning the omelet so that the four sides cook evenly, 3 to 4 minutes. Be careful not to brown it too much; just make sure it's set.

7. Remove the skillet from the heat and transfer the omelet to a cutting board. If you need to shape it into a better rectangle, wrap in a gimbap mat and press and shape it with your hands. Let it cool for 5 minutes, then cut crosswise into ¾-inch slices.

Fluffy Eggs in an Earthenware Pot

TTUKBAEGI-GYERANJJIM 뚝배기계란찜

Serves 2 to 4

When these fluffy eggs, which puff up like a soufflé, come to the table steaming and hissing, no one can resist dipping their spoon into the pot. The dish, which many Korean barbecue restaurants serve as a side, is comfort food at its best. I use a 2½-cup earthenware pot, set directly over a flame. If you don't have one, you can make the dish using a small, heavy stainless-steel saucepan.

4 large eggs

2 teaspoons salty fermented shrimp (sauejeot) or 1 teaspoon kosher salt

½ cup unsalted chicken broth

1 scallion, chopped

1 teaspoon toasted sesame oil

1. Combine the eggs and salty fermented shrimp or salt in a bowl and whisk with a fork or whisk for about 1 minute. Add ¼ cup of the chicken broth and whisk for another minute.

2. Pour the remaining ¼ cup chicken broth into a 2½-cup earthenware pot or a small, heavy stainless-steel saucepan and set over medium-high heat. Bring to a boil, 2 to 3 minutes (less in a saucepan).

3. Reduce the heat to medium-low. Slowly pour the egg mixture into the pot, little by little, whisking constantly with a fork or whisk. Once all the mixture has been added, continue to whisk for another minute.

4. Cover with a dome-shaped heat-safe ceramic or stainless-steel bowl that fits over the pot, so that the egg mixture can expand.

5. Cook for 10 to 12 minutes (about 8 minutes if using stainless steel), until steam begins to escape from under the bowl lip and steamy liquid begins to drip down the sides. The eggs will smell nutty.

6. Carefully remove the lid (avoiding the hot steam) and garnish with the scallion. Drizzle on the sesame oil and serve right away.

NOTE

After cooking, there will probably be a layer of egg stuck to your pot. You can clean it off using a wire scrubber.

Eggs and Green Chili Peppers in Soy Broth

GYERAN-PUTGOCHU-JANGJORIM
계란풋고추장조림

Serves 6

Peeled hard-boiled eggs become a beautiful light brown when simmered for a short time in a mixture of soy sauce and broth. Green and red chili peppers, simmered in the same broth, add a little kick, and the combination makes a great everyday side dish. If you have any leftover broth, eat it with warm rice. The savory eggs also look beautiful in a lunchbox, surrounded by other side dishes and rice.

6 large eggs

4 ounces green and red chili peppers or shishito peppers, washed and cut crosswise into 1-inch pieces

3 garlic cloves, cut into halves

1 cup Anchovy-Kelp Stock (page 74), Vegetable Stock (page 78), or store-bought unsalted chicken or beef stock

¼ cup soy sauce

1. In a medium saucepan, bring 2 quarts water to a boil over medium-high heat. Slowly and gently lower the eggs, one by one, into the boiling water. Cover and cook for 10 to 11 minutes, stirring occasionally with a wooden spoon, so the yolks will set in the center of the eggs.

2. Drain the eggs and immediately transfer to a bowl of cold water. Gently crack the eggs against the bottom or side of the bowl, keeping them submerged in the water. Peel the eggs in the water. The shells will come off clean. Put the eggs in a bowl and set aside.

3. In a medium saucepan, combine the green and red chili peppers, garlic, stock, and soy sauce. Place over medium-high heat, cover, and cook for 10 minutes. Add the peeled eggs and cook, uncovered, stirring occasionally with a wooden spoon to evenly coat, for 5 to 6 minutes, until some of the broth has evaporated and the eggs are light brown.

4. Remove the pan from the heat and let the eggs cool in the broth.

5. To serve, put the eggs on a cutting board and slice crosswise or cut in half lengthwise. Put them on a small plate or in a small shallow bowl with some of the chili peppers. Spoon in some broth, avoiding the bright yellow yolks. Or arrange in a lunchbox, without the stock. The eggs can be refrigerated for up to 1 week.

Fried Gochujang
with Ground Beef and Pine Nuts

GOCHUJANG-BOKKEUM 고추장볶음

Makes about 1 pound (2½ cups)

Ground beef stir-fried with sesame oil, black pepper, garlic, honey, pine nuts, and a lot of gochujang is a great side dish, but also works very well as mitbanchan. I used to put a tiny amount of it in my children's lunchboxes for them to eat with their rice, with chopsticks, and they always finished every bit of it. Why wouldn't they? The combination is irresistible.

3 teaspoons toasted sesame oil	1 cup Korean hot pepper paste (gochujang)
8 ounces ground beef	3 tablespoons honey or sugar
½ teaspoon ground black pepper	½ cup pine nuts
2 garlic cloves, minced	

1. Heat 1 teaspoon of the sesame oil in a large skillet over medium-high heat. Add the ground beef and black pepper and stir-fry with a wooden spoon for about 3 minutes, until the beef is fully cooked. Place a strainer over a bowl and drain, pressing down with the wooden spoon so that the excess fat goes through the strainer. Discard the fat.

2. Wipe out the skillet and return it to medium-high heat. Add the remaining 2 teaspoons sesame oil and the garlic and stir with a wooden spoon for about 1 minute, until the garlic is fragrant and light brown. Add the cooked beef and stir together for 1 minute.

3. Reduce the heat to medium and add the hot pepper paste, honey, and pine nuts. Stir for 3 to 4 minutes, just until the paste becomes shiny and thins slightly. Do not overcook. Remove the skillet from the heat and allow the mixture to cool. Serve or transfer to an airtight container and refrigerate for up to 1 month (the fermented gochujang helps to preserve the meat). To eat, take up a small amount of the paste with chopsticks or a spoon and mix with rice.

Stir-Fried Dried Anchovies

MYEOLCHI-BOKKEUM 멸치볶음

Makes about 4 ounces (2 cups)

You've probably been served these crunchy, sweet, and salty anchovies as a side dish in a Korean restaurant. Every family has their own recipe, and what makes the dish stand out is the crunchiness of the anchovies. I stir-fry them in oil to make them extra crispy before I start adding the seasonings.

Since you eat the entire anchovy, including the tiny bones and the head, myeolchi-bokkeum is an excellent source of calcium. It's especially good for the developing bones of young children, which is why it's one of the most common mitbanchan in Korean lunchboxes.

4 ounces dried small (about 1 inch long) anchovies (about 2 cups)	2 garlic cloves, minced
	1 tablespoon vegetable oil
¼ cup Korean hot pepper paste (gochujang)	1 teaspoon toasted sesame oil
1 teaspoon soy sauce	2 teaspoons toasted sesame seeds
1 tablespoon sugar	

1. Put the dried anchovies in a colander. Shake and toss the anchovies to remove the smallest bits and broken pieces.

2. Combine the hot pepper paste, soy sauce, sugar, garlic, and 2 tablespoons water in a small bowl and mix until the ingredients are well incorporated.

3. Heat the vegetable oil in a skillet over medium heat. Add the anchovies and stir with a wooden spoon until the anchovies are crisp, 3 to 4 minutes.

4. Push the anchovies to the edge of the skillet, leaving the center of the skillet empty, and turn off the heat.

5. Scrape the seasoning sauce into the center of the skillet and stir gently until bubbling (the skillet will be hot enough). Return the skillet to low heat and stir the anchovies into the seasoning sauce. Mix until all the anchovies are well coated. Remove from the heat. Add the sesame oil and sesame seeds and stir well. Serve warm or cool, or transfer to an airtight container and refrigerate for up to 1 month.

Stir-Fried Dried Shrimp

MAREUN-SAEU-BOKKEUM 마른새우볶음

Makes 6 ounces (about 2½ cups)

These nutty-tasting shrimp are sweet, spicy, and pleasantly crunchy. One of the nicest things about this dish is the contrast between the thin, crunchy shells and the savory flesh of the shrimp. Green chili peppers give a fresh-tasting kick.

You can find small dried shrimp at Korean grocery stores and online. Be sure to buy the ones without heads for this recipe. Look for the reddest, plumpest dried shrimp you can find, since those have more meat.

4 ounces dried shrimp, without heads (about 2 cups)

2 tablespoons vegetable oil

2 garlic cloves, minced

2 green chili peppers, shishito peppers, or jalapeños, sliced (about ⅓ cup)

1 tablespoon soy sauce

1 tablespoon sugar

1 tablespoon toasted sesame oil

1 tablespoon toasted sesame seeds

1. Heat a large skillet over medium heat and add the shrimp. Stir with a wooden spoon for 2 to 3 minutes, until the shrimp turn slightly gray and smell fragrant.

2. Add 1 tablespoon of the vegetable oil and continue stirring for 2 to 3 minutes, until the shrimp are shiny and very crisp.

3. Transfer the shrimp to a coarse mesh strainer set over a bowl. Shake the strainer several times and knock it against the bowl to allow the sharp bits of shell to go through. Take up the shrimp little by little and transfer from the strainer to a bowl, leaving behind more sharp bits of shell in the strainer. Discard all the residue from the strainer and bowl.

4. Wipe out the skillet and heat over medium-high heat. Add the remaining 1 tablespoon vegetable oil, the garlic, and green chili peppers and stir for 30 seconds. Turn off the burner, add the soy sauce and sugar, and quickly stir with the wooden spoon for about 1 minute. The soy sauce and sugar will sizzle in the hot skillet even after you remove it from the heat.

5. Add the shrimp, return the skillet to medium heat, and stir together for another minute, until the shrimp are well coated with the seasoning.

6. Remove from the heat and stir in the sesame oil and sesame seeds. Serve or transfer to an airtight container and refrigerate for up to 1 month.

Spicy Shredded Dried Squid

OJINGEOCHAE-MUCHIM 오징어채무침

Makes about 12 ounces

There's hardly any preparation involved for this spicy, sweet, nutty, salty side dish. All you do is combine the ingredients for the seasoning paste and stir in the shredded dried squid. Although it isn't traditional, I use olive oil in the paste because I like the flavor.

Shredded dried squid, called jinmichae, is available in Korean grocery stores in the frozen section. You can eat the white squid strands on their own as well as with the seasoning paste. They make a good snack or side dish and go well with alcohol, especially beer.

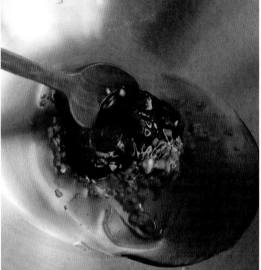

⅓ cup Korean hot pepper paste (gochujang)

2 garlic cloves, minced

¼ cup rice syrup or 3 tablespoons sugar

3 tablespoons olive oil or vegetable oil

1 tablespoon toasted sesame oil

8 ounces shredded dried squid (jinmichae), cut into 2-inch pieces

1 teaspoon toasted sesame seeds

1. Combine the hot pepper paste, garlic, rice syrup, olive oil, and sesame oil in a bowl and mix together with a wooden spoon until well incorporated.

2. Add the squid and mix well by hand until the squid is evenly coated with sauce, shiny, and a little softer. Sprinkle with the sesame seeds. Serve or transfer to an airtight container and refrigerate for up to 1 month.

Seasoned Grated Dried Pollock

BUGEO-BOPURAGI-MUCHIM 북어보푸라기무침

**Makes three 2½-inch fish balls;
serves 4 as a snack or side dish**

Dried pollock is grated, seasoned with sesame oil and sugar, and shaped into balls to make a side dish that looks beautiful on the table. They melt in your mouth, with a salty flavor that is only mildly fishy.

Dried pollock (bugeo) is easy to find in the dried fish section in Korean markets. It is very tough, but for these balls, you grate it into feathery shavings. The dish has its origins in the Joseon dynasty, when it was made for the Korean kings. Legend has it that the cooks grated the bugeo with a spoon and served it as a side dish with a simple porridge.

The fluffy fish balls look like tiny delicate puffs of cotton candy, one reddish, one tan, and one brown. Serve them as part of a meal for special guests; they go well with beer or soju. Or tuck them into a lunchbox for someone you love.

1 large or 2 small dried whole pollock (about 3 ounces)	¼ teaspoon Korean hot pepper flakes (gochu-garu)
1 teaspoon toasted sesame oil	1 teaspoon toasted sesame seeds
1 teaspoon sugar	½ teaspoon soy sauce
¼ teaspoon kosher salt	

1. Cut off the head of the dried pollock with kitchen scissors and discard. Dip the body in cold water for 1 second and put it on a cutting board. Dry it with a paper towel. Check the fish for bones; if there are any, remove them by hand.

2. Hold the skin side of the fish against the palm of your hand and grate the fleshy side with a grater. (The skin can be used for making fish stock; wrap in plastic and refrigerate or freeze.)

3. Transfer the grated fish to a bowl. Add the sesame oil, sugar, and salt. Mix well with a spoon first, then rub the mixture between your palms, a little at a time, until all the mixture is evenly seasoned. Divide the grated pollock evenly among three bowls.

4. To make the red ball, put the hot pepper flakes in a strainer and strain into a small bowl. Discard the dregs and add the strained hot pepper to one of the bowls of grated pollock, along with one-third of the toasted sesame seeds. Rub the mixture well by hand and shape into a ball by squeezing gently with both hands. Put the red ball on a plate.

5. To make the brown ball, add the soy sauce and half of the remaining sesame seeds to the second bowl of grated pollock. Rub the mixture well by hand and shape into a ball by squeezing gently with both hands. Place on the plate next to the red ball.

6. To make the tan ball, add the remaining sesame seeds to the third bowl. Mix well and shape into a ball by squeezing gently with both hands. Place next to the brown ball on the plate and serve. The pollock balls will keep in the refrigerator for up to 1 week.

Stir-Fried Fish Cake

EOMUK-BOKKEUM 어묵볶음

Serves 4 to 8

It's easy to find packaged fish cakes in the freezer section of Korean markets. We cut up the sheets into bite-size pieces and use them in stir-fries like this one. The stir-fry has a good fish flavor, spiced up with a generous amount of gochujang, and makes a substantial accompaniment to rice.

1 tablespoon vegetable oil

8 ounces fish cake, store-bought or homemade (page 182), cut into bite-size pieces

⅓ cup sliced onion

1 garlic clove, minced

2 tablespoons Korean hot pepper paste (gochujang)

1 tablespoon rice syrup or 2 teaspoons sugar

2 teaspoons toasted sesame oil

2 teaspoons toasted sesame seeds

1 scallion, chopped

1. Heat the vegetable oil in a large skillet over medium-high heat. Add the fish cake and, using a wooden spoon, stir-fry for 2 to 3 minutes, until the fish cake is light golden brown.

2. Add the onion, garlic, hot pepper paste, and rice syrup and stir-fry for 2 to 3 minutes, until shiny and fragrant.

3. Remove the skillet from the heat. Add the sesame oil, sesame seeds, and scallion and mix well. Serve. The fish cake can be refrigerated for up to 3 days.

VARIATION
To make a version that is not spicy, substitute 1 tablespoon soy sauce for the hot pepper paste.

Seasoned Sea Squirts

MEONGGE-MUCHIM 멍게무침

Makes about 7 ounces (about ¾ cup)

My father's hometown of Namhae on the South Sea is famous for its springtime sea squirts, and I sometimes get cravings for this sea creature, which Koreans usually eat raw. They're sweet and briny like clams, and also similar in texture. You can't get fresh sea squirts in markets in America, but you can find them frozen in Korean grocery stores, already shelled, cleaned, and cut up.

1 (6-ounce) package frozen sea squirts (about ¾ cup), thawed in the refrigerator

1 tablespoon fish sauce

1 tablespoon soy sauce

2 teaspoons toasted sesame oil

1 garlic clove, minced

1 scallion, chopped

1 tablespoon Korean hot pepper flakes (gochu-garu)

1 teaspoon sugar

1 teaspoon toasted sesame seeds

1. Rinse the sea squirts in cold water and drain. Mix with the fish sauce in a small bowl. Cover and refrigerate for 1 hour.

2. Drain and squeeze out the excess water. Chop the sea squirts into small pieces.

3. Combine the soy sauce, sesame oil, garlic, scallion, hot pepper flakes, sugar, and sesame seeds in a bowl and mix well with a spoon. Add the chopped sea squirts and mix together with the spoon. Transfer to a serving bowl and serve, or transfer to an airtight container and refrigerate for up to 1 week.

Salty Fermented Radish

MU-JANGAJJI 무장아찌

Makes about 5 pounds

Since it has so much soy sauce, you can bet that this is salty. It has to be, so the radish maintains its crisp texture over time. I've toned it down from the traditional version, which calls for salt instead of soy sauce. I add jujubes to give the radish a little sweetness and tanginess, plus dried red chili peppers for a very subtle kick.

My grandmother would slice the jangajji thin, season it, and serve it as a side dish for rice. Sometimes she used it to make a cold soup side dish. That's one of the great things about this recipe—you can use it as a base for other dishes, such as Cold Salty Fermented Radish Soup Side Dish (page 254) and Seasoned Salty Fermented Radish (page 253).

The key is to use good-quality radishes that are firm, heavy, juicy, and very fresh, with smooth, shiny skin. The jangajji doesn't need to be refrigerated. My one-year-old batch is still crisp and delicious.

5 pounds Korean radish or daikon, peeled and cut lengthwise into 4-by-5-inch slices, about 1 inch thick

8 dried jujubes

7 garlic cloves, peeled and sliced

6 or 7 large whole dried red chili peppers or about ½ cup small dried red chili peppers

2 tablespoons thinly sliced peeled ginger

8 cups soy sauce

1. Put the radish slices into a large glass or earthenware jar. (I use a 5-quart earthenware jar, which is the perfect size.) Add the jujubes, garlic, dried red chili peppers, and ginger.

2. Pour the soy sauce into the jar. Press the radish down with your hand and put fermentation weights, a small plate, or a few small, clean rocks on top so that the radish remains completely submerged. Cover and set aside for 3 days.

3. Remove the weights, jujubes, and peppers and reserve. Pour as much of the soy sauce brine as you can into a large, heavy pot, leaving the radish in the jar. Cover, bring the brine to a boil over medium-high heat, and boil for 5 minutes. Remove the pot from the heat and allow the brine to cool thoroughly, then pour the brine back into the jar with the radish slices. Return the jujubes and peppers to the jar, add the weights, cover, and let sit for 1 week.

4. After a week, repeat Step 3. Then cover the jar and allow the radishes to ferment for 1 month before eating. The radishes will turn a beautiful dark brown and become darker and slightly tangy as time passes. Keep the jar in a cool place for 1 year or more.

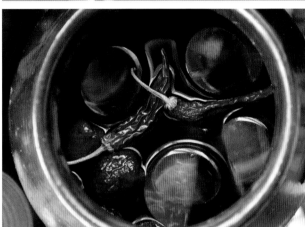

Seasoned Salty Fermented Radish

MU-JANGAJJI-MUCHIM 무장아찌무침

Makes about ¾ cup

With its pungent taste and crisp texture, just a few small pieces of this condiment contribute so much pleasure to each spoonful of rice. It really wakes up your palate between bites of dishes like Braised Beef Short Ribs (page 163) or Pan-Fried Cod Fillets with Sesame Oil (page 172).

4 ounces Salty Fermented Radish (page 250), cut into thin matchsticks (about ½ cup)

2 scallions, chopped

1 garlic clove, minced

2 teaspoons Korean hot pepper flakes (gochu-garu)

1 tablespoon rice syrup or 2 teaspoons sugar

1 tablespoon toasted sesame oil

1 tablespoon toasted sesame seeds

Combine all the ingredients in a bowl. Mix well with a spoon. Serve or transfer to an airtight container and refrigerate for up to 1 month. Serve 1 or 2 tablespoons in a small plate or bowl with rice and other side dishes.

Cold Salty Fermented Radish Soup Side Dish

MU-JANGAJJI-NAENGGUK 무장아찌냉국

Serves 4

"Wow! This is so refreshing!" That's what guests always say when they try this dish for the first time. The sweet, sour, and salty cold soup is another good reason to make Salty Fermented Radish (page 250). The soup goes well with Sweet Potato Starch Noodles with Vegetables and Meat (page 323) and with Steamed Dumplings (page 305), and of course we always serve it with rice.

4 ounces Salty Fermented Radish (page 250), cut into thin matchsticks (about ½ cup)

2 garlic cloves, minced

½ small sliced onion (about ¼ cup)

3 scallions, chopped

1 green chili pepper or jalapeño, thinly sliced

1 tablespoon white vinegar

2 teaspoons sugar

1 cup crushed ice (about 12 ice cubes)

1 tablespoon toasted sesame seeds, ground with a mortar and pestle or in a coffee grinder

1. Combine the fermented radish and 2 cups cold water in a small glass or ceramic bowl. Cover and refrigerate for at least 20 minutes and up to several hours.

2. Uncover and add the garlic, onion, scallions, chili pepper, vinegar, and sugar. Stir well with a spoon until the sugar has dissolved and all the flavors are well incorporated.

3. Add the crushed ice and spoon the ground sesame seeds on top. Serve right away.

HOW TO CRUSH ICE CUBES

Place the ice cubes in a kitchen hemp sack or wrap them in a few layers of folded cheesecloth and pound on the cutting board until broken into small pieces. You can also pulse the ice cubes in a food processor or blender to crush.

Salty Pickled Peppers

GOCHU-JANGAJJI 고추장아찌

Makes about 3 pounds

These are my family's all-time favorite pickles. I make them every summer, when the green chili peppers are at their peak, and we enjoy them all year long. By the time summer rolls around again, I'm almost out of last year's batch and ready to make a new one. I use the mild green chili peppers that I buy at a large Korean market. Other types of mild green chilis, such as Anaheims, will also work. So will jalapeños, if you like spicy food.

My grandmother buried her chili pepper pickles in her salty doenjang (Korean fermented soybean paste) for months, and by the time she served them to us they were incredibly salty and spicy, so much so that I could eat only one or two small ones with my bowl of rice. These days Koreans use much less salt. But too little salt and the peppers go soggy easily, so don't be afraid to use the full cup called for here.

4 pounds mild, crisp green chili peppers (see headnote), rinsed and drained

2½ cups fish sauce

1 cup kosher salt

1. Cut away all but ½ inch of the pepper stems.

2. Using a toothpick, poke a hole in each pepper just under the stem. The holes will allow the brine to seep into the peppers.

3. Put the peppers in heat-safe glass or earthenware jars. (I use two 1-gallon glass jars.)

4. Combine the fish sauce, salt, and 4 quarts water in a large pot. Bring to a boil over medium-high heat. Reduce the heat to medium and boil for 10 minutes. Skim away the foam with a mesh skimmer.

5. Remove the pot from the heat and pour the hot brine directly over the peppers. Keep the peppers submerged in the brine for 24 hours by weighing them down with a small heavy plate, or clean rocks or fermentation weights.

6. Open the jars, remove the weights, and strain the peppers over a pot. Return the peppers to the jars and boil the brine over medium-high heat for 15 minutes.

7. Remove the pot from the heat and let the brine cool thoroughly. Pour over the peppers. Put the weights back on top to keep the peppers submerged, and cover. Do not screw the jar tops on too tightly. Let sit for 1 week.

8. After a week, repeat steps 6 and 7, without the weights. Then cover and store the peppers in the refrigerator.

9. If the peppers are too large to serve, cut them into bite-size pieces just before serving. Do not rinse the peppers—fresh water will make them soggy.

Seasoned Salty Pickled Peppers

GOCHU-JANGAJJI-MUCHIM 고추장아찌무침

Makes 3 pounds

In the summertime, when energy and appetites are low, Koreans sometimes eat these pickles with a bowl of rice for lunch. Spicy foods stimulate the appetite, and we find them cooling in hot weather. We pour cold water into our rice and mix it in.

Whenever I have these seasoned pickled peppers in the fridge, sealed away in an airtight container, I feel comfortable, as when I have lots of kimchi. If the peppers are small, you can eat them whole, but you can also cut them up. You probably won't eat more than two at a time.

3 pounds Salty Pickled Peppers (page 256)

6 garlic cloves, minced

3 scallions, chopped

6 tablespoons Korean hot pepper flakes (gochu-garu)

6 tablespoons fish sauce

6 tablespoons rice syrup or 4 to 5 tablespoons sugar

1 tablespoon toasted sesame seeds

1. Drain the peppers and discard the brine.

2. Combine the garlic, scallions, hot pepper flakes, fish sauce, and rice syrup in a large bowl and mix well with a wooden spoon.

3. Add the pickled peppers and sesame seeds and mix well by hand (wear disposable gloves if you wish) to ensure that the seasonings are incorporated.

4. Transfer the peppers to an airtight container and refrigerate. They will keep for a year in the refrigerator. Never rinse the pickles, as fresh water will make them soggy.

Fermented Clams

JOGAEJEOT 조개젓

Makes about 1 cup

When I was young, my mother used to shop in traditional, sprawling open-air markets every morning at about 6:00 a.m. She always took me along. Because it was so early, I had plenty of time to visit the market, have breakfast, and still get to school on time.

In the early mornings, I would see women sitting on low wooden footstools in front of large basins filled with freshly caught small clams that had been hauled in at dawn. Using small knives, they shucked the clams with speed and grace, and tossed them into small bowls that were sold with them. The clams were very fresh, with the clean, bracing taste of the sea. My mother usually put a handful of them in her soybean paste stew, and she made salted fermented clams with them.

When clams are salted and fermented, their taste intensifies and their flavor deepens. They soften, but their texture is still chewy. Koreans usually make jogaejeot with smaller clams, but in my experiments, I've found that littleneck and topneck clams also work well. I rarely see the smaller varieties in American markets, and even when I do, I find them too difficult to open. I prefer to buy my clams fresh in the shell and shuck them my own way (see page 428), but you can ask your fishmonger to open them for you, or shuck them any way you like.

Rubbing the clams and salt together hastens the fermentation. Without this step, the process would require much more salt and take at least 5 months rather than a single month.

Once the clams have fermented, you can serve them as they are or mix them with seasonings (page 260). Either way, they are intensely flavorful, so serve just a small amount—at most a tablespoon—at a time.

10 ounces shucked (see page 428) fresh raw clams (from about 5¾ pounds clams, such as topneck or littleneck)

5 tablespoons plus 1 teaspoon kosher salt

1. Put the shucked clams in a bowl.

2. In another large bowl, combine 1 quart cold water, 1 tablespoon of the kosher salt, and several ice cubes. Stir well to dissolve the salt.

3. Transfer the clams to the cold salty water. One by one, grab the clams and swish around in the water to remove any residue. Repeat until all the clams are free of sand. Transfer the clams to a strainer, drain, and then rinse the bowl.

4. Return the clean clams to the bowl and add ¼ cup salt. Take up handfuls of clams and salt and squeeze and knead until the clams are slippery and foamy. Transfer the clams to a small earthenware or glass jar. Sprinkle the remaining 1 teaspoon salt over the surface. Cover, refrigerate, and let the clams ferment in the refrigerator for 1 month before serving. They will keep for another 3 months in the refrigerator.

Seasoned Fermented Clams

JOGAEJEOT-MUCHIM 조개젓무침

Makes about 2 cups

When you take a taste of seasoned fermented clams, you will experience many of the signature flavors in Korean cuisine. There is the fermented flavor that might be described as "funky," as well as saltiness, heat from the green chili peppers and the Korean hot pepper flakes, and sweetness from the rice syrup or sugar. You can serve this right away, or refrigerate for up to 3 months.

3 to 5 green chili peppers (3 ounces), chopped

4 garlic cloves, minced

2 teaspoons minced peeled ginger

¼ cup Korean hot pepper flakes (gochu-garu)

¼ cup rice syrup or 2 to 3 tablespoons sugar

1 tablespoon vegetable oil

1 cup Fermented Clams (page 259)

Toasted sesame seeds

1. Combine the chili peppers, garlic, ginger, hot pepper flakes, rice syrup, and vegetable oil in a medium bowl and mix well with a spoon.

2. Put the fermented clams on a large cutting board. Chop them into very small pieces. Transfer to the seasoning mixture and mix well with a spoon.

3. Transfer the mixture to a glass jar, cover, and refrigerate for up to 3 months, or transfer to a bowl if serving right away. Serve 1 to 2 tablespoons of the clams in a very small bowl to be shared at the table. Sprinkle with a pinch of sesame seeds just before serving.

DOSIRAK MADE WITH LOVE

PORTABLE KOREAN LUNCHBOX MEALS

Dosirak, or Korean lunchboxes, are made in the morning and meant to be eaten hours later at school, on the road, at work, or on a picnic. The word can refer to the lunchbox itself or the meal inside it. These make-ahead dishes have endless variety and are delicious, nutritious, economical, and practical. And when made by your mom, they inspire you to get through the rest of the day. My lunchbox was prepared by my mother when I was in elementary and middle school, but when I started high school away from my parents in Seoul, I made my own.

When I became a mom, I was determined to make my children the best lunchboxes. I wanted them to be surprised when they opened the lid. Sometimes I inlaid steamed green peas on top of their freshly cooked fluffy white rice, one by one, to make a heart shape. Sometimes I hid a gooey, soft sunny-side-up egg underneath the rice, so they would discover it as they were eating. A soft egg yolk oozing onto rice that's been sitting for a few hours and has solidified a bit is really something wonderful. Sometimes I put a sweet note like "Help yourself!" or "Enjoy!" in the box. Little things like this were ways to let my children know that I was thinking of them, and that the lunchbox was made with my love. I wanted them to open it and say: "My mom is the best!"

Dosirak from the nineteenth century in the National Folk Museum of Korea in Seoul

Dosirak are deeply ingrained in Korean culture. Centuries ago, the boxes were made with rice straw and bamboo; they were airy enough to keep the food fresh all day and sturdy enough to keep everything intact. Then as now, they were carried by workers, farmers, government officials, school children, and anyone else who needed to eat lunch outside the home.

The lunchboxes were traditionally lined with an edible leaf, such as a squash leaf or lotus leaf, which helped to keep the food, especially the rice, fresh tasting and protected it from the heat in the summer. The leaf was covered with a layer of rice; then, another leaf was placed on top of the rice. Salty side dishes such as fermented salty vegetables or some Korean fermented soybean paste were arranged on that leaf, and then the box was covered with the lid.

Today people buy their lunchboxes. They're made of plastic or stainless steel, and there are special insulated dosirak for use in winter. Thermal dosirak containers usually consist of three pieces: one for rice, one for soup, and one for side dishes. The rice and soup containers are insulated thermoses to keep these items warm, and the container for side dishes is uninsulated plastic.

In this chapter, I share twelve of my favorite dosirak combinations. The first six are new recipes, and the other six are dosirak composed of recipes from elsewhere in this book, things like kimchi, rice, fish, meat, vegetables, banchan, and mitbanchan.

I serve toasted gim (aka nori) in almost every dosirak. It's a crispy treat that tastes like the sea and goes with pretty much any side dish. It should be sealed in a plastic bag to keep it crisp. Koreans used to wrap gim for dosirak in the used foil wrappers from ramyeon (Korean instant noodles, similar to ramen). By lunchtime, the gim would still be perfectly crisp. Some people use the gim to wrap bites of rice, or you can just eat it between bites of side dishes.

RULES FOR MAKING GOOD DOSIRAK

1. Rice is the anchor and main focus of the whole lunchbox, and you'll need to start with rice that has been freshly made that morning. It can be Fluffy White Rice (page 41), Multigrain Rice (page 44), or Barley Rice (page 46), but it has to be fresh. I'm sure you're wondering why you can't make it the night before and then microwave it in the morning. What's the big deal? But it is a big deal. When it comes to taste and texture, reheated rice can't compare with freshly made, so we start our dosirak the right way, every day.

2. Which side dishes will go with the rice? They should complement each other in color, taste, texture, and shape, and create a well-balanced meal together. As a general guide, you can make a lunchbox with rice and one or two mitbanchan, and one or two freshly made side dishes, such as a rolled omelet, a pancake, or vegetables.

3. The side dishes you choose should not be too wet, because the lunchbox has to stay fresh all morning, and wet side dishes will make everything else in the box soggy. If you want a soupy side dish, put it in its own airtight container.

4. If your side dish is hot, let it cool before adding it to the box.

5. Kimchi should be wrapped separately in an airtight container. Otherwise, its pungent smell will mix with the other side dishes.

Other Ideas for Dosirak

Seaweed Rice Rolls

GIMBAP DOSIRAK 김밥 도시락

Makes 4 rolls; serves 2

Gimbap, seaweed rolls filled with rice and colorful fillings, is one of Korea's all-time favorite dishes. There are many variations, with different fillings, but they are always bright and tasty, with a mix of chewy and crispy textures. In this version, I use homemade steamed fish cake, but you can also use store-bought.

Because they are so portable, like sandwiches, Koreans often prepare gimbap for lunchboxes. I used to wake up before 5:30 a.m. to make them for my children's lunchboxes. I would never make the rolls ahead of time: You can't refrigerate them because the rice dries out, making the texture unappealing.

FOR THE RICE

1 teaspoon vegetable oil

½ teaspoon toasted sesame oil

¼ teaspoon kosher salt

4 cups freshly cooked Fluffy White Rice (page 41)

FOR THE EGGS

3 large eggs

¼ teaspoon kosher salt

1 teaspoon vegetable oil

FOR THE VEGETABLES

1 (1-pound) English cucumber

Kosher salt

1 teaspoon vegetable oil

4 strips yellow pickled radish (use precut or cut a whole radish into 8-by-⅓-inch strips)

1 large carrot, cut into matchsticks

½ teaspoon sugar

FOR THE FISH CAKE

8 ounces fish cake, either 4 store-bought thin rectangular sheets or homemade (page 182)

2 teaspoons vegetable oil

1 garlic clove, minced

1 tablespoon brown or white sugar

1 teaspoon soy sauce

2 teaspoons toasted sesame oil

FOR THE GIMBAP

2 teaspoons toasted sesame oil

4 sheets seaweed paper (gim; aka nori), toasted (see page 425)

MAKE THE RICE

Mix the vegetable oil, sesame oil, and salt in a large, shallow bowl. Add the freshly made warm rice. Gently fold in with a rice scoop or a wooden spoon. Let the rice cool down until it's no longer steaming. Cover and set aside.

MAKE THE EGGS

1. Whisk the eggs and salt in a bowl, then strain into another bowl. Discard the stringy bits remaining in the strainer.

2. Heat the vegetable oil in a large nonstick skillet over medium-high heat and swirl to coat evenly. Wipe out the excess oil with a paper towel. Turn off the heat, add the egg mixture to the skillet, and tilt the skillet to spread the egg into a large circle that covers the bottom. Let it sit for a few minutes, until the bottom of the egg pancake is cooked by the heat remaining in the skillet. Flip the egg pancake and turn the heat to medium. Cook just until the bottom side is set, without allowing the egg to brown. Remove from the heat and transfer to a cutting board.

3. Let the pancake cool for a few minutes, then cut into ¼-inch strips. Transfer to a large plate or baking sheet. Cover with plastic wrap to keep the egg strips from drying out.

MAKE THE VEGETABLES

1. Cut the cucumber crosswise into 2-inch-long sections. Cut each section lengthwise into ⅛-inch-thick slices, starting at the edge, until you get to the seedy core. When you can see the seeds, turn the cucumber so the cut side is down and slice again from the edge to the core. Continue with the other two sides, then discard the core and the seeds. Cut the strips into matchsticks.

2. Put the matchsticks in a bowl, sprinkle with a pinch of salt, and toss. Let stand for 5 to 10 minutes. Squeeze the cucumber tightly with both hands to remove the excess water.

Recipe Continues

3. Heat ½ teaspoon of the vegetable oil in a skillet over medium-high heat. Add the cucumber and stir with a wooden spoon for 30 seconds. Transfer to the plate next to the egg strips.

4. Add the yellow pickled radish strips to the plate next to the cucumber.

5. Put the carrot matchsticks in a bowl, toss with a pinch of salt, and let stand for 5 to 10 minutes.

6. Heat the remaining ½ teaspoon vegetable oil in the same skillet over medium-high heat. Add the carrots and stir with a wooden spoon for 30 seconds. Add the sugar and stir for another 30 seconds to glaze the carrots. Remove from the heat and transfer to the plate next to the yellow pickled radish.

MAKE THE FISH CAKE

1. **If using homemade fish cake:** Cut the roll in half lengthwise. Cut one half in quarters lengthwise. Refrigerate or freeze the other half for later use.

If using store-bought: Cut the sheets into matchsticks.

2. Heat the vegetable oil in a large skillet over medium-high heat and swirl to coat evenly. Add the fish cake strips and cook, turning with tongs occasionally, until all sides are light golden brown. Remove the skillet from the heat.

3. Add the garlic, sugar, and soy sauce to the skillet. Using tongs or a wooden spoon, move the fish cake strips around in the skillet and turn them over a few times to mix with the seasonings, until the sugar has melted and the strips are nicely glazed. Add the sesame oil and toss together. Leave the fish cake in the skillet.

ROLL AND CUT THE GIMBAP

1. Put the sesame oil in a small bowl and have a basting brush handy.

2. Place a sheet of gim on a bamboo gimbap mat, with the shiny side down. Evenly spread 1 cup seasoned rice over the gim, leaving a 1-inch margin uncovered along the top edge.

3. Divide the carrot, cucumber, egg, yellow pickled radish, and fish cake into 4 portions. Put a portion

of each item in a horizontal row on top of the rice, with the rows slightly overlapping. Use both hands to pick up the bottom edge of the mat and use it to roll the gim up and over the fillings so the rice surrounds them. Squeeze the mat gently, then continue rolling up the gim, using the mat and squeezing to get a tight roll. Unroll the mat and remove the roll from the mat. Using the basting brush, gently brush a small amount of sesame oil over the roll. (This will not only make the roll more delicious and shiny but also protect it from becoming soggy.) Repeat with the remaining ingredients to make 3 more rolls. Cut each roll into ⅓- to ½-inch slices. (For easier slicing, wipe your knife often with a wet towel.)

4. Arrange the slices on a plate or pack in a lunchbox. The gimbap will keep for several hours at room temperature. Do not refrigerate.

LEFTOVER GIMBAP

Gimbap is supposed to be served fresh, but if you have leftovers, you can refrigerate, then pan-fry. Heat a small amount of vegetable oil in a nonstick skillet over medium-high heat. Dip the gimbap slices in beaten egg and fry them until nicely browned on both sides.

Layered Three-Color Bibimbap Dosirak

SAMSAEK-BIBIMBAP DOSIRAK
삼색비빔밥 도시락

Serves 1

Sometimes a plate, bowl, or container inspires me to create a recipe. That's what happened when I found a cylindrical glass container at a kitchenware store. I made this simple, colorful layered bibimbap for serving in it, but of course you can serve it in any lunchbox container you have.

Carrot, cucumber, and soybean sprouts give a beautiful mix of colors and textures. Each vegetable is sandwiched between layers of rice, with a bright yellow fried egg on top, in a see-through container. Pack with another small container filled with soy-scallion seasoning sauce. Don't forget a spoon!

You can double or triple this recipe.

1½ cups soybean sprouts (4 ounces), cleaned (see page 421) and drained

Kosher salt

1 teaspoon toasted sesame oil

¾ cup thinly sliced cucumber

1 small carrot, cut into thin matchsticks (about ¾ cup)

1¼ teaspoons vegetable oil

1½ cups freshly cooked Fluffy White Rice (page 41)

1 large egg, cooked sunny-side up or over easy

¼ cup Soy-Scallion Seasoning Sauce (page 130)

1. Put the soybean sprouts in a small saucepan and add ¼ cup water and a pinch of salt. Cover and cook over medium-high heat for 5 minutes, until the bean sprouts are cooked through and have a nutty aroma. Remove from the heat and drain. Transfer to a bowl and mix with the sesame oil.

2. Put the sliced cucumber in another bowl and toss with a pinch of salt. Let the cucumber slices sit for 5 minutes, until slightly softened.

3. Put the carrot matchsticks in another bowl and toss with a pinch of salt. Let the carrot sit for 5 minutes, until slightly softened.

4. Heat ¼ teaspoon of the vegetable oil in a skillet over medium-high heat. Add the cucumber and sauté for 30 seconds, until slightly softened and bright green. Transfer to the bottom of a wide 3-cup (or a little larger) glass container (about 4½ inches wide by 3½ inches tall) and spread in an even layer. Add half the rice and spread it in an even layer on top of the cucumber.

5. Heat the skillet over medium-high heat. Add the remaining 1 teaspoon vegetable oil and the carrot. Stir-fry for 1 minute, until slightly softened. Transfer to the container and spread over the rice in an even layer.

6. Add the remaining rice to the container and spread in an even layer. Add the seasoned soybean sprouts and spread in an even layer. Add the egg on top.

7. Cover the container. Put the seasoning sauce in a separate container and add a spoon. To eat, pour the seasoning sauce into the container and mix everything together with your spoon.

Omelet-Rice Dosirak

OMEU-RAISEU DOSIRAK 오므라이스 도시락

Serves 1 generously

Ever since I first uploaded this recipe to YouTube, it's been crazy-popular. Millions of people love the simple combination of stir-fried rice with vegetables, ham or other meat, butter, soy sauce, and ketchup (yes, ketchup!), topped with a thin egg omelet. Koreans adapted the dish from the Japanese, who themselves were inspired by Western omelets. I ate omeu-raiseu for years without knowing what the name meant. Only when I learned English did I realize that the Japanese had borrowed words from English—*omeu* from omelet, and *raiseu* from rice.

Even though it's at its most delicious when served right after it's made, omeu-raiseu still tastes great after a few hours. It's easy to eat because all you need to do is scoop up each bite with a spoon—no chopsticks needed, and no other side dishes needed either, although I usually include a separate container of grapes or peeled orange.

I've simplified the recipe from the original, but I always add as many vegetables to the fried rice as I can. You can use either freshly made rice or cold rice. Freshly made is easier to mix during stir-frying, since the grains separate more readily, whereas cold rice tends to stick together in a clump.

FOR THE EGG PANCAKE

1 large egg

Pinch of kosher salt

1 teaspoon vegetable oil

FOR THE STIR-FRIED RICE

1 tablespoon unsalted butter

¼ cup cubed or chopped ham

⅓ cup chopped mushrooms (shiitake, oyster, or white button)

⅓ cup chopped onion

¼ cup chopped yellow bell pepper

¼ cup chopped red bell pepper or chopped carrot

1½ cups Fluffy White Rice (page 41), freshly made or cold

2 tablespoons ketchup

1 teaspoon soy sauce

Pinch of ground black pepper

MAKE THE EGG PANCAKE

1. Whisk the egg and salt in a small bowl, then strain into another small bowl. Discard the stringy bits remaining in the strainer.

2. Heat the vegetable oil in a large nonstick skillet over medium-high heat and swirl to coat evenly. Wipe out the excess oil with a paper towel. Turn off the heat, add the egg mixture to the skillet, and tilt the skillet to spread the egg into a 6- to 7-inch circle. Let it sit for a few minutes, until the bottom of the egg pancake is cooked by the heat remaining in the skillet. Flip the egg pancake and allow it to set for another minute. If it's still slightly uncooked, turn on the heat to low for 30 seconds to 1 minute. Set the egg aside in the skillet or transfer to a plate.

STIR-FRY THE RICE

1. Heat the butter in a large skillet over medium-high heat. Add the ham, mushrooms, onion, yellow bell pepper, and red bell pepper and cook, stirring with a wooden spoon, for 1 minute, until the onion is slightly translucent.

2. Add the rice and stir together for 3 to 4 minutes for freshly made rice, 6 to 7 minutes for cold rice from the fridge, pressing the rice down into the skillet with the back of your wooden spoon to separate the grains.

3. Stir in the ketchup, soy sauce, and pepper and cook, stirring, for another 1 to 2 minutes, until well mixed into the rice. Remove from the heat. Transfer the rice and vegetables to a plate or a lunchbox container. Cover them with the omelet pancake, tucking the edges of the omelet in tightly underneath the rice.

Old-Days Dosirak

YET-NAL DOSIRAK 옛날 도시락

Serves 1

Rice, Korean-style sausage, braised soybeans, a little kimchi, and stir-fried anchovies: This is the kind of dosirak I had when I was in elementary school. I top it with an egg in this recipe, but that would have been too expensive when I was a child.

Not long ago, I was surprised to see this dish on the menu at a popular Korean barbecue restaurant in New York. They called it "old-days dosirak." Seeing it on the menu made me nostalgic and brought back a lot of memories. When I was a kid, we often made a quick bibimbap. Halfway through eating, when there was some empty space in the lunchbox, we would add some gochujang and kimchi, put the lid back on, and shake it all up vigorously, then remove the lid and finish eating. When I went to the barbecue restaurant, the waiter shook the dosirak for me, just as I used to do!

In those days, everybody had a metal lunchbox. My mom would pack my lunch in it every day, and later I used it for my own family. The one in the photo has been in my family for decades.

The sausage in this recipe is sold in Korean grocery stores. The brand name is Good Memories Sausage. It's not made with meat; Koreans invented it at a time when meat was too expensive and rare to use in sausage. Instead, food companies developed a meatless product using a bit of fish, starch, soybean powder, and vegetables, plus some red food coloring.

FOR THE SAUSAGE

1 large egg

Pinch of kosher salt

2 teaspoons vegetable oil

3 ounces Korean old-style sausage, sliced into 8 to 12 thin (¼-inch) disks

FOR THE DOSIRAK

1½ cups freshly cooked Fluffy White Rice (page 41)

About 3 tablespoons Stir-Fried Dried Anchovies (page 241)

About ¼ cup Braised Soybeans and Walnuts (page 218)

1 large egg, cooked over easy

¼ cup kimchi (any kind)

COOK THE SAUSAGE

1. Whisk the egg and salt a small bowl.

2. Heat the vegetable oil in a skillet over medium heat and swirl to coat.

3. Dip each slice of sausage into the egg mixture and then place it in the skillet. Cook for a few minutes on each side, until both sides are light brown. Transfer to a plate.

ASSEMBLE THE DOSIRAK

Spread the rice over about two-thirds of the lunchbox container. In the other third, arrange the cooked sausage, stir-fried dried anchovies, and the soybeans and walnuts. Put the over-easy egg on top of the rice. Cover. Pack the kimchi in a separate container.

HAPPY MEMORIES OF HOME

When she was a newlywed, my good friend Jihyeon would prepare dosirak for her doctor husband, with lots of lunch items, including good-quality sausage. Then he asked her if she could give him the cheap Korean-style sausage instead. "Can you believe he actually prefers that?" she said. "It's because that's what his mom used to make for him!"

Memories do play a huge role in our tastes. The food we love sometimes has more to do with our personal history than with anything else.

Lettuce-Wrapped Bulgogi Rice Dosirak

BULGOGI-SSAMBAP DOSIRAK 불고기쌈밥 도시락

Serves 1

When I lived in Gwangju, in the southern part of South Korea, a big Japanese hotpot restaurant opened in town. It was packed with people enjoying shabu-shabu, which was very good. But I was much more impressed by one of the side dishes that came with the set menu: bulgogi leafy lettuce wraps. The cupped bright green leaves with the rice and a bit of bulgogi tucked inside looked so pretty. I knew I could make them at home, and they seemed like the perfect thing for a modern healthy lunchbox. The meat is marinated in a simple bulgogi marinade and seared for just a couple of minutes. The wraps are very easy to assemble.

1½ teaspoons soy sauce

1 teaspoon toasted sesame oil

1 teaspoon sugar

1 garlic clove, minced

½ scallion (white or green part), chopped

½ teaspoon toasted sesame seeds

Pinch of ground black pepper

4 ounces beef sirloin or tenderloin, sliced thin

1 cup freshly cooked Fluffy White Rice (page 41)

6 leaf lettuce leaves

2 tablespoons Soybean Paste Dipping Sauce (page 134)

Cherry tomatoes, halved, for garnish

1. Combine the soy sauce, sesame oil, sugar, garlic, scallion, sesame seeds, pepper, and 1 tablespoon water in a bowl and mix well until the sugar has dissolved. Add the beef and mix well with a spoon or by hand.

2. Heat a medium skillet over high heat, add the marinated beef, and cook for 2 to 3 minutes, stirring with a wooden spoon, until the beef is no longer pink and the marinade has evaporated.

3. Remove the skillet from the heat and allow the meat to cool. Divide into 6 equal portions.

4. Divide the rice into 6 equal portions.

5. Put a lettuce leaf in your palm, add a portion of rice, 1 teaspoon of the dipping sauce, and a portion of the bulgogi, and place it in the lunchbox. Make 5 more wraps to fill the lunchbox and garnish with cherry tomatoes.

Tuna Sandwich
with Hard-Boiled Egg Dosirak

CHAMCHI-GYERAM SAENDEUWICHI DOSIRAK
참치계란샌드위치 도시락

Serves 2

If you and your kids are fans of tuna sandwiches, you will love my Korean version. It's true that a tuna sandwich is not traditional Korean food; I never had it when I was growing up. But when my kids were young, they sometimes asked me to make sandwiches for their lunchboxes. I don't remember where I learned the recipe, but my Korean friends and I used to make these for our kids.

When I mix the hard-boiled egg and tuna into the seasoned cucumber and onion, I take care not to mash them too much, so the tuna mixture won't become mushy. You should be able to see the bits of egg, tuna, and vegetable when you're done.

⅓ cup chopped cucumber

2 tablespoons chopped onion

¼ teaspoon kosher salt

1 (5-ounce) can tuna, preferably oil-packed Korean tuna, drained

¼ cup mayonnaise

1 hard-boiled egg, peeled

¼ teaspoon ground black pepper

4 slices multigrain or white bread, toasted

2 lettuce leaves

1 medium tomato, sliced

1. Combine the cucumber and onion in a small bowl and mix with the salt. Let it sit for 5 to 10 minutes. Squeeze out any excess water with your hands and transfer to a medium bowl.

2. Add the tuna, mayonnaise, egg, and black pepper. Mix with a spoon, gently cutting and crushing the egg into pieces with the spoon. Break the egg white into small pieces. Break the egg yolk into coarse chunks, so the yellow bits are visible and pretty.

3. Place 2 slices of bread on the cutting board. Top each slice with a piece of lettuce and a few tomato slices. Top the lettuce and tomato with the tuna mixture and spread evenly with a spoon. Top with the remaining bread slices. Cut each sandwich in half and pack in a sandwich box.

Other Ideas for Dosirak

Many of the most popular side dishes in the other chapters in this book, especially recipes from the Banchan and Mitbanchan chapter (page 214 to 261), are also lunchbox favorites. See the following pages for some dosirak I love to make.

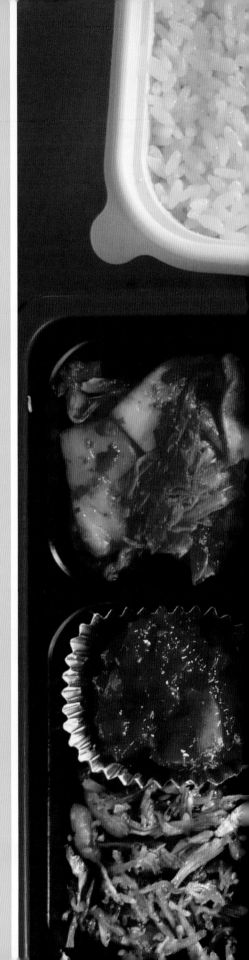

Stir-Fried Kimchi
with Tuna Dosirak

KIMCHI-CHAMCHI-BOKKEUM DOSIRAK
김치참치볶음 도시락

Stir-fried kimchi with tuna makes a perfect dosirak because the kimchi dries out a little when you stir-fry it, so it's juicy but not too wet for a lunchbox. The cod adds a balance of color and protein, and the braised soybeans and walnuts are a sweet, nutty, high-protein snack between bites of the hearty multigrain rice and the kimchi. Chive pancakes are among my all-time favorite side dishes. Soft on the inside and crispy on the outside, they're packed with fresh green chives that contribute lots of vitamins and a gorgeous green color. You're supposed to eat the lettuce last, when you've finished the other side dishes.

Clockwise from top left: **Pan-Fried Cod Fillets with Sesame Oil (page 172), Braised Soybeans and Walnuts (page 218), Chive Pancake (page 225), Stir-Fried Kimchi with Tuna (page 220), freshly cooked Multigrain Rice (page 44), a few leaves of lettuce, and a cherry tomato**

Deep-Fried Fish Fillet Dosirak

SAENGSEON-KKASEU DOSIRAK 생선까스 도시락

Hot kimchi stew and multigrain rice make for a comforting winter dosirak. You can spoon some of the warm, spicy, sweet-and-sour broth over the rice, or eat half the stew to clear some room and then spoon all of the rice into the container and mix it with the remaining stew, one-bowl-meal style. The fish fillets remain crunchy for hours in the lunchbox. To add some color to this dosirak, I finish it off with fresh lettuce and tomato.

Clockwise from top left: **Kimchi Stew (page 99), freshly cooked Multigrain Rice (page 44), Deep-Fried Fish Fillets (page 180)**

Tuna Pancake Dosirak

CHAMCHIJEON DOSIRAK 참치전 도시락

When I lived in Canada and brought my own lunch to work, my coworkers all raved about my tuna pancake dosirak. I shared the pancakes with everyone and eventually they started making their own. The best way to eat the sweet, rich fried gochujang is to take a dollop with your chopsticks, mix it briefly with a bit of rice, and eat.

    The colors in this lunchbox are well balanced. Since a number of the items are slightly dry, a bit of kimchi between bites will help everything go down pleasantly. Give the kimchi its own container so the pungent aromas and juices don't mix with the other items. The orange pieces also get their own container. Don't forget to include a toothpick for the oranges so your hands don't get sticky!

Top left: Orange slices; *Top right:* Traditional Napa Cabbage Kimchi (page 112); *In lunchbox, top left:* Fried Gochujang with Ground Beef and Pine Nuts (page 238); *Bottom left:* Seasoned Grated Dried Pollock (page 246); *Middle:* Tuna Pancakes (page 228) and lettuce; *Right:* freshly cooked Multigrain Rice (page 44)

Glazed Meatball Dosirak

WANJA-JORIM DOSIRAK 완자조림 도시락

This healthy dosirak combination is full of protein, with meatballs, tofu, shredded dried squid, and eggs all in one lunchbox. It's a balance of textures: The meatballs are juicy, the tofu is soft, and the dried shredded squid is slightly chewy. It also has a spicy kick and some red to balance out the colors. Don't use too much sauce for the tofu, or it will mix with the other dishes. Before I close the lid, I like to sprinkle toasted sesame seeds over the top.

Left box, top to bottom: freshly cooked Fluffy White Rice (page 41), Glazed Meatballs (page 166); *Right box, top to bottom:* Spicy Shredded Dried Squid (page 244), Rolled Omelet (page 232), cherry tomato, Pan-Fried Tofu with Soy-Scallion Seasoning Sauce (page 207)

Bullet Train Dosirak

KTX 도시락

When I took the Korean bullet train (Korea Train eXpress, or KTX) for the first time to go to Yeosu from Seoul, the train sold a nice warm lunchbox on board. It was only about US$10, but it was the most delicious lunchbox I'd ever bought. All the side dishes were tasty and colorful, and they were beautifully packed with warm rice. When I got home, I re-created the lunchbox, using the photo I'd taken on my iPhone (see page 281). The dosirak is elaborate, but none of the dishes is difficult. Normally I keep my kimchi in a separate container, but to replicate my KTX lunch, I keep it in this dosirak.

Bottom: **Freshly cooked Fluffy White Rice (page 41), sprinkled with toasted black sesame seeds;** *Bottom right section of box, clockwise from top left:* **Sautéed Cucumber (page 200), Fried Gochujang with Ground Beef and Pine Nuts (page 238), Traditional Napa Cabbage Kimchi (page 112); Stir-Fried Fish Cake (page 248);** *Top right section of box, clockwise from top left:* **Seasoned Salty Fermented Radish (page 253), Braised Soybeans and Walnuts (page 218), Stir-Fried Dried Anchovies (page 241), Rolled Omelet (page 232);** *Left section of box:* **Glazed Meatball patty from Glazed Meatballs (page 166), Eggs and Green Chili Peppers in Soy Broth (page 236), cherry tomatoes, and lettuce**

Stir-Fried Potato and Ham Dosirak

GAMJA-HAEM-BOKKEUM DOSIRAK
감자햄볶음 도시락

Crunchy stir-fried dried shrimp and soft, juicy stir-fried fish cake, with its spicy kick, make great companions in this dosirak. The two items are separated with a fresh lettuce leaf to keep them apart. The two halves of the egg braised in soy broth below these dishes look like a pair of eyes; they create a little surprise when the lunchbox is opened. The slightly dry eggs are nicely complemented by the other juicy side dishes, including the chili pepper, which goes well with rice. Below that is the stir-fried potato and ham that gives this dosirak its name. Of course, freshly made fluffy white rice is part of the mix, garnished with some cherry tomatoes for color and a few extra milligrams of vitamin C.

Left box: Top: Stir-Fried Dried Shrimp (page 242), lettuce, Stir-Fried Fish Cake (page 248); *Middle:* Eggs and Green Chili Peppers in Soy Broth (page 236); *Bottom:* Stir-Fried Potato and Ham (page 230); *Right top:* Traditional Toasted Gim (page 216); *Below that:* freshly cooked Fluffy White Rice (page 41) with a cherry tomato and black sesame seed garnish

DRINKS AND PARTY FOOD

EMBRACE YOUR GUESTS

Korea has a highly developed drinking culture that revolves around hospitality, kindness, respect, harmony, and fun. For us, drinking is always social; it's the best way to get to know someone new, catch up with an old acquaintance, show your appreciation and respect, or just have fun with people you like. Alcohol is always served with a dish or two—or three. Called anju, these foods are as essential as the drink itself and consist of a wide array of easy, addictive nibbles that are constantly evolving. If there's no food, there's no party.

In traditional society, alcoholic beverages were made at home. All housewives knew how to ferment and distill using seasonal grains, flowers, herbs, and mountain vegetables. Of the 146 recipes in the first cookbook written in Korean, *Eumsik-dimibang* (1870), 51 of them are for making alcohol! Then, during the Japanese occupation (1910 to 1945), the practice was outlawed and it pretty much disappeared. Now it's coming back, and in this chapter, I'll show you how to make a traditional alcohol called yakju. I'll also share a modern-style cocktail, Watermelon Soju.

You'll find a variety of party foods in this chapter. Some, like Seafood Scallion Pancake and Steamed Dumplings, are on the lighter side; others, like Spicy Garlic Fried Shrimp and Sweet, Spicy, and Sour Baby Back Ribs, are more substantial.

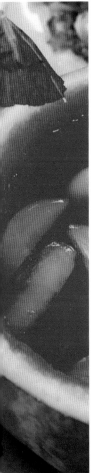

Yakju

YAKJU 약주

Makes 8 cups clear yakju

Korea's long history of homemade alcoholic drinks is not surprising, given our experience with fermenting. The word *ju* (Chinese for alcohol) is used in the names of many types of alcoholic drinks—brewed drinks like beer (maekju), distilled drinks like Korea's most popular drink, soju, or fermented and filtered drinks like yakju, a clear liquor whose main ingredient is rice.

The alcohol level of yakju is high, around 15 percent, and you can keep it for months in the fridge. Traditionally it was filtered using a long, narrow bamboo basket called a yongsu. The basket is not easy to find anymore, so I developed the straining method in this recipe.

Yakju is traditionally made with herbs and roots to increase its medicinal properties and to flavor it. I add dried bellflower roots, long used to treat bronchitis and other inflammatory diseases. If you've never made alcohol at home before, try this! You'll be surprised at how easy it is.

You will need a large steamer, a cotton cloth or steamer liner, an 8-quart earthenware jar, and a coarse strainer.

4½ pounds short-grain rice (aka sushi rice)	4 teaspoons active dry yeast (2 packets)
3 cups starter culture (nuruk)	1 ounce dried bellflower roots (about 1 cup)

STEAM THE RICE

1. Wash and drain the rice several times. Cover with cold water and soak for 3 hours. Drain.

2. Fill a large steamer with 3 inches water and bring to a boil. Put a large cotton cloth or steamer liner in the steamer basket and arrange the rice on top of it in an even layer. Pull the edges of the cloth up over the rice. Cover and steam over medium-high heat for 1 hour.

3. Reduce the heat to low and simmer for another 10 minutes. Remove from the heat.

FERMENT THE RICE

1. Transfer the steamed rice to a large bowl or container. Stir and fluff it with a rice scoop or wooden spoon to cool down for 10 minutes. Add 4 quarts cold water and stir well so that the temperature goes down even more. When it is lukewarm, add the nuruk, yeast, and dried bellflower roots. Stir well.

2. Transfer the mixture to an earthenware jar. Cover with a cotton cloth and close the lid. Let sit for 6 to 7 hours.

3. Stir the mixture with a wooden spoon. The mixture will be very thick because the rice will have absorbed some of the water and expanded. Cover and let sit at room temperature. Twice a day, each day, uncover, remove the cloth, and stir the mixture with a wooden spoon, then replace the cloth and cover. After 2 or 3 days, small bubbles will pop up to the surface. After 5 or 6 days, the mixture will begin to separate, with clear liquid on top and a milky brown substance on the bottom. Stir and mix it two or three times a day until it is no longer bubbling, which should be 8 or 9 days from the time you began the recipe.

STRAIN THE LIQUID

1. Carefully ladle the clear liquid on the top into a bowl. You will have about 5 cups clear liquor, which is yakju. Transfer to a bottle or jar and cover. It is ready to drink now, or you can save it for later when all the yakju is made. Refrigerate.

2. To extract the remaining yakju, place a coarse strainer over a large bowl and put the remaining mixture through the strainer. It will be very thick. Stir the mixture in the strainer with the wooden spoon and press down so that the liquid goes through. Transfer the mash in the strainer to another bowl. You can use this for making makgeolli (page 298), a coarsely filtered alcohol.

3. Strain the thick liquid in the bowl one more time through a coarse strainer. You will get about 3 quarts.

Recipe Continues

4. Transfer the resulting mash in the strainer to the bowl of mash from Step 2 if you want to make makgeolli. Pour the liquid into a large jar, cover, and refrigerate for 2 weeks. Be sure not to shake or move it while it sits.

5. After 2 weeks, the yakju will separate, with clear yakju on top and all the sediment on the bottom. Carefully ladle all but about 1 inch of the clear yakju into a bowl. You will have about 3 cups. Add it to the yakju (if you still have it) or drink it. Discard the sediment.

HOW TO MAKE MAKGEOLLI

Add 4 cups water to the mash and massage, then squeeze the liquid out and strain. Add sugar to taste if desired. Makgeolli can be refrigerated for up to 2 weeks.

Watermelon Soju Cocktail

SUBAK-SOJU 수박소주

Serves 4

This super easy recipe is really popular on my YouTube channel and website. I've been making it ever since I saw it years ago at a Manhattan Koreatown bar called Pocha 32.

If you drink this punch, you'll get drunk before you know it. You can make it less strong by substituting Sprite for some of the soju, and you can also make a nonalcoholic version by using only Sprite instead of soju and adding chunks of other fruits such as melon, grapes, and honeydew.

One of the best things about this is that the watermelon is your bowl, so cleanup is easy!

1 large seedless watermelon (8 to 10 pounds), refrigerated

2 (12-ounce) bottles soju *or* 1 (12-ounce) bottle soju plus 1 (12-ounce) can Sprite

12 ice cubes

1. Cut 3 to 4 inches off the top of the watermelon.

2. Scoop out the watermelon flesh with a large spoon and put it in a blender. Reserve the empty hollow watermelon bowl and fill it with water to see how many cups of liquid it will accommodate (usually about 8 cups). Pour out the water.

3. Blend the watermelon flesh for 1 to 2 minutes, until very smooth. Set a fine-mesh strainer over a large bowl and pour the blended watermelon through it. Stir and press down with a spoon to strain it well. Discard the pulp. Remove the foam from the top with a spoon. You should have about 7 cups juice.

4. Combine 4 cups of the juice and the soju (or soju and Sprite). Stir and mix the cocktail well and pour into the watermelon bowl. Add the ice cubes and use a ladle to serve.

Seafood Scallion Pancake

HAEMUL-PAJEON 해물파전

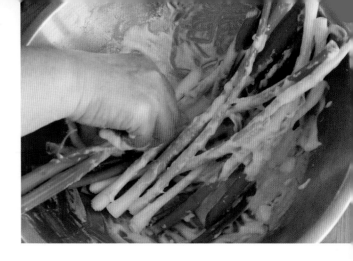

Serves 2

You'll love this fragrant, crispy, golden-brown pancake. It's usually served with alcohol, but it makes for a good snack, too. It's served whole, and everyone helps one another get a piece. One person holds the pancake with their chopsticks so the other person can tear off a tidbit with their chopsticks, then the favor is returned.

I make my pancakes with whole scallions that I dip into the batter, but if they're too long for your skillet, you can cut them into 2- or 3-inch pieces and mix them in before cooking. Or you can make a batch of smaller pancakes. Make sure to use a generous amount of vegetable oil so that your pancake will be as crunchy and golden-brown as possible.

Serve on its own, or with soju, Yakju (page 296), or beer.

½ cup all-purpose flour

¼ teaspoon kosher salt

4 tablespoons vegetable oil

12 scallions, roots trimmed, tops trimmed to 8 to 9 inches long

1 ounce peeled and deveined (see page 427) shrimp, chopped

2 ounces squid, cleaned (see page 431) and sliced or chopped

1 large egg, beaten in a small bowl

Soy-Vinegar Dipping Sauce (page 132)

1. Combine the flour, ½ cup plus 2 tablespoons water, and the salt in a bowl large enough to accommodate the scallions. Mix with a wooden spoon until smooth.

2. Heat 3 tablespoons of the vegetable oil in a large nonstick skillet over medium-high heat and swirl to coat evenly.

3. Add the scallions to the batter to coat them. Using tongs or your hand, place them side by side in the skillet, alternating white end to green end, so they form a neat rectangle.

4. Add the seafood to the leftover batter in the bowl. Using your hands, spread the seafood and batter on top of the battered scallions, scraping out any batter remaining in the bowl. Quickly wash your hands.

5. Reduce the heat to medium and cook for about 3 minutes, until the bottom is light brown and crispy. Turn the pancake over with a spatula. Cook for another 3 minutes, or until both sides are nicely browned and crisp.

6. Turn the pancake over again and pour the beaten egg over the top. Cook for 2 minutes, or until the bottom turns a darker golden brown and the scallions are soft.

7. Turn the pancake over again. Drizzle the remaining 1 tablespoon vegetable oil around the edges of the skillet. Lift one edge of the pancake with the spatula and tilt the skillet so that the oil flows underneath the pancake. Cook for 1 minute, or until the egg is nicely cooked. Transfer to a large plate, with the egg and seafood side up. Serve right away with the dipping sauce.

Steamed Dumplings

JJIN-MANDU 찐만두

Makes 12 shrimp dumplings and 20 to 25 meat dumplings

No Korean cookbook would be complete without a recipe for dumplings (mandu). This recipe makes two kinds of dumplings that go well together: one with a traditional meat and vegetable filling, and one with shrimp on top of the same filling. I first tasted this type of shrimp dumpling in a small, crowded mandu spot in Seoul—it was the most popular item on the menu. It's unusual and striking, featuring a whole steamed shrimp (not chopped, as in most dumplings), with the pink tail peeking out of one end of the dumpling skin.

8 ounces ground beef and/or pork

3 garlic cloves, minced

4 teaspoons toasted sesame oil

1½ teaspoons kosher salt

½ teaspoon ground black pepper

12 large shrimp, peeled but with tails intact, and deveined (see page 427)

8 ounces mung bean sprouts

2 ounces Asian chives or 3 scallions, chopped (about ⅔ cup)

1 small zucchini, cut into 1½-inch matchsticks (about 1 cup)

1½ teaspoons vegetable oil

1 small onion, chopped (¾ cup)

4 ounces medium-firm tofu

12 (4½-inch) dumpling skins and 20 to 25 (3½-inch) dumpling skins

Soy-Vinegar Dipping Sauce (page 132)

MAKE THE FILLING

1. Combine the ground meat, garlic, 2 teaspoons of the sesame oil, ½ teaspoon of the salt, and ¼ teaspoon of the black pepper in a bowl. Mix well with a spoon. Cover and refrigerate while you prepare the other ingredients.

2. Combine the shrimp, ¼ teaspoon of the salt, and the remaining ¼ teaspoon pepper in a bowl. Mix well by hand. Cover and refrigerate.

3. In a saucepan, bring 4 cups water to a boil over high heat. Add the bean sprouts and blanch for 2 minutes, stirring with a wooden spoon. Drain and rinse in cold water. Drain and squeeze tightly to remove the excess water. Transfer to a large bowl. Add the chives or scallions.

4. Toss the zucchini in a bowl with ¼ teaspoon of the salt. Let sit for 10 minutes. Squeeze out the excess water. Heat ½ teaspoon of the vegetable oil in a skillet over medium-high heat. Add the zucchini and sauté for 1 minute, until bright green and slightly soft, then transfer to the bowl with the sprouts and chives.

5. Return the skillet to medium-high heat. Add the remaining 1 teaspoon vegetable oil and the onion. Stir-fry for 2 minutes, until the onion is semi-translucent and fragrant. Transfer to the bowl with the other vegetables.

6. Squeeze the tofu to remove excess water and add to the vegetables.

7. Remove the marinated meat from the refrigerator. Heat the skillet over medium-high heat and add the meat. Cook, stirring, until the meat is no longer pink, 2 to 3 minutes. Transfer to the bowl with the tofu and vegetables. Add the remaining ½ teaspoon salt and the remaining 2 teaspoons sesame oil and mix well with a wooden spoon or by hand.

Recipe Continues

SHAPE AND STEAM THE SHRIMP DUMPLINGS

1. Remove the 4½-inch dumpling skins from the package. Set out a small bowl of water. Remove the bowls of meat filling and shrimp from the refrigerator. Line a platter, baking sheet, or cutting board with plastic wrap.

2. Lay a dumpling skin flat on your palm. Dip your index finger in the water and wet the edges of the skin so that it will seal easily. Spoon 1 or 2 teaspoons meat filling into the center and place 1 shrimp, belly up, on top of the filling, leaving a 1-inch margin between the edge of the wrapper and the head end of the shrimp, with the tail extending off the dumpling skin. Gather the sides of the skin up around the shrimp, leaving the edge at the head end loose, and press them together all the way along the body of the shrimp. Fold the top edge down over the head end of the shrimp and the sides to seal the dumpling, and leave the tail sticking out the end. Place it on the plastic-lined platter. Repeat with the remaining 11 shrimp.

3. Fill a steamer with 3 inches water and bring to a boil. Remove the basket from the steamer and line with cotton cloth or cheesecloth. Arrange the shrimp dumplings side by side in the basket and put the basket back in the steamer. Cover and steam over medium-high heat for 15 minutes, or until the shrimp turn bright pink, the filling is cooked through, and the dumpling skins are shiny and translucent. Remove from the heat. Transfer the dumplings to a plate. Serve right away with the dipping sauce.

SHAPE AND STEAM THE MEAT DUMPLINGS

1. While the shrimp dumplings are steaming, remove the 3½-inch dumpling skins from the package. Set out a small bowl of water. Line a large platter, baking sheet, or cutting board with plastic wrap.

2. Lay a dumpling skin flat on your palm. Dip your index finger in the water and wet the edges of the skin so that it will seal easily. Spoon a heaping tablespoon of the meat filling into the center and fold the skin over the filling. Press the edges to seal, and make 8 to 10 small pleats to give the dumpling a pretty appearance and seal it more tightly. Place it on the plastic-lined platter. Repeat with the remaining filling and dumpling skins. You will make 20 to 25 dumplings.

3. Fill a steamer with 3 inches water and bring to a boil. Remove the basket from the steamer and line with cotton cloth or cheesecloth. Arrange the dumplings side by side in the basket and put the basket back in the steamer. Cover and steam over medium-high heat for 15 minutes, or until the filling is cooked through and the dumpling skins are shiny and translucent. Remove from the heat. Transfer the dumplings to a plate. Serve right away with the dipping sauce.

DUMPLING SKINS

You'll find various sizes of round dumpling skins. A large skin is 4½ inches in diameter and a medium is 3½. For the shrimp dumplings, you'll need 4½-inch skins to enclose the shrimp; the medium skins are for the meat dumplings. If you have any leftover skins, wrap them a few times in plastic wrap and freeze them for future use. They will thaw at room temperature in 1 hour.

Mussel Soup

HONGHAP-TANG 홍합탕

Serves 4

Honghap-tang is a regular on the menu of almost every soju bang (soju bar). It's not just for accompanying drinks, though—it makes a great family dish as well. During peak mussel season in Korea, I'd hear trucks driving through the neighborhood with voices booming over loudspeakers: *"Honghap wasseoyo! Honghap wasseoyo!"* ("Mussels are here! Mussels are here!") Fresh from the sea, they were sold by the bucket. I'd head out with my pail and they'd fill it up. Since mussels don't keep, we would have them all day, served with kimchi and rice.

2 pounds mussels

1 medium onion, sliced thin

½ green chili pepper, sliced

2 garlic cloves, minced

2 scallions, chopped

½ red chili pepper, sliced

1. Put the mussels in a large bowl. Tap the mussels that are open and discard any that don't close. Remove the beards by pulling them down toward the hinge of the shell and outward. Wear rubber gloves and wash the mussels in cold running water, rubbing the mussels against each other and changing the water several times to clean thoroughly. Drain, return the mussels to the bowl, and fill with cold water. Soak for 1 hour so they breathe and spit out sand and mud.

2. Put the onion and green chili pepper in a large pot.

3. Drain the mussels, rinse them again with cold water, and drain. Place them in the pot, on top of the onion and chili.

4. Add 3 cups water and cook, uncovered, over medium-high heat for 15 minutes, until all the mussels open, the broth turns a little milky, and the onion looks a little translucent. Using tongs, transfer the cooked mussels to another large pot.

5. Place a strainer over a bowl and strain the broth. Discard the onion and green chili pepper.

6. Slowly pour the broth into the pot with the mussels. (Don't dump it all in, because there will be some sand in the bottom of the bowl, which you will discard.) Sprinkle with the garlic and heat over high heat for 3 to 4 minutes, until bubbling. Sprinkle the scallions and red chili over the mussels, remove from the heat, and serve right away. You can serve the pot on the table and everyone can dig in with their spoons, or you can ladle some broth and mussels into individual bowls.

Spicy Garlic Fried Shrimp

KKANPUNG-SAEU 깐풍새우

Serves 6 to 8

This Chinese-influenced Korean dish features large shrimp deep-fried and finished in a spicy garlic sauce. Sometimes it's made with chicken instead of shrimp; then it's called kkanpunggi (*gi* means "chicken" in Chinese).

I make kkanpung-saeu along with other dishes when I have a big party. It's always popular. I cook the shrimp in their shells, which become nicely coated with the scrumptious sauce. When shrimp are fried in the shell, they look great and stay plump and juicy, and the shells become crisp and chewy. They are great to chew on. If you prefer, though, you can easily remove them with chopsticks or your fingers, since they have been cut along the back before cooking.

FOR THE SHRIMP

1 pound large shrimp (16 to 20), in the shell

¼ teaspoon kosher salt

¼ teaspoon ground black pepper

2 tablespoons potato starch

FOR THE SPICY GARLIC SAUCE

¼ cup rice syrup or 3 tablespoons sugar

2 tablespoons soy sauce

2 tablespoons white vinegar

1 tablespoon potato starch

⅓ cup vegetable oil

8 garlic cloves, peeled and cut in half lengthwise

½ cup thinly sliced leek (about ½ leek)

4 teaspoons crushed red pepper flakes

½ cup chopped onion

1 green chili pepper, stemmed, seeded, and sliced thin lengthwise

1 red chili pepper, stemmed, seeded and sliced thin lengthwise

7 or 8 small dried red peppers

FOR FRYING

2 cups vegetable oil

1 large egg

1 tablespoon potato starch

1 teaspoon toasted sesame oil

PREPARE THE SHRIMP

1. Using scissors, cut down the back of each shrimp shell and make a shallow slit down the length of it, exposing the dark vein that runs down the center. Gently open it up and pull out the vein. (You can do this by hand or use a toothpick or wooden skewer.) Remove the sharp spike above the tail. Place the cleaned shrimp in a bowl and rinse several times with cold water. Drain well and return to the bowl. Add the salt and pepper and mix by hand. Refrigerate for 10 minutes.

2. Drain the shrimp and transfer to a cutting board. Pat dry with paper towels. Dry the bowl and return the shrimp to it. Add the potato starch and mix well by hand to coat. Cover and refrigerate until ready to fry.

Recipe Continues

MAKE THE SPICY GARLIC SAUCE

1. Combine ¼ cup water, the rice syrup, soy sauce, vinegar, and potato starch in a small bowl and mix well. Set aside.

2. Heat the vegetable oil in a large skillet over medium-high heat. Add the garlic and leek and stir gently with a wooden spoon until the garlic is light brown and the leek is crunchy and golden brown, 3 to 4 minutes. Remove from the heat and strain the oil into a bowl. Transfer the garlic and leek to a separate bowl and set aside. Add the red pepper flakes to the oil and stir a few times. Let sit for 5 minutes. Strain the oil and discard the pepper flakes.

3. Return the infused oil to the skillet and heat over medium-high heat. Add the onion, green and red chili peppers, and dried red chili peppers and stir until the onion is light brown, 2 to 3 minutes. Add the reserved soy sauce mixture and stir for 20 to 30 seconds, until bubbling. Remove the pan from the heat and set aside.

FRY AND SERVE THE SHRIMP

1. In another large skillet, heat the vegetable oil over medium-high heat to 350 degrees F, 7 to 8 minutes. Meanwhile, remove the shrimp from the refrigerator. Combine the egg and potato starch in a bowl. Beat with a fork until well mixed, and add the mixture to the shrimp. Mix together with a fork or by hand.

2. When the oil reaches 350 degrees, working in batches, add the shrimp one by one to the hot oil and deep-fry, turning with tongs from time to time. Fry until the shrimp turn red, 2 to 3 minutes. Remove from the oil and drain in a mesh strainer set over a bowl.

3. When all the shrimp are done, let the oil come back up to 350 degrees F, about 1 minute. Return the shrimp to the skillet and fry again for 2 to 3 minutes, until the shells turn golden brown and crunchy.

4. Reheat the sauce over high heat until bubbling. Add the fried shrimp and the reserved fried garlic and leek. Mix well with the wooden spoon and tongs to coat nicely. Remove from the heat and stir in the sesame oil. Transfer to a large platter and serve right away.

Clams
with Beef Steamed on the Half-Shells

DAEHAPJJIM 대합찜

Serves 4

I asked my daughter which of my dishes from home she particularly loves. She said, "The clams cooked on the shells!" This aromatic combination of chopped clams, beef, garlic, onion, and green chili pepper is traditionally served for special occasions. It's one of my signature party dishes. The compliments begin even before guests taste it, because the shells look so pretty with the clam and beef topping, which is bound with beaten egg white, brushed with egg yolk, and steamed until it sets in the shell.

You can find natural scallop baking shells at cookware stores and online.

8 to 10 littleneck clams, shelled, cleaned (see page 428), and chopped

2 ounces ground beef (about ⅓ cup)

½ teaspoon kosher salt

¼ teaspoon freshly ground black pepper

¼ teaspoon sugar or honey

1 teaspoon toasted sesame oil

1 garlic clove, minced

1 tablespoon chopped onion

1 scallion, chopped

1 green chili pepper, seeded and chopped

1 large egg, separated, white and yolk beaten separately

3 tablespoons all-purpose flour

4 natural scallop baking shells (see headnote)

A few pieces of sliced red chili pepper and scallion matchsticks, for garnish (optional)

1. Combine the clams, beef, salt, black pepper, sugar, sesame oil, garlic, onion, scallion, chili pepper, egg white, and 2 tablespoons of the flour in a bowl and mix well with a spoon.

2. Place the baking shells on your cutting board and sprinkle evenly with the remaining 1 tablespoon flour. (This will help the clam mixture stick to the shells.)

3. Fill each shell with an equal portion of the clam mixture. Brush the top of the clam mixture with the beaten egg yolk.

4. Pour 2 inches water into the bottom part of a steamer large enough to accommodate all the shells (or work in batches) and bring to a boil over medium-high heat. Place the filled shells in the steamer basket and place the basket in the steamer. Cover and steam for 25 minutes.

5. Uncover the steamer and remove from the heat. Let cool for a few minutes, then transfer the filled shells to a platter. Garnish, if you wish, with sliced red chili pepper and scallion matchsticks and serve. The steamed clams will keep in a covered container in the refrigerator for up to 3 days or in the freezer for up to 1 month. To reheat, return to the steamer and steam for 5 minutes.

Raw Sea Squirts

MEONGGE-HOE 멍게회

Serves 4

Sea squirts are my favorite seafood. They're very popular in Korea, but to non-Koreans who have never seen them before, they probably look a little weird. Because of their appearance, they are also called sea pineapples. They have a sweet briny flavor and a rubbery texture, though some parts are a bit crunchy.

8 fresh sea squirts or 1 (8-ounce) package frozen sea squirts

Sweet, Sour, and Spicy Dipping Sauce (page 133)

PREPARE FRESH SEA SQUIRTS

1. Cut off the siphons on the upper side of the sea squirts and set aside; they are good to eat. Insert your knife where the tip was and cut along the bottom of the sea squirt, then pull it open.

2. Insert your thumb between the flesh and outer skin and move it around to separate the skin from the insides.

3. If there is a dark line of mud running through the middle, cut it out, taking care not to cut too deeply into the flesh.

4. Repeat with the rest of the sea squirts. Rinse them in cold water a couple of times, then drain and pat dry.

PREPARE FROZEN SEA SQUIRTS

1. Thaw the package overnight in the refrigerator.

2. Remove from the package and rinse in cold water. Drain and pat dry.

SERVE

Cut each sea squirt into bite-size pieces and put them on a plate. Eat with chopsticks, dipping a piece into the sauce in between sips of your drink.

Top left: fresh sea squirts in a Korean market; *bottom left:* raw sea squirt siphons; *right:* cleaned raw sea squirts

Spicy Whelks
with Noodles

GOLBAENGI-MUCHIM-GUKSU 골뱅이무침국수

Serves 4

This is one of Korea's quintessential drinking dishes and it goes well with soju or beer, though you can also serve it as a snack or light meal without alcohol at all. The taste and texture of whelks is similar to that of conch. Canned whelks are easy to get at Korean grocery stores, and they're inexpensive.

The textural contrast of the chewy whelks, crunchy vegetables, and smooth, slippery noodles is one of the things that makes this dish so popular. It's important to soak the shredded daepa in water first so that it's springy and curly, with a milder, less oniony taste.

1 ounce daepa (large green onion) or 4 to 5 scallions, cut into 3-inch matchsticks

1 (14-ounce) can whelks or 8 ounces canned conch

2 garlic cloves, minced

¼ cup Korean hot pepper paste (gochujang)

1 tablespoon Korean hot pepper flakes (gochugaru)

2 tablespoons plus 1 teaspoon white vinegar

2 tablespoons rice syrup or 5 teaspoons sugar

¼ teaspoon kosher salt

4 ounces thin wheat-flour noodles (somyeon)

½ English cucumber, cut into 3-inch matchsticks (1 cup)

1 green chili pepper, sliced

1 small carrot, peeled and cut into 3-inch matchsticks

1 tablespoon toasted sesame oil

1 teaspoon toasted sesame seeds

1. Put the daepa or scallion matchsticks in a bowl, add 4 cups cold water, and soak for 10 minutes. Drain, rinse under cold running water, and drain again; they will curl a little. Put them on a plate.

2. Drain the whelks. Rinse them briefly under cold running water and drain. Transfer to a bowl. Cut any large whelks into bite-size pieces.

3. Combine the garlic, hot pepper paste, hot pepper flakes, vinegar, rice syrup, and salt in a bowl and mix well.

4. Pour 3 to 4 inches water into a large saucepan and bring to a boil over medium-high heat. Add the noodles and stir with a wooden spoon to prevent them from sticking to each other. Cover and cook for 2 to 3 minutes, until the water starts to boil over. Stir the noodles and cook, uncovered, for 2 to 3 more minutes. The noodles will float to the surface and look a little translucent. You can take a few samples with tongs or chopsticks and put them in a bowl of cold water, then taste. They should be chewy and cooked through. Drain through a large strainer and rinse under cold running water, rubbing the noodles with your hands until they are cold and no longer slippery. Drain and transfer to a large bowl.

5. Add the daepa or scallion matchsticks, cucumber, green chili pepper, and carrot to the bowl with the noodles. Add the whelks and the sauce. Gently mix everything together by hand. Mix in the sesame oil and transfer to a large platter. Sprinkle with the sesame seeds. Serve right away.

SERVING SUGGESTION

Place some ice cubes on a large platter or plate and put the serving dish in the center, on top of the ice cubes. The ice will keep the dish cold until everyone finishes eating it, and it makes a beautifully icy centerpiece.

Eight-Treasure Seafood and Vegetables

PALBOCHAE 팔보채

Serves 4

This Chinese-Korean dish is what to make when you have a party where you want to impress people. *Pal* is the number 8, and *bo* means "treasure," but there are more than eight treasures in my version: several varieties of seafood and crispy vegetables, all stir-fried in smoky chili oil and finished in a thick, slightly sticky sauce.

I used to make palbochae in Korea when I'd have a housewarming party, which was a big deal in the old days. Many guests would come, bringing traditional Korean gifts like matches, toilet paper, and detergent to bless the new house and wish my family a good future. These parties are a great opportunity for the lady of the house to show off her cooking skills. For me, making Korean food wasn't enough; I always wanted to make some special Chinese-Korean dishes as well.

I judge a good palbochae by the presence of sea cucumber. It's the most expensive ingredient, and it takes quite a bit of time to prepare, so it has to be in the dish to get my approval. You can buy it presoaked, but buying the dried sea cucumber and soaking it yourself is worth doing, even though it takes a couple of days, because it's cheaper and has a better taste and texture.

I use cuttlefish in this recipe because it's thick enough to score with a deep crisscross pattern, which looks pretty when the cuttlefish is cooked. But if it's not available, you can use squid. I blanch everything first to reduce the stir-frying time.

FOR THE CHILI OIL

¼ cup vegetable oil

12 small dried red chili peppers

4 garlic cloves, minced

1 teaspoon minced peeled ginger

1 tablespoon Korean hot pepper flakes (gochu-garu)

FOR THE VEGETABLES AND MUSHROOMS

2 dried shiitake mushrooms, rinsed, soaked in cold water until soft (about 4 hours), and drained

1 small onion, sliced (about ½ cup)

3 ounces canned bamboo shoots, rinsed in cold water and drained (1 cup)

4 ounces trimmed bok choy, cut into 3-inch pieces (about 2 cups)

8 ounces mixed red, green, and yellow bell peppers, seeded and cut into 1-inch squares (about 1½ cups)

FOR THE SEAFOOD

8 ounces cuttlefish or cleaned squid body (to clean squid, see page 431)

4 ounces soaked dried sea cucumber (see page 430; from 1 small dried sea cucumber)

4 ounces shrimp, peeled and deveined (see page 427)

4 ounces conch meat, cut into 1½-inch pieces

4 large sea scallops (about 4 ounces), rinsed

FOR BLANCHING AND FINISHING

1 teaspoon kosher salt

2 tablespoons potato starch

2 tablespoons oyster sauce

½ cup unsalted chicken broth

1 teaspoon toasted sesame oil

MAKE THE CHILI OIL

Heat the vegetable oil in a small pan over medium-high heat for 1 minute. Add the chili peppers, garlic, and ginger and stir for about 2 minutes, until the garlic turns crunchy and golden brown. Remove from the heat and add the hot pepper flakes. Stir a few times, then strain into a bowl.

Recipe Continues

PREPARE THE VEGETABLES AND MUSHROOMS

Cut away the stems from the mushrooms and use for another recipe. Cut the caps into quarters and put them on a plate. Put the bell peppers, bok choy, bamboo shoots, and onion on the same plate.

PREPARE THE SEAFOOD

Cut a crosshatch pattern on the surface of the cuttlefish without cutting all the way through. Cut into 1½-inch pieces. Place on a plate. Put the sea cucumber, shrimp, conch meat, and scallops on the same plate.

BLANCH THE VEGETABLES AND SEAFOOD

1. In a large pot, bring 3 quarts water to a boil over medium-high heat. Add the salt and stir. Blanch the bok choy and bell pepper for 30 seconds, stirring with a large slotted spoon. Transfer to a bowl with the slotted spoon.

2. Bring the water back to a boil and blanch the cuttlefish, sea cucumber, and scallops for 1 minute. Return to the plate.

3. Blanch the conch meat and shrimp for 2 minutes and return them to the plate with the other seafood.

4. Slice the sea cucumber crosswise into ¼-inch-thick pieces.

FINISH THE DISH

1. Combine the potato starch and 2 tablespoons water in a small bowl.

2. Heat the chili oil in a large pan over high heat. Add the onion and mushrooms and stir-fry until the onion is semi-translucent, about 2 minutes. Add all the seafood and vegetables and stir. Add the oyster sauce and stir for 2 to 3 minutes.

3. Add the chicken broth and cook, stirring with the wooden spoon, for a few minutes, until the broth is boiling. Add the potato starch slurry and mix all the ingredients for 1 to 2 minutes, until the broth thickens and glazes the seafood and vegetables.

4. Remove the pan from the heat and stir in the sesame oil.

5. Transfer to a large platter and serve right away.

Sweet Potato Starch Noodles

with Vegetables and Meat

JAPCHAE 잡채

Serves 4 to 6

Japchae is a beautiful dish of translucent sweet potato noodles, lots of colorful vegetables, mushrooms, and meat. Along with kimchi and bulgogi, it's one of the most popular and best-known Korean dishes. My readers tell me it's always a hit when they bring it to a party.

In the past, I cooked each ingredient separately and then combined them, which is traditional, but in this recipe, I simplified the process without losing any flavor or changing the appearance of the dish. I coat all the vegetables except for the spinach with a thin layer of oil and cook them all together. The photo on page 324 shows how to arrange the ingredients in the pot.

If you are vegetarian or vegan, you can modify the recipe—simply skip the meat and the egg yolk garnish.

8 ounces pork belly, beef tenderloin, or boneless, skinless chicken breast, cut into 2½-inch-long strips

3 tablespoons plus 2 teaspoons brown sugar

1 tablespoon plus 1 teaspoon toasted sesame oil

7 or 8 dried wood ear mushrooms, soaked in cold water for at least 30 minutes (optional)

8 ounces sweet potato starch noodles (dangmyeon), soaked in cold water for 40 minutes

¼ cup plus 2 teaspoons soy sauce

5 garlic cloves, minced

½ teaspoon ground black pepper

8 ounces mushrooms (oyster, king oyster, portobello, shiitake, and/or white button), sliced

1 large onion, sliced

1 large carrot, peeled and cut into 1- to 2-inch matchsticks

4 to 6 scallions, cut into 2½-inch pieces

¼ cup vegetable oil

8 ounces bunch spinach, roots cut away and leaves cut into 4-inch pieces

1 tablespoon toasted sesame seeds

Yellow Egg Paper Strips (optional; page 136)

1. Combine your choice of meat, 2 teaspoons of the soy sauce, 2 teaspoons of the brown sugar, and 1 teaspoon of the sesame oil in a bowl and mix well with a spoon or by hand. Cover and refrigerate.

2. If using the dried wood ear mushrooms, drain and transfer to the cutting board. Cut off the tough stems and discard. Cut the caps into bite-size pieces.

3. Drain the noodles and, using scissors, cut into 5- to 6-inch lengths.

4. Combine the remaining ¼ cup soy sauce, garlic, remaining 3 tablespoons brown sugar, and black pepper in a bowl and mix well until the sugar has dissolved.

5. Heat a skillet over high heat and add the marinated meat. Stir with a wooden spoon until the meat is thoroughly cooked and glazed and all the liquid has evaporated, 4 to 5 minutes. Remove the skillet from the heat.

6. In a large, heavy pot, combine the wood ear mushrooms (if using), fresh mushrooms, onion, carrot, scallions, vegetable oil, and ¼ cup water. Mix well with both hands so that all the vegetables and mushrooms are nicely coated with oil. (This will not only prevent the ingredients from turning brown from the seasoning sauce, but will also keep them from burning.)

Recipe Continues

7. Add the spinach and spread in an even layer. Place the noodles on top. Drizzle the seasoning sauce on top of the noodles. Cover and cook for 10 minutes over medium-high heat. Stir and toss all the ingredients with a wooden spoon and tongs for 1 to 2 minutes, until all the liquid has evaporated and the noodles are nicely cooked and shiny.

8. Remove the pot from the heat and add the meat, the remaining 1 tablespoon sesame oil, and the sesame seeds. Toss the mixture so that all the ingredients are evenly distributed. Transfer to a large platter. Garnish with the egg paper strips (if using) and serve. The dish can be refrigerated for up to 3 days. To reheat, stir-fry in a skillet with a few tablespoons water or vegetable oil.

Sweet, Spicy, and Sour Baby Back Ribs

DWAEJI-DEUNGGALBI-JORIM 돼지등갈비조림

Serves 4

This style of ribs is somewhat new to Korean cuisine. They are inspired by those I had at a popular Korean restaurant in Los Angeles called Ham Ji Park. There was a long line to get in, and the place was filled with diners eating huge plates of ribs. I paid close attention to the flavors, knowing that the owner would never give me her recipe.

The ribs are not nearly as spicy as you might imagine, despite a generous amount of Korean hot pepper paste. The apple, brown sugar, ketchup, and rice syrup make them sweet. They are marinated in mirim, then dusted with potato starch and cooked in oil before being finished in the sauce, which gives them a thick, glossy coating. Serve them with soju, beer, soda, or a glass of ice water.

FOR THE RIBS

2 pounds pork baby back ribs, separated

¼ cup mirim (aka mirin)

1 teaspoon soy sauce

¼ cup potato starch or cornstarch

2 cups vegetable oil

1 scallion, chopped

FOR THE SEASONING SAUCE

1 small apple, peeled, cored, and cut into chunks

1 small onion, cut into chunks

6 garlic cloves, peeled

1 teaspoon coarsely chopped peeled ginger

½ cup ketchup

¼ cup Korean hot pepper paste (gochujang)

2 tablespoons brown or white sugar

¼ teaspoon ground black pepper

¼ cup rice syrup or 3 additional tablespoons sugar

PREPARE THE RIBS

Rinse the ribs in cold water. Drain and place in a bowl. Add the mirim and soy sauce and toss well by hand to coat evenly. Cover and refrigerate for at least 1 hour, tossing a few more times during the process.

MEANWHILE, MAKE THE SEASONING SAUCE

1. Combine the apple, onion, garlic, ginger, and ¼ cup water in a food processor, pulse a few times, then process to a puree.

2. Transfer the puree to a large skillet. Add the ketchup, hot pepper paste, sugar, and pepper and mix well. Cook over medium-high heat, stirring occasionally with a wooden spoon, for 10 minutes, or until the sauce thickens slightly and becomes shiny. Remove from the heat and stir in the rice syrup or additional sugar.

FRY THE RIBS

1. Drain the ribs, pat dry, and put them in a zipper-lock plastic bag. Add the starch and mix well, shaking the bag so that the ribs are evenly coated.

2. Heat the vegetable oil in a large, deep skillet over medium-high heat until the temperature reaches 350 degrees F and it bubbles briskly when you dip the tip of a rib into it, 4 to 5 minutes.

3. Using tongs, carefully add the ribs to the oil one by one. I can fit 2 pounds of baby back ribs in my 12-inch pan if I place them side by side, but if you need to, cook in batches. Fry, turning the ribs often with tongs, until golden brown and crunchy on all sides, 12 to 13 minutes. If the ribs seem to be cooking too fast and start to burn on the surface before they are cooked on the inside, moderate the heat.

4. When the ribs are done, transfer to a strainer set over a bowl to drain the excess oil. Reserve 2 tablespoons of the frying oil.

FINISH THE RIBS

Reheat the sauce over medium heat. Add the reserved frying oil. When the sauce begins to sizzle, add the ribs and mix with a wooden spoon or tongs to coat. Transfer the ribs to a platter and sprinkle with the scallion. Serve.

Korean-Style Fruit Salad

GWA-IL-SAELEODEU 과일샐러드

Serves 4

You may wonder whether this fruit salad in a creamy dressing is really Korean. Yes, it is! It's a special salad, always served at celebrations and feasts, and on special occasions like our biggest holidays. It's so colorful and pretty that it always draws attention to the table. After I wrote my first cookbook, my editor came for dinner and asked me if I was going to put it in my next book. Here it is!

I like to make this salad in the fall, whenever I find fresh, crisp Fuyu persimmons. Pears and apples, also at their best in the fall, are important, too. The raisins can be any color, but they have to be there, along with crunchy roasted peanuts.

I always make a large amount, because it keeps well in the refrigerator. If tomorrow is a busy day, you can get all the cutting and chopping done ahead of time, toss everything together, and put it in an airtight container until dinnertime the next day. It won't get soggy at all.

⅓ English cucumber, cut into ½-inch cubes (¾ cup)

½ Korean pear or any crisp, juicy pear, peeled and cut into ½-inch cubes (1¼ cups)

1 medium, crisp Fuyu persimmon, peeled and cut into ½-inch cubes (1 cup)

1 small Fuji apple or any crisp apple, peeled, cored, and cut into ½-inch cubes (1 cup)

8 large green seedless grapes

¼ cup raisins

¼ cup roasted peanuts

2 large hard-boiled eggs

⅓ cup mayonnaise

1 tablespoon yellow mustard

1. Combine the cucumber, pear, persimmon, apple, grapes, raisins, and peanuts in a large bowl. Cut one of the eggs into quarters and add to the bowl.

2. Separate the white and yolk from the other egg. Set aside the egg yolk, put the white in the bowl, and gently tear it into pieces.

3. Add the mayonnaise and mustard and, using a spoon, mix together the ingredients. Transfer the mixture to a serving plate or bowl. Press the egg yolk through a mesh strainer over the salad. Serve or refrigerate for up to 24 hours.

KOREAN BUDDHIST TEMPLE CUISINE

VEGAN SIMPLICITY

Buddhism is one of Korea's oldest religions, with more than 1,600 years of history; some active temples have been in the same spot for more than a thousand years. With strict rules about preparation and ingredients passed down from generation to generation, meals that the monks and nuns prepare for themselves are healthy and uniquely Korean.

The Buddhist teaching of compassion for all living things forbids the use of meat. Onions, garlic, chives, and scallions are also off-limits because they are considered to be too stimulating and would prevent monks and nuns from achieving enlightenment through meditation. Within these bounds, Buddhist monks and nuns have developed their own cuisine that is influenced by the vegetables that surround their mountain temples. They are keen foragers and know all about which vegetables

are best in what season, where to find them, and how best to prepare them. They make their own doenjang (fermented soybean paste), gochujang (fermented hot pepper paste), and soy sauce, and their own kimchi, too, just without the banned ingredients.

I went to the remote Goun temple in the province of Gyeongsangbudko to learn more about temple cuisine. I spent time with Wonhae, a Buddhist nun and the head cook of the temple, who was very generous with her time and knowledge. She taught me all about her cooking, answered my many questions, and took me into the mountains to forage. She was very charismatic and had strong hands, sparkling eyes, an outgoing personality, and a booming voice that could fill the mountainside when she called out to other monks. When we worked together, however, she was shy and soft-spoken.

When I got to the temple, Wonhae was waiting for me with some other nuns, and our lunch was ready on the table. It consisted of just a few simple dishes, but when I tasted the food I was amazed by how delicious it was. The flavors were deep, complex, and varied, yet subtle and delicate. That lunch stands out as the best meal I had during my trip.

I learned that for the monks, blandness is another flavor to be used like sweet, sour, spicy, bitter, fermented, and salty. Their focus is not on making the dishes tasty, but rather on the mindfulness it takes to gather the ingredients and to make and eat the food, and to prepare just as much as they need so they can continue with their meditations. For them, this process is all part of their path to enlightenment.

The monks put a lot of time and effort into tending their fermented sauces and pastes.

Outside, behind the kitchen, I saw rows and rows of huge Korean earthenware pots (onggi) organized by year. Every morning, if the weather is fine, the monks open the pots so that the sauces and pastes can ferment in the mountain sunshine, and every evening or whenever clouds appear, they close them to protect them from the elements.

A typical meal at Goun temple consists of hot fluffy rice, a flavorful soybean paste soup, and a large selection of side dishes, such as Pan-Fried Shiitake Mushrooms, Temple-Style Sautéed Cucumbers, Sautéed Zucchini with Perilla Seeds, and the lovingly tended sauces and pastes.

You may never make it to a Korean temple, but in this chapter, you can learn many lessons about food from the monks and nuns. With these easy recipes, it won't be difficult to create a temple-style meal in your own home.

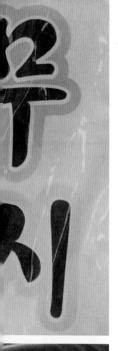

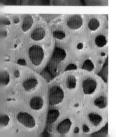

Steamed Rice in Lotus Leaf Wrap

YEONNIP-BAP 연잎밥

Serves 4

At Goun temple, the nun named Wonhae told me that she and the other nuns prepare these wraps in bulk and freeze them when lotus leaves are in season. Then, when they want to eat them, they take them from the freezer and steam them. In the past, when they walked long distances from temple to temple, monks and nuns would take along a steamed lotus leaf wrap. Accompanied by Korean fermented vegetables, such as Salty Fermented Radish (page 250), this makes for an easy lunchbox.

After steaming in the aromatic lotus leaves, the rice is infused with the vegetal flavor of the lotus leaf, which is similar to good green tea.

1 whole lotus root or 4 slices packaged lotus root (optional)

1 tablespoon white vinegar

8 fresh or frozen chestnuts, shelled and skinned (see page 418)

1 pound white glutinous rice, soaked in cold water for 3 hours or overnight and drained

Kosher salt

4 dried lotus leaves, rinsed, soaked in cold water for 2 to 3 hours, and drained

¼ cup fresh shell beans, such as cranberry beans (optional)

20 ginkgo nuts, shelled and cooked (see page 419)

20 pine nuts, tips removed (see page 421)

4 dried jujubes, pitted (see page 423)

1. If you are using a whole lotus root, peel it with a potato peeler and rinse in cold water. Cut it crosswise to get four ¼-inch-thick slices. (Reserve the rest of the lotus root for another use.) Put the packaged or fresh-cut slices in a bowl and add 6 cups water and the vinegar. Soak for 30 minutes, then drain.

2. Bring 3 cups water to a boil in a small saucepan and add the lotus slices and chestnuts. Cook for 5 minutes, until the lotus slices and chestnuts are barely tender. Drain and set aside.

3. Fill a large steamer with 3 inches water. Remove the steamer basket and line it with a large cotton cloth or steamer liner. Add the drained rice and spread it in an even layer. Bring the water to a boil over medium-high heat. Return the steamer basket to the steamer, cover, and steam for 30 minutes. Remove from the heat and uncover. Let the rice cool for 5 minutes, then transfer to a large bowl. Add ¼ cup water and ½ teaspoon salt. Mix well with a rice scoop or wooden spoon. Divide the rice into 4 portions.

4. Line a 4- to 5-inch bowl with one of the lotus leaves, positioning the leaf so that the base (where the stem was cut) is in the center. Add 1 portion of the rice. Top with 1 lotus root slice, 2 chestnuts, a few beans (if using), 5 ginkgo nuts, 5 pine nuts, and 1 jujube.

5. Lift the bottom side of the leaf and fold it over to the top, enclosing the rice mixture. Fold both sides, one at a time, over the first fold, then fold over the remaining leaf to enclose the rice. Transfer to the steamer. Repeat with the remaining leaves, rice, and vegetables.

6. Cover the steamer and steam the lotus wraps over medium-high heat for 30 minutes, or until the filling is fully cooked and the rice is infused with the flavor of the lotus leaf. Serve hot or at room temperature. Lotus wraps can be stored in an airtight container in the refrigerator for up to 3 days or in the freezer for up to 3 months.

Temple-Style Sautéed Cucumbers

OI-BOKKEUM 오이볶음

Serves 4

I was served these cucumbers as a large side dish at Goun temple. The slices were very crisp, dark green, and nearly free of liquid. The trick is to slice the cucumbers very thinly and squeeze out as much water as you can after they have been salted. Then, instead of sautéing them in oil right away as is usually done, the Buddhist nuns tossed the cucumbers in a bowl with toasted perilla seed oil.

1 pound seedless cucumbers, sliced paper thin

1½ teaspoons kosher salt

1 tablespoon toasted perilla seed oil or toasted sesame oil

1 tablespoon vegetable oil

1 tablespoon toasted sesame seeds, ground with a mortar and pestle or coffee grinder

1. In a large bowl, toss the sliced cucumbers with 1 teaspoon of the salt. Let sit for 10 minutes.

2. Drain the cucumber, wrap in a few layers of folded cheesecloth, and squeeze out the excess water. Return to the bowl and add the perilla seed or sesame oil. Mix by hand.

3. Heat the vegetable oil in a large skillet over medium heat. Add the cucumber and the remaining ½ teaspoon salt. Increase the heat to medium-high and stir for 2 to 3 minutes, until the cucumber is very green and crispy. Remove from the heat and stir in the ground sesame seeds. Transfer to a plate or bowl and serve.

Sautéed Zucchini
with Perilla Seeds

AEHOBAK-DEULKKAE-BOKKEUM 애호박들깨볶음

Serves 4

Before I visited the Buddhist temple, I made sautéed zucchini with flavorings like fish sauce, salty fermented shrimp, and garlic. The vegetarian monks prepare theirs with red and green chili peppers, a little soy sauce, and toasted perilla seed powder. I was surprised to find that it was just as tasty as mine, even though it has no garlic.

1 large or 2 small zucchini (about 11 ounces total)

½ teaspoon kosher salt

2 teaspoons vegetable oil

½ teaspoon soy sauce

1 red chili pepper, sliced

1 green chili pepper, sliced

1 tablespoon toasted perilla seed powder or toasted sesame seeds, ground with a mortar and pestle or coffee grinder

2 teaspoons toasted perilla seed oil or toasted sesame oil

1. Cut the zucchini in half lengthwise and cut each half crosswise into ¼-inch-thick slices. Put the zucchini in a large bowl and toss with the salt. Let sit for 10 minutes.

2. Heat the vegetable oil in a large skillet over medium heat. Add the zucchini and cook, stirring, for 7 to 8 minutes, until it softens slightly and becomes translucent.

3. Add the soy sauce, chili peppers, and perilla or sesame seed powder. Stir for 1 minute and remove from the heat. Stir in the perilla seed oil or sesame oil. Transfer to a bowl or plate and serve.

Cilantro Salad

GOSU-MUCHIM 고수무침

Serves 4

I had never eaten cilantro until I went to Thailand, and the first time I tasted it, I didn't like its strong flavor. But after a few weeks of trying many delicious dishes made with cilantro, I eventually came to love it.

I had never seen any of my family or relatives eating cilantro in the southern part of Korea where I grew up, although recently my mom told me that she had this cilantro salad at the house of a friend whose parents had come from North Korea.

At Goun temple, the Buddhist monks and nuns often make cilantro salad. The manager of the temple-stay program told me that cilantro is so popular with the monks that they grab a few stems from the garden on their way back to meditation from the restroom, put them in their mouths, and go right back to meditating!

2 teaspoons soy sauce

2 teaspoons toasted sesame oil

½ teaspoon white vinegar

1 teaspoon Korean hot pepper flakes (gochu-garu)

1 large bunch cilantro with crisp stems (about 4 ounces), cut into 2-inch-long sprigs

2 teaspoons toasted sesame seeds, ground with a mortar and pestle

Combine the soy sauce, sesame oil, vinegar, and hot pepper flakes in a bowl and mix well with a spoon. Add the cilantro and mix well by hand to coat the cilantro evenly. Transfer to a plate. Sprinkle with the ground sesame seeds and serve.

Mushrooms and Peppers Rolled in Cilantro

GOSU-GANGHOE 고수강회

Serves 6 to 8

Koreans make pretty vegetable packages tied together with scallions or the crispy stems of green herbs. These dishes stand out at a Korean party because of the stunning color contrasts. I remember my mother making a dish like this for my father when I was young. She blanched scallions and, instead of wrapping them around other vegetables, she coiled the scallions and put them on a plate. Then she added seasoning sauce.

Be sure your cilantro has long, plump, crisp stems. You could also use water dropwort (minari).

3 or 4 king oyster mushrooms with long stems (3 to 4 ounces)

1 (3- to 3.5-ounce) package fresh enoki mushrooms

1 yellow bell pepper

1 red bell pepper

22 to 25 cilantro sprigs with long, plump stems

Sweet, Sour, and Spicy Dipping Sauce (page 133)

1. Cut off the tops and base ends from the king oyster mushrooms. Discard the bases and reserve the tops for other dishes. Cut the stems into 2½-by-⅓-inch pieces. Reserve the excess stems for other dishes. You will need 22 pieces.

2. Cut off the brown roots from the enoki mushrooms and trim the ends so that they are about 2½ inches long.

3. Cut away the tops and bottoms of the red and yellow bell peppers. Cut them in half and remove the seeds and membranes. Slice lengthwise into ¼-inch-thick strips. You will need at least 22 strips of each pepper. Trim the strips to 2½ inches long. Transfer the pepper strips to a large platter and cover with plastic wrap so they don't dry out. Reserve the excess bell pepper for other dishes.

4. In a medium saucepan, bring 1 quart water to a boil over medium-high heat. Blanch the king oyster mushroom strips for 30 seconds. Remove with a slotted spoon or tongs and transfer to a platter.

5. Blanch the cilantro for 1 minute. Drain and rinse under cold running water. Gently squeeze out the excess water and put the cilantro on the platter.

6. Make a small bundle with 1 piece of king oyster mushroom, a few pieces of enoki mushrooms, and 1 or 2 strips of red and yellow bell pepper. Hold it in one hand and wrap a sprig of blanched cilantro around the middle to tie the bundle together. Gently tuck in the ends of the sprig and place on a large serving plate. Repeat with the remaining ingredients. Serve right away with the dipping sauce or cover and refrigerate for up to several hours.

Pan-Fried Shiitake Mushrooms

PYOGO-BEOSEOT-BOKKEUM 표고버섯볶음

Serves 4

These glazed stir-fried mushrooms are marinated in a sweet-salty mix of soy sauce and sesame oil and cooked with mildly spicy green chili peppers. They make a substantial side dish. Dried shiitakes require 12 hours of soaking to reach the proper tenderness. The soaking water will be very flavorful, so don't throw it away! Use it instead of water for making Soybean Paste Stew (page 90) or any other soup.

2 ounces dried shiitake mushrooms (about 10 large or 20 small dried mushrooms), soaked in 3 cups cold water for 12 hours, *or* 10 ounces fresh shiitake mushrooms

1 tablespoon soy sauce

1 tablespoon toasted sesame oil

1 teaspoon sugar

Pinch of ground black pepper

½ teaspoon potato starch

1 tablespoon vegetable oil

4 large mild green chili peppers (about 4 ounces), stemmed, halved lengthwise, and sliced diagonally into 2 inch pieces

½ teaspoon kosher salt

1 teaspoon toasted sesame seeds

1. If using dried mushrooms, remove them from the soaking water and squeeze out the excess water over the bowl. Reserve the soaking water. Cut away the stems from the soaked or fresh mushrooms and use for another recipe. Cut the mushroom caps in half if small or in quarters if large, to obtain bite-size pieces. Put the mushrooms in a bowl, add the soy sauce, sasame oil, sugar, and black pepper and mix together by hand to coat the mushrooms well.

2. Combine ½ cup of the mushroom soaking water (or fresh water if using fresh mushrooms) and the potato starch in a small bowl and mix well to make a slurry.

3. Heat the vegetable oil in a large skillet over medium heat. Add the marinated mushrooms and stir-fry until light brown, about 2 minutes. Add the green chili peppers and stir-fry for about 1 minute, until the peppers begin to soften. Add the salt and the slurry and stir for 1 to 2 minutes, until the mushrooms are glazed and tender. Sprinkle with the sesame seeds, transfer to a plate, and serve.

Spicy Burdock Root Salad

UEONG-MUCHIM 우엉무침

Serves 4

On one of my visits to Seoul, I ate at Balwoo Gongyang, a Michelin-starred restaurant run by the Jogye order of Buddhist monks, who serve their interpretation of Korean temple food. One of the dishes I enjoyed was this spicy raw burdock root. I had always thought that burdock root was supposed to be cooked, but I loved this fresh, salad-like preparation in which the burdock root was very thinly sliced and coated with a spicy sauce. The texture of the burdock reminded me of carrots, and the flavor was sweet, crisp, and herbal.

   When I came home to New York, I remade the recipe, but I added vinegar to make it just a little bit acidic. The vinegar water also prevents the burdock root slices from turning brown. Soaking them for 20 to 30 minutes is a key step in the recipe.

1 tablespoon white vinegar

8 ounces burdock root

Sweet, Sour, and Spicy Dipping Sauce (page 133)

½ teaspoon toasted sesame seeds

1. In a bowl, combine 3 cups water and the vinegar. Peel the burdock root with a potato peeler. Cut it crosswise into 2-inch-long pieces, then cut those pieces lengthwise into ⅛-inch-thick pieces. Transfer to the vinegar water and soak for 20 to 30 minutes.

2. Drain the burdock, pat dry, and transfer to a large bowl. Add the dipping sauce and toss well with a spoon. Transfer to a bowl, sprinkle with the sesame seeds, and serve.

Pan-Fried Chinese Yam Slices

MA-GUI 마구이

Serves 2

The yams used in this recipe are not the kind you're probably thinking of, the ones that are similar to sweet potatoes. These yams are called *ma* in Korean, and are long, white, cylinder-shaped tubers with a light brown skin. They are sometimes called Chinese yams. Cooked, they are a bit like a potato, but crisper, sweeter, and less starchy.

Raw yams have a texture similar to jicama and taste a little like it, but they are a bit slippery. Don't let that deter you, because the slime disappears when the ma is cooked.

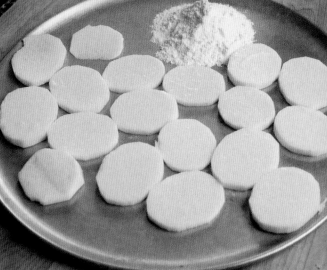

8 ounces Chinese yam (ma), peeled and sliced into ¼-inch-thick pieces

2 tablespoons glutinous rice flour or all-purpose flour

2 tablespoons vegetable oil

1 tablespoon toasted sesame oil

¼ teaspoon kosher salt

1. Toss the yam slices with the flour to coat evenly.

2. Combine the vegetable and sesame oils in a small bowl.

3. Heat 2 tablespoons of the oil mixture in a large skillet over medium heat and swirl to coat the pan. Add each piece of yam one by one to make a single layer. Cook for 3 to 4 minutes, until the bottom is slightly crisp, then flip them over. Add the remaining 1 tablespoon oil mixture and cook for 3 to 4 minutes, until the other side is crisp; do not let them brown. Transfer to a serving plate. Sprinkle with the salt and serve right away.

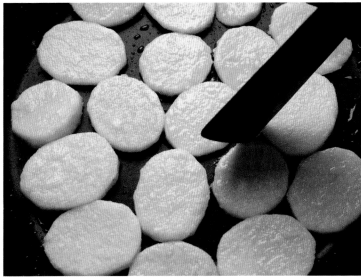

Steamed Chinese Yams

MA-JJIM 마찜

Serves 2

This is a common dish in Korean Buddhist temples, where it is served at breakfast, lunch, or dinner as a side dish, with rice. It's like a thick porridge, very soft, smooth, comforting, and pretty.

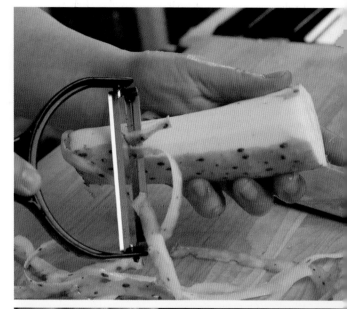

1 pound Chinese yams (ma), peeled and grated

¾ to 1 teaspoon kosher salt

1 fresh shiitake mushroom or 1 dried shiitake mushroom, soaked in cold water for 3 to 4 hours, stem removed and cap sliced thin

1 red chili pepper or ¼ red bell pepper, cut into thin matchsticks

2 teaspoons toasted sesame oil

1. Bring 2 inches water to a boil in the bottom of a steamer. Remove from the heat.

2. Put the grated yam in a heat-resistant bowl. Add the salt and mix well with a spoon. Add the shiitake mushroom and stir. Arrange the red pepper strips on top. Drizzle on the sesame oil and place the bowl in the steamer basket.

3. Reheat the water in the steamer over medium-high heat until boiling. Add the steamer basket to the steamer. Cover and cook for 15 minutes. Remove from the heat and serve.

Pepper and Perilla Leaf Pancakes

GOCHU-KKAENNIP-JANGTTEOK 고추깻잎장떡

Serves 2

I often add jangs like hot pepper paste (gochujang) and soybean paste (doenjang) to my pancakes instead of salt. These pancakes, made with both, are called jangtteok. They are supposed to be a little salty, so they go well with rice. When I tasted the Korean Buddhist version, I was struck by their simplicity and tastiness, although they contain none of the usual garlic, scallions, or onions. Instead, the nuns use a combination of perilla leaves and green chili peppers. The perilla leaves give the pancakes a fresh, minty flavor.

¾ cup all-purpose flour

2 tablespoons Korean fermented soybean paste (doenjang)

2 teaspoons Korean hot pepper paste (gochujang)

4 to 5 large mild Korean green chili peppers (about 4 ounces), chopped

12 to 16 perilla leaves (about ½ ounce), chopped

3 tablespoons vegetable oil

1. Combine the flour, soybean paste, hot pepper paste, and ¾ cup water in a bowl. Mix well with a spoon or whisk until smooth. Add the chili peppers and perilla leaves. Mix well with a spoon.

2. Heat 1 tablespoon of the vegetable oil in a large nonstick skillet over medium heat and swirl to coat the skillet. Scoop up the mixture with a large spoon, place it in the skillet, and flatten and round the edges to make a 3-inch circle. Repeat with the rest of the mixture to make a total of 5 or 6 pancakes. If your skillet is small, work in batches.

3. Cook for about 2 minutes, until the bottom turns golden brown and crispy. Turn and press down with a spatula to spread the pancakes to about 3½ inches. Add the remaining 2 tablespoons vegetable oil and shake the skillet so that the oil runs underneath the pancakes. Cook for another 2 to 3 minutes, until both sides are golden brown. Transfer to a plate and serve.

PERILLA LEAVES

I love the taste of perilla leaves and grow them fresh on my apartment balcony every year. July and August are the peak time to harvest. I pick them every morning and add them to my green smoothie. They grow very easily. Some of my plants' seeds even fell into the planters of the apartment below mine, so now my neighbor is growing perilla leaves, too! They are easy to find at Korean markets, though sometimes they are mislabeled as sesame leaves.

Sweet and Crunchy Tofu

TOFU-GANGJEONG (DUBU-GANGJEONG) 두부강정

Serves 4

There were several side dishes on the table when I visited the dining hall at Goun temple, but this one was the first to disappear. The monks loved it!

When you taste this dish, you'll be surprised at how meaty the tofu is. Twice-frying transforms it, so it becomes crunchy outside while remaining soft inside. It's time to show off your magic and turn almost tasteless tofu into something so sweet and spicy that even Buddhist monks can't resist it.

¼ cup ketchup

¼ cup rice syrup or 3 tablespoons sugar

3 tablespoons Korean hot pepper paste (gochujang)

1 pound medium-firm or firm tofu, patted dry with a kitchen towel

¼ cup potato starch

2 cups vegetable oil

1 tablespoon toasted pumpkin seeds

1. Combine the ketchup, rice syrup, and hot pepper paste in a large skillet. Heat over medium-high heat, stirring with a wooden spoon, until bubbling, 1 to 2 minutes. Remove from the heat.

2. Cut the tofu into 1-inch dice and put the pieces in a plastic bag. Add the potato starch, seal the bag, and gently turn the bag over until the tofu is well coated. Remove each piece from the bag individually and transfer to a large plate or a cutting board lined with plastic wrap, leaving some space between the pieces.

3. Heat the vegetable oil in a large nonstick skillet over medium-high heat to 330 to 340 degrees F, 4 to 5 minutes. Place the tofu pieces, one at a time, on a spatula and add to the oil, or do this carefully by hand. Reduce the heat to medium. Fry the tofu until the surface turns a little crispy, 2 to 3 minutes. Turn the tofu pieces with a spatula or slotted spoon—they should be firm enough to turn without breaking—and fry for another 2 to 3 minutes, occasionally turning so that all sides cook evenly. When the tofu is light brown and slightly crisp all over, remove from the pan and set in a strainer set over a bowl.

4. Reheat the oil for 1 minute over medium-high heat. Add all the fried tofu pieces and fry one more time, turning the pieces with a slotted spoon, until golden brown and crunchy on all sides, 4 to 5 minutes. Transfer to the strainer set over a bowl to drain the excess oil.

5. Put the pumpkin seeds in the slotted spoon and dip into the hot oil for 10 seconds. Transfer the seeds to a small bowl.

6. Reheat the sauce over medium-high heat until bubbling. Add the fried tofu and gently mix together to coat. Sprinkle with the pumpkin seeds. Transfer to a serving plate and serve.

SWEETIES

FOR PLEASURE AND GOOD HEALTH

On festival days long ago, I remember going to my grandmother's house in the countryside and seeing the mound of traditional Korean cookies she had prepared for us there, waiting. They were hand-cut in simple shapes, piled in a mountain and covered in sticky, sweet, and shiny sauce. She made them for everyone, but mostly for her grandchildren. When I bit into one, it was flaky and crispy with a sweet coating, melting in my mouth. I never forgot them!

Traditionally Korean sweets are homemade and served on special occasions like weddings, birthdays, and Korean holidays, or as refreshing snacks between meals or with tea. They are light, restorative, and usually grain-, herb-, and/or fruit-based, made to improve health and refresh the body and mind. We avoid artificial sweeteners and colors, and use natural seasonings, ice, honey, beans, and fruits like pear and dried persimmon, as well as ginger. You enjoy these sweets for dessert, though Korean meals don't usually include a dessert course. (If we have anything sweet after a meal, it's often fresh seasonal fruit.)

It's been fun for me to share Korean sweets on YouTube with a whole new group of people who have never had them before, and in this chapter, I show you some of the best. There are recipes for high-quality traditional Korean sweets (called han-gwa in Korean), which include deep-fried honey-soaked cookies like the ones I had at my grandmother's house and Candied Ginger. You'll also find my traditional summertime favorite, Shaved Ice with Sweet Red Beans and Fruits, as well as a modern interpretation of an ancient classic, Persimmon Punch Slush. And no discussion of Korean sweets would be complete without talking about the gorgeous Rice Cakes Steamed on Pine Needles that we eat at Chuseok, the Korean harvest holiday that resembles Thanksgiving.

Steamed Pear
with Honey

KKULBAEJJIM 꿀배찜

Serves 1 or 2

This is a nice, warm treat for a cold winter day. The pear is flavored with cinnamon and ginger, sweetened with honey, filled with pine nuts and jujube, and then steamed for a long time. It becomes translucent and so soft that it can be eaten with a spoon along with the juice. Before serving, the rich, pear is crowned with ginkgo nuts. A delicious dessert or snack, it's also a home remedy for treating colds, sore throats, and coughs.

2 teaspoons grated ginger

1 large Korean pear (1 to 1½ pounds)

1 tablespoon pine nuts

1 dried jujube, pitted (see page 423)

2 tablespoons honey

¼ teaspoon ground cinnamon

5 ginkgo nuts, shelled (see page 419)

1. Wrap the ginger in a double thickness of cheesecloth and squeeze over a bowl. Reserve the juice and discard the spent ginger.

2. Slice off the top of the pear, about 1 inch down from the stem, to make a lid. Scoop out the core and the seeds with a small spoon and discard, making sure not to cut through the bottom of the pear.

3. Fill the hollow with the ginger juice, pine nuts, and jujube. Drizzle in the honey and sprinkle with the cinnamon.

4. Put the lid back on the pear and place it in a heat-resistant bowl that will fit into your steamer.

5. Pour 2 inches water into the steamer and bring to a boil over medium-high heat. Place the bowl with the pear in the steamer basket. Cover and steam for 1 hour and 10 minutes, or until the pear is translucent. (There will be a pool of juice in the bowl.) Remove the steamer from the heat but keep it covered.

6. While the pear is steaming, bring 2 cups water to a boil in a saucepan. Add the ginkgo nuts and cook for 2 minutes, stirring with a wooden spoon, until the papery skins are loose. Drain, remove the skins, and set the ginkgo nuts aside.

7. Remove the lid of the pear and spoon the ginkgo nuts on top. Replace the lid and serve right away. To eat, use a spoon to scoop up the pear flesh, and enjoy with the flavorful juice in the bowl.

Candied Ginger

SAENGGANG-JEONGGWA 생강정과

Makes about 8 ounces (1¼ cups)

This chewy jellied candy coated in white sugar tingles in your mouth and makes a delicious accompaniment to hot green tea. You can also use it as a home remedy for colds, sore throats, and stomachaches. Ginger has an anti-inflammatory agent that always calms my stomach when it's upset.

We make this on special occasions like Chuseok, the Korean equivalent to Thanksgiving. That's when all the children come back to their hometowns to visit, usually from the city to the countryside. It's customary for the adult children to go visiting from house to house, stopping in on their neighbors to tell them all about their lives in the city. Their neighbors greet them and prepare a little table with drinks and desserts like Honey Cookies (page 363), fresh fruits, Rice Cakes Dusted with Soybean Powder (page 373), and this delightful candy.

8 ounces peeled ginger, cut into ⅛-inch-thick slices (about 1¼ cups)

¾ cup sugar

¼ cup rice syrup

1. Bring 5 cups water to a boil in a medium saucepan.

2. Rinse the sliced ginger in cold water to remove the excess starch. Drain. Add the ginger to the boiling water. Cover and boil for 5 minutes. Drain and rinse with cold running water to remove the excess starch and reduce the spiciness. Drain again and transfer the ginger to a bowl. Add enough water to cover the ginger by 3 inches and soak for 3 hours to further reduce the spiciness.

3. Drain the ginger and transfer to a small, heavy saucepan. Add ½ cup of the sugar and ½ cup water. Stir a few times, make sure the ginger is submerged, and cover. Simmer over low heat for 30 minutes.

4. Stir in the rice syrup, bring back to a boil, cover, and simmer over very low heat, stirring from time to time with a wooden spoon, for 30 minutes, or until the syrup is gooey and the ginger is quite sticky. Remove from the heat.

5. Put the remaining ¼ cup sugar on a sheet of parchment paper. Transfer the ginger slices to the sugar-covered parchment paper and, using tongs or chopsticks, toss the slices to coat with the sugar. When the ginger has cooled slightly, separate each slice by hand and press in any remaining sugar. Spread the slices out on the parchment side by side and cool for about 20 minutes. Serve or transfer to an airtight container and refrigerate for up to 1 month.

NOTE

The sticky syrup left in the pot can be diluted for a delicious tea (it's also a great way to clean the pot). Add cold water, bring to a boil, and serve.

Honey Cookies

YAKGWA 약과

Makes about 24

Yakgwa are deep-fried honey-soaked cookies made with flour, honey, and soju, a type of Korean alcohol (see page 34). Rich and flaky, they are delicately flavored with ginger and cinnamon, and they soak overnight in a mixture of honey and rice syrup.

In the old days, these traditional Korean sweets were reserved for the upper classes, as Korea grew very little wheat, so flour was a luxury. Honey was also valuable, not only as a sweetener but also for its medicinal properties. In fact, the Korean word for medicine is *yak*, so yakgwa cookies are considered to be healthy.

Today most people purchase their yakgwa readymade, but some still make them at home for special occasions. Store-bought cookies don't use top-quality ingredients as this traditional recipe does.

I suggest using a deep 12-inch skillet to fry the cookies so that you can make them all in one batch.

FOR THE DOUGH

2 cups all-purpose flour

½ teaspoon ground cinnamon

¼ teaspoon kosher salt

¼ teaspoon ground black pepper or white pepper

4 teaspoons toasted sesame oil

¼ cup chopped or grated ginger

¼ cup honey

¼ cup soju

FOR THE DIPPING SYRUP

¼ cup chopped or grated ginger

1 cup rice syrup or corn syrup

¼ cup sugar

¼ cup honey

¼ teaspoon ground cinnamon

Vegetable oil, for frying

Pumpkin seeds or pine nuts, for garnish (optional)

MAKE THE DOUGH

1. Combine the flour, cinnamon, salt, pepper, and sesame oil in a bowl. Rub handfuls of the mixture briskly between your palms to distribute the oil evenly through the flour. The flour mixture will darken in color slightly. Sift through a sieve or mesh strainer into a bowl and discard any bits that don't go through.

2. Wrap the ginger in a double thickness of cheesecloth and squeeze over a bowl. Discard the spent ginger. Add the honey, soju, and ¼ cup water to the bowl with the ginger juice. Mix well with a spoon.

3. Add the liquid mixture to the flour mixture and mix until the dough comes together. Knead very lightly in the bowl, just until the dough is cohesive. You do not want to develop the gluten in the flour, so do not knead until smooth, otherwise the cookies will be hard and heavy when you fry them. Cover the dough with plastic wrap and set aside for 10 minutes.

MEANWHILE, MAKE THE DIPPING SYRUP

1. Wrap the ginger in a double thickness of cheesecloth and squeeze over a bowl. Pour the juice into a large saucepan and discard the spent ginger.

2. Add the rice syrup, sugar, and 1 cup water to the saucepan with the ginger juice. Bring to a boil over medium-high heat and boil until small bubbles form on the surface, about 10 minutes. Stir, remove from the heat, and stir in the honey and cinnamon. Mix well and set aside.

SHAPE AND FRY THE COOKIES

1. Using a rolling pin, roll out the dough on a large cutting board until it is about ¼ inch thick. Cut it in half, then put one half on top of the other half. (This will give the cookies their flaky layers.) Repeat two more times. Roll out the final stack to a ¼-inch-thick rectangle, about 9 inches wide by 11 inches long.

Recipe Continues

2. Using a cookie cutter or a cookie stamp, cut the dough into small cookies, about 1½ inches in diameter. With a stainless-steel chopstick or a wooden skewer, poke several small holes, right through to the cutting board, in the center of each cookie. (The hole will help the cookies cook evenly and maintain their shape, and will also allow them to absorb more syrup.)

3. In a deep 12-inch-skillet or sauté pan, heat 1½ to 2 inches oil over medium-high heat until it reaches 200 degrees F. Reduce the heat to low and add the cookies one by one to the oil. Work in batches if you are using a smaller pan so that you don't overcrowd the pan. It will take about 2 minutes for the cookies to float to the top. When all of the cookies float, carefully turn them over with tongs or a skimmer. Keep cooking until all the cookies are light brown, 12 to 13 minutes. Using tongs or a slotted spoon, transfer the cookies as they are done to a large mesh strainer set over a bowl or to a wire rack set over a baking sheet.

4. Raise the heat to medium-high and heat the oil until it reaches 330 degrees F. Reduce the heat to medium and, working in batches if necessary, add the cookies and fry them for 4 to 5 minutes, turning with the tongs or a slotted spoon, until all the cookies are evenly golden brown. Strain and shake the cookies to remove excess oil. Transfer the hot cookies to the dipping syrup in the pan. You will hear a hissing sound as you dip the hot cookies into the syrup. Turn the cookies over a few times in the syrup, then cover the pan and soak for 8 to 12 hours at room temperature, turning them over a couple of times.

5. Remove the cookies from the syrup, drain, and serve. If you wish, garnish with pumpkin seeds or pine nuts just before serving. Store the cookies in an airtight container at room temperature for up to 1 week or in the refrigerator for up to 1 month.

A SPOONFUL OF HEALTH

Koreans' love of honey goes back thousands of years. Honey has always been considered precious, not only because it's delicious but also because it has many medicinal properties, including vitamins and minerals that can improve everyday health. It's been used in both cooking and traditional medicine for centuries. Many Koreans eat it regularly. A spoonful a day will boost your immune system, give you a shot of antioxidants, and bring you many other health benefits.

Korean households always keep honey on hand. Go to any Korean grocery store and you will find a large selection on the shelf. It's expensive in Korea, so many Koreans traveling to the U.S. buy honey to take back to Korea as gifts.

Fluffy Pine Nut Rice Cake

JATSEOLGI 잣설기

Serves 4 to 8

This fluffy white rice cake is perfect for any special occasion. It has a chewy texture and just seems to get nuttier and sweeter as you eat. We like to serve this cake with tea.

We typically serve jatseolgi at a baek-il, the celebration of a baby's first one hundred days, a major milestone. The rice cake represents purity and a wish for good health in the future. But it isn't just for babies! Anyone is happy to get this cake on their birthday.

Be sure to use Korean frozen short-grain rice flour for this. It's sold in the freezer section of Korean groceries. Do not use regular rice flour.

½ cup pine nuts

4 cups Korean frozen short-grain rice flour (see headnote), thawed overnight in the refrigerator

1 teaspoon kosher salt

3 tablespoons honey

1 dried jujube, pitted (see page 423) and sliced (optional)

Several pumpkin seeds (optional)

1. Put the pine nuts on a piece of parchment paper on a cutting board and fold the parchment over them. Using a rolling pin, crush the nuts by rolling over them a few times. Open the paper and use your hands to gather up the sticky nuts in a pile, then fold the paper over again and crush again with the rolling pin. Repeat until all the pine nuts are completely crushed. Transfer the crushed nuts to a bowl.

2. Place a medium-mesh sieve over a large bowl and sift the rice flour through it by gently rubbing it with a wooden spoon or your hand. Sift it twice and discard any chunks that don't go through.

3. Combine the salt, honey, and 3 tablespoons water in a small bowl. Mix well to dissolve the salt. Add this mixture to the rice flour and mix with your hands. Press out the lumps between your palms to break them up. Repeat until you have a fine flour that's uniformly damp. (If there are still some lumps, press them through the sieve to break them up.) Add the crushed pine nuts and gently mix in, using both hands.

4. Fill a large steamer with 8 cups water. Line the steamer basket with a large cotton cloth or a few layers of cheesecloth; the cloth needs to extend over the edges of the basket with a generous overhang. Remove the bottom from an 8-inch springform pan and place the ring in the center of the steamer basket. Add the rice flour mixture to the cake ring. Flatten it out so it sits level in the ring.

5. Use your knife to divide the uncooked rice cake into 8 wedges, like a pizza. This will make it easier to separate when it's cooked. If you are using the jujube and pumpkin seeds, scatter them over the middle of the cake.

6. Bring the water in the steamer to a boil over medium-high heat, then add the basket. Place another cloth over the top of the basket so no moisture will drip onto the rice cake. Cover and steam for 30 minutes.

7. Uncover and remove the top cloth. Let the cake cool for 10 minutes.

8. Grab the extra cloth hanging over the edges of the steamer basket and pull it up over the rice cake so you can gently lift it out and keep the cake level. Place the cake on a baking sheet and use a large spatula to lift it up gently so you can pull the cotton cloth out from underneath it. Remove the springform ring. The rice cake is already divided, so each portion should come out nicely. If it doesn't, you may need to help it out a bit with your knife.

9. Serve the cake immediately, or keep it at room temperature for several hours. Freeze the leftover cake when it is still fresh, double-bagging it. Thaw at room temperature for 10 to 15 minutes or reheat in a microwave.

Rice Cakes Steamed on Pine Needles

SONGPYEON 송편

Makes 14 to 15 songpyeon

These chewy, slightly sweet, nutty rice cakes are traditionally eaten on Chuseok, the Korean harvest moon festival, when the whole family comes together from far and wide to celebrate. We steam them on fresh pine needles, which infuse the cakes with their woodsy, herbal aroma.

The dough is made with flour ground from newly harvested rice, which is very meaningful in Korea. It represents the fruit of many months of farmers' labor and means that the new crop is finally here. For properly chewy cakes, the rice flour must be wet when you make the dough. The wet rice flour is made by washing and soaking the rice grains in cold water, draining, and bringing them to a local mill to be ground into wet flour. In the U.S., Korean grocery stores sell convenient packages of ground wet short-grain rice flour. You'll find them in the freezer section. Do not use regular dried rice flour: No matter how long you steam it, the rice cake will never cook properly and there will be hard lumps inside.

I make songpyeon for every Chuseok. In Korea we use many different fillings, which we enclose in the dough. Part of the fun of eating the delicate, ridged walnut-size rice cakes is not knowing what filling you will get until you bite into them. My favorites are pine nuts with honey and sesame seeds with honey—sweet and nutty surprises hidden inside a chewy cake that is not sweet at all.

Korean rice cakes come in different colors—white, green, purple, red, yellow—and we decorate them with delicate flowers that we make with some of the dough. For this recipe, I've chosen to make white and green songpyeon, and I decorate them with red flowers. I use mugwort powder, which has an herbal flavor, for the green songpyeon. I forage mugwort and dry it, but you can find the powder in Korean groceries. If you can't locate it, green tea powder works.

3 cups plus 2 tablespoons Korean frozen short-grain rice flour (see headnote), thawed overnight in the refrigerator

Kosher salt

1 teaspoon mugwort powder or green tea powder

⅛ teaspoon raspberry Jell-O powder

¼ cup pine nuts

2 tablespoons honey

¼ cup toasted sesame seeds, ground with a mortar and pestle or spice grinder

Fresh long pine needles, such as white pine needles, washed, rinsed, and patted dry (optional; see note)

1 tablespoon toasted sesame oil

NOTE

If fresh pine needles aren't available, you can make the songpyeon without. Lay them directly on the cotton cloth in the steamer.

MAKE THE DOUGH

1. Place a medium-mesh sieve over a large bowl and sift the rice flour through it by gently rubbing it with a wooden spoon or your hand. Sift it twice and discard any chunks that don't go through.

2. To make the white dough, transfer 1½ cups of the rice flour to another large bowl. Add ¼ teaspoon salt and ¼ cup hot water. Mix with a wooden spoon until the ingredients come together into a lumpy dough. Knead by hand until smooth, about 1 minute. Wrap the dough in plastic wrap to prevent it from drying out.

3. To make the green dough, transfer another 1½ cups of the rice flour to another large bowl. Add the mugwort powder or green tea powder, ¼ teaspoon salt, and ¼ cup plus 2 teaspoons hot water. Mix well with a wooden spoon until the ingredients come together into a lumpy dough. Knead by hand until smooth, about 1 minute. Wrap the dough in plastic wrap to prevent it from drying out.

Recipe Continues

4. To make the red dough, combine the remaining 2 tablespoons rice flour, a pinch of salt, the raspberry Jell-O powder, and 1¼ teaspoons hot water. Mix well with your fingers until smooth. Shape into a ball and wrap in plastic wrap.

MAKE THE FILLINGS

1. Put the pine nuts on a sheet of parchment paper on your cutting board and fold the parchment over them. Using a rolling pin, crush the pine nuts by rolling over them a few times. Open the paper and use your hands to gather up the sticky nuts in a pile, then fold the paper over again and crush again with the rolling pin. Repeat until all the pine nuts are completely crushed. Transfer to a small bowl. Add a pinch of salt and 1 tablespoon of the honey. Mix well with a spoon and set aside.

2. Combine the toasted sesame seed powder, a pinch of salt, and the remaining 1 tablespoon honey in a small bowl and mix well.

SHAPE THE RICE CAKES

1. Set aside a walnut-size piece of white dough for decorating the rice cakes and wrap it in plastic wrap so it won't dry out. Take another walnut-size piece of white rice dough and roll it between your palms to make a ball. Press your thumb into the center of the ball to shape it into a cup. Fill the cup with about 2 teaspoons of the sesame seed mixture or the pine nut mixture and bring the edges together to seal gently. Roll between your palms to make a ball. Make a ridge along the top half of the ball by pinching it slightly with your thumb and index finger. Repeat with the rest of the white dough, the green dough, and the fillings. You should get 7 white songpyeon and 8 green.

2. Using the red dough and the reserved white dough, pinch off little pieces to make flowers or other decorations. Stick them onto the rice cakes.

STEAM THE RICE CAKES

1. Fill your steamer with about 2½ inches water and bring to a boil over medium-high heat. Place a cotton cloth or folded cheesecloth in the steamer basket and spread the pine needles evenly over the cloth. Add the songpyeon side by side, leaving a little gap between them. Place the steamer basket in the steamer and cover with a large cotton cloth or folded cheesecloth so that the steam doesn't drip back onto the songpyeon. Cover and steam for 25 minutes. Reduce the heat to low and simmer for an additional 5 minutes.

2. Remove from the heat, uncover, and let stand for a few minutes, until cool enough to handle. Transfer the songpyeon to a platter. Brush each one with a little sesame oil and serve. You can freeze freshly made songpyeon for up to 1 month. Thaw at room temperature and serve or reheat in a microwave.

SIBLING RIVALRY

My mom made the dough for rice cakes on the night before Chuseok, and my sisters and I would shape them. She told us, "If you can make beautiful songpyeon, you will have a beautiful baby someday." As carefully as we could, we pinched off walnut-size pieces of dough, rolled them into balls, and indented them with our thumbs. We put some filling in them, pulled the sides over the filling, and pinched them together to form a neat ridge. Then we fashioned pretty little flowers out of dough and stuck them onto the cakes. My mother would steam them on pine needles. When they were ready, we teased each other: "Who made this ugly one?"

Rice Cakes Dusted with Soybean Powder

INJEOLMI 인절미

Serves 4

One of the most popular rice cakes in Korea, injeolmi are made for special occasions like weddings, New Year's Day, family birthdays, and Chuseok (Korean Thanksgiving). The chewy cakes are generously coated with roasted yellow soybean powder, which gives them a nutty, toasty flavor.

To make injeolmi, you steam the dough, then pound it with a mortar and pestle until it's smooth. Then you shape the cakes and coat them with the roasted soybean powder. For the best results, make sure that the roasted soybean powder is very fresh, since it loses its nuttiness over time. Once you open the packet, store in the freezer and use within 1 month. You can use some of the leftover powder as a flavoring for rice.

Homemade rice syrup is delicious for dipping the cakes in, but you can use store-bought.

2 cups glutinous rice flour

3 tablespoons sugar

½ teaspoon kosher salt

⅓ cup roasted yellow soybean powder

Honey or rice syrup (for homemade, see page 376), for dipping (optional; see headnote)

1. Fill the bottom of a steamer with 2 inches water, bring to a boil, and turn off the heat.

2. In a bowl, combine the glutinous rice flour, 2 tablespoons of the sugar, the salt, and 1 cup water. Stir and mix well with a large spoon until the dough comes together. Knead the dough for a few minutes, first with the spoon and then with your hands. It should be wet and sticky, but the consistency should be smooth.

3. Place the steamer basket in the steamer. Line it with a large cotton cloth or a few layers of cheesecloth. Set the dough on top of the cloth and poke a hole in the center with the handle of your wooden spoon, then pull it apart slightly so the dough resembles a donut. This will allow it to steam evenly. Gather the edges of the cloth and fold over the dough.

4. Cover the steamer, bring to a boil, and steam for 25 minutes over medium-high heat. Turn the heat to low and steam for another 5 minutes. Remove from the heat.

5. Meanwhile, place a small bowl of cold water next to the workspace so that you can wet your hands to prevent them from sticking to the rice cake.

6. Remove the cloth and transfer the hot rice cake to a mortar. Pound the dough with the pestle for 3 to 5 minutes, until the dough is smooth and you see bubbles.

7. Put the soybean powder on a cutting board and shape it into an approximately 7-inch square. Spoon the rice cake out of the mortar and place it on top of the powder. Wet your hands with the cold water and gently spread and shape the rice cake into an approximately 5-by-7-inch rectangle. Sprinkle some of the soybean powder over the rice cake. Cut the rice cake into 10 equal pieces with a spatula and shape each piece into rectangle. Coat each piece with some of the soybean powder.

Recipe Continues

8. Transfer the injeolmi to a plate. Sprinkle all the remaining soybean powder over the top of the injeolmi, then sprinkle with the remaining 1 tablespoon sugar. Serve right away. If you can't serve the rice cakes immediately, freeze them while still fresh and soft. Thaw at room temperature to restore their soft, chewy texture. If the rice cakes harden, place under the broiler in the middle of the oven and heat until the top blisters and turns golden brown. Watch carefully; it will be ready quickly. If desired, dip the broiled rice cakes in honey or rice syrup.

PAYING RESPECTS

Injeolmi was my father's favorite rice cake, so my mother used to make or buy it often, for any special occasion. I went to Namhae Island, in the very south of Korea, a couple of years ago, to visit my father's grave in the mountains. It's customary to pay respects to deceased family members by bringing food, flowers, and alcohol to their graves. So I prepared some of his favorite dishes, including injeolmi, and I brought soju. I placed the food and alcohol in front of his grave. I bowed to him just as if he were sitting there in front of me and talked to him as if he were listening. I knew that he was very happy to see me and that he appreciated my work.

Homemade Rice Syrup

SSAL-JOCHEONG 쌀조청

HERE IS YOUR TIMELINE FOR MAKING THIS DELICIOUS SYRUP:

Rice soaking time: **1 hour**

Rice cooking time: **22 minutes**

Fermenting time: **6 hours**

Boiling time: **2 hours**

Makes 3½ to 4 cups (if using the stovetop method) or 1½ cups (if using a rice cooker)

Rice syrup has been used as a sweetener in Korean cuisine for a long time. In the old days, before we imported rice, we had to rely on our small domestic production, so rice was very precious. The syrup was an ingredient used only in the kitchens of the royal court and the very wealthy.

Now rice syrup is a common ingredient, available in Korean supermarkets everywhere. But homemade rice syrup tastes much deeper and richer than commercial syrup. The sweet, earthy flavor of this syrup makes it a perfect match for rice cakes. You can also use it instead of store-bought rice syrup in other dishes.

This recipe starts with the traditional method of making rice syrup on the stovetop. This is a great project for a weekend, since turning the cooked rice into a sweet golden liquid takes about 10 hours. I also offer a modern method for making a smaller amount of rice syrup using a large (at least 10-cup) rice cooker with a warm function. It's very easy, and much quicker. In both methods, the conversion of starch to sugar is accomplished with the help of the enzyme amylase, found in barley malt powder.

TO MAKE THE SYRUP ON THE STOVETOP

2¼ pounds short-grain white rice (about 5 cups)

2 cups barley malt powder or flakes

1. Put the rice in a large, heavy pot and cover with cold water. Soak for 1 hour, then drain the rice through a strainer.

2. Return the soaked rice to the pot. Add 5 cups water. Cover and cook over medium-high heat for 12 minutes, or until the rice is bubbling and beginning to boil over. Stir the rice with a rice scoop or wooden spoon to make sure that none is sticking to the bottom of the pot. Cover, reduce the heat to medium-low, and cook for another 10 minutes, until the rice is fully cooked. Remove from the heat. Uncover and fluff the cooked rice with the wooden spoon. It may be a little crunchy on the bottom, but that's fine.

3. Add 8 cups water and stir well with the wooden spoon. Insert an instant-read thermometer. The temperature should be about 140 degrees F. Add the barley malt powder and mix well. Let sit for 1 hour. Uncover and stir. Place over medium heat and insert the thermometer. Stir with a wooden spoon until the temperature reaches 137 degrees, 2 to 4 minutes, then turn off the heat right away, before it climbs to 140 degrees, and let it cool to 127 degrees. (If the temperature rises to 140 degrees or above, the enzyme that converts the starches into sugars won't work well.) Cover and let stand for 1 hour. Repeat this process—heating to between 137 and 140 degrees and then letting it cool to 127 degrees—every hour for 4 more hours. The mixture needs to ferment for 6 hours total, maintaining a temperature between 110 and 140 degrees.

Recipe Continues

4. Stir the mixture well. Line a large strainer with a large piece of muslin or a cotton sheet. Place the strainer over a large bowl. Pour the rice mixture into the cloth-lined strainer. Let it drain for about 10 minutes, until some cloudy liquid has seeped into the bowl and the cloth is cool enough to handle. Lift the edges of the cloth and twist together to seal in the rice so that nothing leaks out, then slowly twist and squeeze out the rest of the liquid. This is time-consuming, but you don't want to lose any of the precious liquid, so squeeze out as much as you can. You will have 3 to 3½ quarts. Discard the solids.

5. Wash the pot and pour in the strained liquid. Bring to a boil over medium-high heat and boil for about 2 hours, until the amount reduces to approximately 1 quart. You don't have to stir until it's been boiling for about 1½ hours. After about 1½ hours, small bubbles will appear on the surface. Stir from time to time and keep boiling for 20 to 30 minutes, until large bubbles appear. Soon after the large bubbles appear, the entire surface of the syrup will be full of bubbles. Insert a thermometer and do not allow the temperature to go higher than 220 degrees F. Remove from the heat. The syrup should be stickier, sweeter, and darker. It should drizzle off a spoon in a thick, steady stream, like maple syrup. Be sure not to cook longer at this point because the hot syrup will get stickier and thicker as it cools and end up like hard candy. If this happens, thin it by adding a little bit of water, bring to a boil, then remove from the heat.

6. Allow the syrup to cool. Transfer to an airtight container and refrigerate for up to 3 months.

TO MAKE THE SYRUP IN A RICE COOKER

1 pound short-grain white rice (about 2½ cups)

1 cup barley malt powder or flakes

1. Put the rice in a bowl. Cover with cold water, then drain. Swish the wet rice around in the bowl with one hand, then rinse and drain a few more times, until the water runs clear. Drain and put the rice in the rice cooker. Add 2 cups water and cook the rice.

2. Fluff the rice with a wooden spoon. Add 4 cups cold water and stir well. Add the barley malt powder and mix well.

3. Set the rice cooker on the warm setting, cover, and let stand for 6 hours.

4. Open the rice cooker and stir the rice mixture well. Line a large strainer with a large piece of muslin or a cotton sheet and place the strainer over a large bowl. Pour the rice mixture into the cloth-lined strainer. Let it drain for about 10 minutes, until some cloudy liquid has seeped into the bowl and the cloth is cool enough to handle. Lift the edges of the cloth and twist together to seal in the rice mixture so that nothing leaks out, then slowly twist and squeeze out the rest of the liquid. This is time-consuming, but you don't want to lose any of the precious liquid, so squeeze out as much as you can. You will have 5 to 6 cups. Discard the solids.

5. Wash the inner pot of the rice cooker and put it back in the rice cooker. Add the strained liquid.

6. Set the rice cooker on cooking with the lid open and cook for 30 minutes, or until large bubbles appear. Stir with a wooden spoon. Turn off the rice cooker. You will have about 1½ cups rice syrup. If your rice syrup is too sticky, thin it by adding a bit of water, bring to a boil, then remove from the heat.

Persimmon Punch Slush

SUJEONGGWA SEULLEOSWI 수정과 슬러쉬

Serves 4

Made with dried persimmons, ginger, and cinnamon and sweetened with honey, persimmon punch is a traditional Korean drink, often served at the end of a meal. It's been a favorite since ancient times.

In this contemporary version, which I enjoyed at a popular cafe in Insadong, Seoul, an area that has long been associated with Korean art and culture, the punch is served ice cold, with icy slush made from the same mixture. It's sweet and thirst quenching, with the bonus of a soft, creamy persimmon in each serving.

½ cup sliced peeled ginger (2 ounces)

4 cinnamon sticks

½ cup white or brown sugar

½ cup honey

4 dried persimmons, stemmed and seeded

¼ cup pine nuts, tips removed (see page 421)

1. Combine 7 cups water, the ginger, and the cinnamon sticks in a large saucepan. Cover and cook over medium heat for 20 minutes.

2. Lower the heat to medium-low and simmer for another 30 minutes, until the liquid is golden brown and infused with the ginger and cinnamon. Meanwhile, set a strainer over a bowl and line with cheesecloth or a cotton cloth.

3. Pour the contents of the pan into the strainer; discard the solids. Add the sugar and honey to the liquid and stir well. You will have about 6 cups punch. Let it cool down to room temperature.

4. Transfer about 2 cups of the punch to an airtight container and freeze.

5. Add the persimmons to the punch. Cover and refrigerate for at least 8 hours or overnight. The persimmons will swell and become very soft.

6. To serve, remove the frozen punch from the freezer and let sit at room temperature for 10 to 15 minutes. Scrape with a fork. Pour ½ to 1 cup punch into each glass. Add a big spoonful of the shaved frozen punch and top with 1 soaked persimmon. Put several pine nuts on top of the persimmon and serve with a spoon.

Shaved Ice
with Sweet Red Beans and Fruits

PATBINGSU 팥빙수

Serves 1

Offered in the summer by Korean bakeries, patbingsu is made with shaved ice and chunks of fruit, sweet red beans, a little milk, and sweetened condensed milk. (In Korean, *pat* means "red beans"—aka adzuki beans—and *bingsu* is "shaved ice.") These days Korean bakeries try to outdo each other with new bingsu creations every year, but I love the traditional style with red beans, which is the recipe I'm giving you here.

When I lived in the city of Gwangju, in the southwest corner of the country, a popular bakery downtown was well known for its patbingsu. The shaved ice was like a mountain of snow, filled with delicious morsels like sweet red beans, colorful fruits, and chewy rice cakes. I can still picture my children's big smiles when I suggested we go for patbingsu, served in one big portion with spoons. We were so eager to dig in that we'd get "brain freeze," a feeling I associate with summer.

Canned sweet red beans are sold in every Korean grocery store, so you can make this very easily if you have an ice shaver. You can also prepare your own sweet red beans at home using the recipe below.

3 cups shaved ice (from about 2 cups water)

½ cup sweet red beans, canned or homemade (recipe follows), refrigerated

¼ cup whole milk

5 or 6 strawberries (about 1 cup), cut into small pieces

⅓ cup cubed mango, kiwi, peach, or plum

1 or 2 Rice Cakes Dusted with Soybean Powder (page 373), cut into ½-inch cubes (optional)

3 tablespoons cold sweetened condensed milk

Refrigerate a 2- to 3-cup serving bowl. When it is cold, put 1½ cups of the shaved ice in the bowl. Add ¼ cup sweet red beans and gently drizzle on the whole milk. Arrange the remaining shaved ice on top, building it up to make it look like a mountain. Add the fruits and rice cakes (if using). Drizzle on the condensed milk and serve right away. Gently mix everything together and eat with a spoon.

How to make sweet red beans

Makes a little more than 2 cups

1 cup dried red beans (adzuki beans)

1 cup sugar

1 teaspoon vanilla extract

½ teaspoon kosher salt

1. Pick out any broken or brownish beans and discard. Put the beans in a strainer. Rinse them under cold running water, then transfer to a large, heavy saucepan.

2. Add 4½ cups water and cover. Place over medium-high heat and cook for 10 minutes. Reduce the heat to low and simmer for 1 hour 20 minutes, until the beans are soft and tender but not mushy.

3. Remove from the heat and drain. Return the beans to the pot and add the sugar, vanilla extract, and salt. Stir and crush the beans lightly with a wooden spoon. Allow the beans to cool thoroughly, transfer to an airtight container, and refrigerate for up to 2 weeks.

Peach Omija Punch

BOKSUNGA-OMIJA-HWACHAE 복숭아오미자화채

Makes about 10 cups

Omija, or five-flavored-fruits, are small red berries, prized for being at once sweet, sour, bitter, salty, and spicy. They are thought to contain antioxidants, and Koreans believe that they are good for fatigue and boost the immune system. I add omija to my green smoothie every morning for their health benefits.

This punch is like nothing you've tasted before. It's both sweet and sour, with a gorgeous red color, the result of soaking the omija. The chopped peaches add even more sweetness. Delicate pine nuts are the crowning touch.

1 ounce dried omija (a generous ¼ cup)

4 or 5 ripe white or yellow peaches (about 2 pounds)

1 cup honey

¼ cup sugar

12 ice cubes

12 pine nuts, tips removed (see page 421)

1. Put the omija in a fine-mesh strainer and rinse under cold running water to remove any dust. Transfer to a large glass container and add 6 cups cold water. Cover and leave at room temperature for 24 hours.

2. Meanwhile, peel and pit the peaches, then slice them thinly. Cut the slices into bite-size pieces or cut into shapes with a vegetable cutter. Transfer to another container, add ¼ cup of the honey and the sugar, and gently toss together. Cover and refrigerate for 24 hours.

3. Place a strainer over a large bowl and line it with a clean cotton cloth or a few layers of cheesecloth. Strain the omija water through the cloth-lined strainer. Discard the omija.

4. Add the remaining ¾ cup honey to the omija water and stir well with a wooden spoon. Serve right away or refrigerate for up to 1 week. To serve, ladle some omija water into a bowl or glass, then add some marinated peaches with their juice. Stir in a few ice cubes, sprinkle with a few pine nuts, and serve.

WASTE-NOTHING PEACH JAM

If you have some leftover bits of peach flesh clinging to the pits and scraps from cutting the shapes, you can make a sugar-free jam. Put all the bits in a small, heavy saucepan and discard the pits. Cover and cook over low heat, stirring a few times with a wooden spoon, for 20 to 25 minutes, until it reduces to soft and sticky jam.

Ginseng Milkshake

SUSAM MILKSHAKE 수삼밀크셰이크

Serves 2

I often made this zesty, energy-boosting blender drink for my family in the morning. It has an earthy, herbal flavor, sweet but with a bitter undertone from the ginseng.

Ginseng root has been used in traditional Korean medicine for thousands of years, since long before recorded history. It cures a variety of ailments. According to traditional Korean medicine, people have hot or cold attributes. People with cold attributes are apt to have cold hands and feet, low energy, and aching knees, and they're advised to eat foods with hot attributes, such as ginseng. My collaborator, Martha, reports that she never has knee pain from arthritis the day after she drinks this.

1 fresh ginseng root (1¼ to 1½ ounces)

2 cups cold milk

4 ice cubes

1 tablespoon honey (optional)

Cut off the top knob of the ginseng root and cut away any blemishes from the skin. Slice and combine with the milk, ice cubes, and honey (if using) in a blender. Blend at high speed for 1 minute, until smooth and frothy. Serve at once.

STREET FOOD AND MODERN KOREAN DISHES

NEW CLASSICS

Korean inventiveness never ceases to amaze me. We have an incredible capacity for change. Each time I go to my home country, I discover something new. Our food is always evolving, with new dishes appearing alongside traditional, authentic ones.

One place I see this is among the street food vendors. They learn from tradition, from their customers, and from each other, and they're always striving to create the next most delicious, popular thing. The busy Myeongdong shopping district of Seoul, known for its food, fashion, and cosmetics, is crammed with street vendors vying for customers' attention. They appear around sunset and fill every street and every corner. It's fun to watch them cooking and preparing all kinds of foods, and the people moving excitedly from cart to cart so they can try everything. The vendors use intense flavors and enticing textures to attract people. For just a few dollars

you can sample all kinds of things, one cart after another, from rice cakes to cheese skewers to candied sweet potatoes to fish cake soup.

Many dishes in this book have been around for thousands of years, but the food in this chapter dates back only a hundred years or so. Some dishes are much more recent and reflect international influences. Noodles and Black Bean Sauce Platter came from the wave of immigration from China. Army Base Stew is a Korean War–era fusion of American military rations and Korean classic cooking techniques. Bread Rolls and Doughnut Twists reflect the period after the war when the country was becoming receptive to Western-style food.

The recipes in this chapter will give you a sense of the vibrancy and innovation of our food and show that we are always open to new tastes and ideas.

불고기 烤肉 焼き肉 Bulgogi	매운불고기 辣烤肉 辛くている焼肉 Spicy bulgogi	오징어포 凉拌鱿鱼干 スルメ Squid	멸 치 炒小鱼干 カタクチイワシ Anchovy	스 팸 午餐肉 スパム Spam	치 즈 乳酪 チーズ Cheese

Spicy Rice Cakes in Broth
with Ramyeon Noodles

RABOKKI 라볶이

Serves 2 to 4

This is a modern take on one of Korea's most popular street snacks, a spicy rice cake dish called tteokbokki. The classic version consists of chewy rice cakes cooked in a sweet, spicy, and savory gochujang broth. Tteokbokki vendors can be found waiting for customers on streets, stirring the rice cakes and thick, red sauce together in a huge rectangular pan.

These days instant ramyeon noodles are sometimes added to tteokbokki a few minutes before it's served. Ramyeon is the Korean version of the popular Japanese ramen, the instant noodles that come with packaged soup stock. It is relatively new to the country; the president of Samyang Foods brought two ramyeon-making machines over from Japan in 1963. Now you will find many different flavors made by many companies in Korean markets. In this recipe, you will use only the noodles and make your own tasty stock, so there is no need to use the flavoring packet that comes with the noodles.

NOTE

You can use 5 cups homemade or store-bought chicken stock instead of making the anchovy stock below. Vegetarians and vegans can substitute Vegetable Stock (page 78) and skip the fish cake and/or eggs.

1 pound fresh or frozen cylinder-shaped rice cakes for making tteokbokki, thawed in the refrigerator overnight if using frozen

⅓ cup Korean hot pepper paste (gochujang)

1 to 2 tablespoons Korean hot pepper flakes (gochu-garu)

1 tablespoon sugar

8 to 10 large dried anchovies, cleaned (see page 427)

4 ounces fish cake, cut into bite-size pieces, or homemade fish cake (page 182), thinly sliced and cut into bite-size pieces

4 scallions, cut into 3-inch pieces

Half or all the noodles from 1 (4-ounce) package Korean dried instant ramyeon (seasoning packet discarded)

2 hard-boiled eggs, peeled

1. Separate the rice cakes and soak in cold water for 30 minutes, until slightly softened. If you are using long, thick, cylinder-shaped rice cakes, cut them into bite-size pieces.

2. Combine the hot pepper paste, hot pepper flakes, and sugar in a bowl and mix well with a spoon. Set aside.

3. Bring 6 cups water to a boil over medium-high heat in a wide, shallow pot. Add the anchovies and boil for 20 minutes. Remove the anchovies with a slotted spoon or chopsticks and discard. You will have about 5 cups stock.

4. Add the rice cakes, fish cake, scallions, and seasoning paste to the boiling stock. Cook, stirring occasionally with a wooden spoon, for 10 minutes, or until the rice cakes soften and the broth gets a little thick.

5. Shortly before serving, add the Korean ramyeon. Cook, stirring occasionally, for 4 to 5 minutes, until the ramyeon noodles are cooked and separated and the broth is bubbling and thick. Be sure not to overcook the noodles because they will swell and soak up all the broth. Stir in the hard-boiled eggs and serve (cut the eggs in half when you serve).

6. To serve, place the pot on the table with a large spoon. Everyone can spoon some of everything into their bowls to eat with forks or chopsticks.

Fish Cake Soup

EOMUKGUK 어묵국

Serves 2

This wintertime street snack used to warm me up on the coldest days in Seoul. Eomukguk vendors set up small tents on the street with a simmering pot of broth in the middle. The pot is filled with eomukguk skewers, with the ends pointing outward, ready for you to grab. You don't need to say anything or order; you just pull out a skewer and eat. The vendors provide paper cups so customers can serve themselves some of the broth, too. After you've eaten all the fish cakes you want, the vendor counts your empty skewers, and you pay, leave the tent, and go on your way. The broth is free.

You can find many different kinds of fish cakes in Korean grocery stores, some finger-size, some flat, some round, some rectangular. They are mostly starch, although the more expensive ones have a higher fish content; you can tell because they are chewier and more savory, and they cost more. I encourage you to experiment with different fish cakes—or make your own.

This dish goes beautifully with Spicy Rice Cakes in Broth with Ramyeon Noodles (page 392) because the soup clears your palate after the spicy rice cakes. Invite a friend over—the price per skewer is up to you!

You'll need four 10-inch wooden skewers.

12 to 14 ounces assorted store-bought small fish cakes and/or rectangular thin fish cakes, or Steamed Fish Cake (page 182), cut into bite-size pieces

8 cups Anchovy-Kelp Stock (page 74)

1 teaspoon kosher salt

1 teaspoon soy sauce

1 scallion, chopped

Soy-Scallion Seasoning Sauce (page 130)

1. Thread 6 to 8 fish cakes on each skewer. If you are using rectangular fish cakes, cut them in half lengthwise and then fold each in half a few times. Insert a skewer through the center of the folded fish cake.

2. In a wide, shallow pot, combine the stock, salt, and soy sauce and stir. Add the skewers and bring to a boil over medium-high heat. Continue to cook for 5 minutes, until each fish cake softens and expands slightly. As they cook, spoon the boiling stock over the top of the fish cakes. Sprinkle with the scallion.

3. Bring the pot to the table and ladle some soup into individual bowls. Take one or two skewers and add to each bowl. Take some sauce with a small spoon, put it on the fish cake, and eat.

Army Base Stew

BUDAE-JJIGAE 부대찌개

Serves 4

When the war ended in 1953, much of Korea was in bad shape, and food was hard to find. Some Koreans could get canned items like beans and Spam from the U.S. Army bases. They brought them home and prepared them with kimchi, garlic, gochujang, and gochu-garu, creating a Korean-style stew with American ingredients.

The stew began to show up at bars. It was usually cooked at a table for two or more people, and soon every table in the bar would have a bubbling pot. It became increasingly popular, especially over the last few years. Now there are large budae-jjigae franchise chains with restaurants in every city.

6 garlic cloves, minced

2 tablespoons Korean hot pepper flakes (gochu-garu)

1 tablespoon Korean hot pepper paste (gochujang)

½ teaspoon ground black pepper

1 teaspoon soy sauce

8 ounces cabbage (½ medium head), cut into bite-size pieces

½ medium onion, sliced

2 scallions, cut into 1-inch-long pieces

8 ounces pork belly or pork shoulder, cut into thin, bite-size pieces

½ cup fermented Traditional Napa Cabbage Kimchi (page 112), cut into bite-size pieces, or Bite-Size Napa Cabbage Kimchi (page 120)

4 ounces Spam, sliced about ¼ inch thick

4 ounces cocktail sausages, or any cooked sausage (cut larger sausages into bite-size pieces)

6 ounces cylinder-shaped rice cake, cut if necessary into 1½-inch-long pieces

8 ounces medium-firm tofu, cut into bite-size pieces

¼ cup canned baked beans (optional)

2 ounces cheddar cheese, sliced

2 ounces sweet potato starch noodles (dangmyeon), soaked in cold water for 30 minutes and drained

1 (4-ounce) package dried instant ramyeon noodles (seasoning packet discarded)

5 cups Anchovy-Kelp Stock (page 74), chicken stock, or beef stock (homemade or store-bought)

1. Combine the garlic, hot pepper flakes, hot pepper paste, black pepper, soy sauce, and 2 tablespoons water in a small bowl. Mix well with a spoon.

2. Spread the cabbage, onion, and scallions evenly in a wide, shallow pot or skillet. Top with the pork, kimchi, and the garlic-pepper paste. Add the Spam, sausage, rice cake, tofu, baked beans (if using), and cheese.

3. Cut the sweet potato starch noodles in half with scissors and add to the pot. Place the block of ramyeon on top, in the middle.

4. Add 4 cups of the stock and set the pot over high heat. (The Korean style is to cook the dish at the table on a portable burner. If you don't have a tabletop burner, cook it on the stove away from the table.) When the mixture comes to a rolling boil, about 15 minutes, press down on the ramyeon to submerge it in the boiling broth and stir all the ingredients with tongs and a large spoon, turning them over so they cook evenly. Cook for another 5 minutes, or until the pork is fully cooked and the broth is flavorful. If the stock boils down too much, add the remaining 1 cup stock. Serve in bowls.

Noodles and Black Bean Sauce Platter

JAENGBAN-JJAJANGMYEON 쟁반짜장면

Serves 2 to 4

Jjajangmyeon is a Koreanized version of a noodle dish created by Chinese immigrants in Incheon, Korea, in 1905. You'll find it in every basement food court of every department store, and it's especially popular for home delivery in under 30 minutes. Sooner or later, on one of the many Korean TV dramas that are easy to find online (they have translated captions), someone orders these substantial noodles in creamy black bean sauce. The delivery man even comes back later to pick up the empty bowls!

The dish is usually made with pork or beef, but this recipe is a variation that also includes seafood. I serve it already mixed together on a big platter (*jaengban* means "tray").

FOR THE SAUCE

⅓ cup vegetable oil

3 scallions, cut into 1-inch pieces

⅓ cup black bean paste (chunjang)

8 ounces pork belly, cut into ½-inch cubes

1 large onion, cut into bite-size pieces

6 ounces cabbage, cut into bite-size pieces

1 medium potato, peeled and cut into ½-inch cubes

1 small zucchini, cut into ½-inch cubes

4 ounces squid, cleaned (see page 431) and cut into bite-size pieces

4 ounces shrimp, peeled, deveined (see page 427), and cut into a few pieces if desired

1 teaspoon sugar

FOR THE NOODLES

2 bunches (18 ounces) jjajangmyeon noodles

2 tablespoons potato starch

1 teaspoon toasted sesame oil

MAKE THE SAUCE

1. Heat the vegetable oil in a small, heavy pan over medium-high heat for 1 minute. Reduce the heat to medium and add the scallions. Fry until crisp and brown, 2 to 3 minutes. Strain the oil into a bowl. Discard the fried scallions. You will get about 5 tablespoons oil.

2. Heat 3 tablespoons of the infused oil in the same skillet for 1 minute. Add the black bean paste and stir quickly with a wooden spoon for about 1 minute, until fragrant. Remove from the heat.

3. Heat the remaining 2 tablespoons infused oil in a large skillet over medium-high heat. Add the pork and stir occasionally until the surface turns golden brown and crunchy, 5 to 6 minutes.

4. Increase the heat to high and stir in the onion, cabbage, potato, and zucchini. Cook, stirring, for 5 minutes, or until all the vegetables look soft and the cabbage turns a little translucent.

5. Push the vegetables and pork to the edges of the skillet, leaving a little oil in the center. Add the squid, shrimp, and fried black bean paste to the center of the skillet. Add the sugar and stir for 3 to 4 minutes, until the squid and shrimp are cooked.

6. Reduce the heat to medium-high. Add 3 cups water and stir. Cover and cook for 7 to 8 minutes, until the bubbling broth is very flavorful and the seafood and vegetables are cooked through and tender. Remove the skillet from the heat.

Recipe Continues

COOK THE NOODLES AND SERVE

1. Bring a large pot of water to a boil over medium-high heat. Put the noodles on a cutting board. Uncoil and spread them apart with your hands. Add them to the boiling water and stir with a wooden spoon. Cover and cook for 2 to 3 minutes, until the water starts to boil over. Uncover, stir, and cook for 3 to 4 minutes, until they are cooked through. To check to see if the noodles are done, remove one with chopsticks or tongs, dip into a bowl of cold water to cool, and taste. It should be chewy but cooked through. Drain the noodles. Rinse them under cold running water, rubbing them with both hands to remove the excess starch. Drain again.

2. Combine the potato starch and ¼ cup water in a bowl and mix well with a spoon.

3. Reheat the sauce over high heat until bubbling. Stir the potato starch slurry with a spoon and slowly add to the sauce, stirring with a wooden spoon, until the sauce thickens and becomes shiny.

4. Add the noodles and sesame oil. Stir with the wooden spoon for about 1 minute, until the sauce is bubbling. Transfer the noodles and sauce to a large platter and serve right away. Give everybody a bowl or plate and let them serve themselves using tongs.

Fire Chicken
with Cheese

CHEESE BULDAK 치즈불닭

Serves 2

The video of this modern fiery chicken dish covered with gooey cheese is one of the top five on my YouTube channel. Why? Because it's cheesy and red? Does it remind people of lasagna?

But it's a far cry from Italian. *Buldak* means "fire chicken," and the original dish, chunks of chicken in a thick, spicy sauce, was cooked on a rotisserie over flames in a makeshift barbecue pit. Buldak has evolved beyond the fire pit, and it now includes cheese, a very trendy ingredient. My version is super cheesy. Some of my viewers cook it once a week. One of my favorite comments came from one who wrote, "Today, my boyfriend, who is simply the worst cook I've ever known, made this recipe. It came out delicious!"

¼ cup Korean hot pepper flakes (gochu-garu)

2 tablespoons Korean hot pepper paste (gochujang)

1 teaspoon soy sauce

3 tablespoons vegetable oil

¼ teaspoon ground black pepper

¼ cup rice syrup or 3 tablespoons sugar

3 garlic cloves, minced

1 teaspoon minced peeled ginger

1 pound boneless, skinless chicken breast, cut into ¾-inch cubes

3 ounces sliced rice cakes

8 ounces mozzarella cheese, sliced thin

1. Combine the hot pepper flakes, hot pepper paste, soy sauce, 2 tablespoons of the vegetable oil, the black pepper, rice syrup, garlic, and ginger in a large bowl and mix well. Add the chicken and mix well with a large spoon until it is well coated.

2. Heat a large oven-safe skillet over medium-high heat. Add the remaining vegetable oil and the rice cakes. Cook for 3 to 4 minutes, turning often with a spatula, until both sides of the rice cakes are a little crunchy. Transfer the rice cakes to a small bowl.

3. Add the chicken and ¼ cup water to the skillet. Cover and cook, stirring occasionally, for 7 to 8 minutes. Stir in the rice cakes. Reduce the heat to low, cover, and cook for 5 minutes, until the chicken is fully cooked.

4. Meanwhile, preheat the broiler in the oven, with the rack positioned in the middle.

5. Cover the top of the chicken with the sliced mozzarella cheese and slip the skillet under the broiler. Broil for just a few minutes, until the cheese is bubbling. Remove from the heat, bring to the table, and serve.

Rice Cake and Grilled Cheese Skewers

TTEOK-CHEEJEU-GUI 떡치즈구이

Serves 2

Of all the street foods in the Myeongdong shopping district, this skewer of chewy white rice cakes alternating with gooey, golden-brown melted cheese in between was the most irresistible to me. The vendor placed it in a paper cup so it would be easy to eat and drizzled sweetened condensed milk over the top for added richness and sweetness.

You'll need two 8- to 10-inch wooden skewers and, if you want to be like the street vendors, a paper cup.

6 to 8 (3-inch-long) pieces cylinder-shaped rice cake

6 to 8 mozzarella sticks, cut into 2½-inch-long pieces

1 tablespoon unsalted butter

2 tablespoons sweetened condensed milk

1. Alternate 3 or 4 rice cake pieces with 3 or 4 mozzarella sticks side by side on a cutting board. Push a skewer through the center of the formation and press the pieces together tightly. Make another skewer with the remaining rice cakes and cheese.

2. Melt the butter in a large nonstick skillet over medium heat and swirl the skillet to evenly coat it with the butter.

3. Put the two skewers in the skillet side by side (or work in batches if the skillet isn't big enough). Cook for 3 to 5 minutes, until the bottom of the cheese turns light brown. Turn the skewers over. Cook, turning the skewers over a few times, until both sides of the cheese are crusty and golden brown, 3 to 5 minutes.

4. Remove the skillet from the heat. Drizzle 1 tablespoon sweetened condensed milk over each skewer and serve right away. Or put each skewer in a paper cup just like Korean street vendors do, then drizzle the sweetened condensed milk over the top.

Candied Sweet Potatoes

GOGUMA-MATTANG 고구마맛탕

Serves 2 to 4

Candied sweet potato was one of my favorite street snacks when I was young, and you can still get it in the streets of Seoul, exactly as I enjoyed it years ago when vendors waited outside my junior high school for us to finish school in the afternoon. The vendors put the wedges into a paper cup using tongs and add a wooden skewer so their customers can eat the wedges easily.

The snack is a hot sweet potato wedge with a candied coating, sweet and crunchy outside and creamy inside. The wedge shape allows it to have more sides and a larger crunchy surface area. It's one of the most delicious things in the world, especially right after it's made, when the smooth, creamy insides are still hot. It's a favorite with children. Best of all, it's easy to make at home!

Korean sweet potatoes look like American sweet potatoes on the outside, but inside they are starchier, with a creamy color and a somewhat chestnutty texture.

Vegetable oil

1 pound Korean sweet potatoes (see headnote) or regular sweet potatoes

⅓ cup sugar

¼ cup shelled, roasted peanuts (optional)

1 teaspoon toasted pumpkin seeds (optional)

1. Heat 3 inches vegetable oil in a large saucepan over medium-high heat until the temperature reaches 330 to 340 degrees F.

2. While the oil is heating, peel the sweet potatoes and cut them into wedges, about 2 inches thick at the wide end and ½ inch thick at the narrow end.

3. Add the sweet potato wedges to the hot oil. (If you don't have a cooking thermometer, you can tell if the oil is hot enough by grabbing one piece of sweet potato with tongs and dipping it in the hot oil. The oil should bubble right away around the sweet potato.) Turn down the heat to medium and fry the sweet potatoes, turning and rotating them with a large slotted spoon or tongs, until they are cooked through and a little crispy on the outside, 6 to 7 minutes. Transfer to a strainer set over a bowl to drain the excess oil.

4. Bring the oil back up to 330 to 340 degrees F over medium-high heat, then reduce the heat to medium and return the sweet potatoes to the oil. Fry again until golden brown and very crunchy on the surface, 3 to 5 minutes. Transfer to the strainer to drain.

5. In a large skillet, heat 2 tablespoons vegetable oil over medium heat and swirl to coat evenly. Sprinkle the sugar over the oil in an even layer and heat, without stirring, until the edges of the sugar layer begin to melt and color lightly. Do not disturb the sugar, or it will crystallize. Reduce the heat to medium-low and continue to cook, swirling the skillet but not stirring the sugar, until all the sugar has melted and caramelized, 6 to 8 minutes. Immediately remove from the heat. Add the sweet potatoes and the peanuts and pumpkin seeds (if using). Stir and mix everything together with tongs and a spatula until each piece of sweet potato is well coated and shiny.

6. Transfer the sweet potatoes to a large platter lined with parchment paper and allow to cool for 1 minute. Using tongs and a spatula, pull apart the wedges and allow them to cool down a little more before serving.

Sweet Pancakes
Filled with Syrup and Seeds

SSIAHT-HOTTEOK 씨앗호떡

Makes 5 pancakes

The hot yeasted Korean pancake that I used to buy on the streets after school as a kid was a simple, fluffy pancake filled with hot melted sugar. Over time this simple snack has shrunk and added new fillings and cooking methods.

The current popular style is a fried pancake filled with seeds mixed into the syrup, mostly toasted sunflower seeds and pumpkin seeds. Frying in oil gives the cake a sweet, crispy crust.

Vendors serve ssiaht-hotteok in a paper cup because it's too hot to hold with your hands. This is a smart idea because you also don't have to worry about the hot syrup dripping; the cup catches it.

Hotteok are easy to make. Take care that your yeast isn't old and that the water in the dough isn't too hot or it will kill the yeast. I get the temperature right by bringing ¼ cup water to a boil in a small saucepan, then adding enough cold water from the tap to make 1 cup. The temperature is perfect for activating the yeast, about 105 degrees F. Use this method and you will never fail to produce fluffy hotteok.

FOR THE DOUGH

2 tablespoons sugar

2¼ teaspoons active dry yeast (1 packet)

½ teaspoon kosher salt

1 tablespoon vegetable oil

2 cups all-purpose flour

FOR ASSEMBLING AND FRYING

2 tablespoons plus 1 cup vegetable oil

¾ cup mixed toasted pumpkin seeds and sunflower seeds

¾ cup brown or white sugar

MAKE THE DOUGH

1. In a large bowl, combine the sugar, yeast, and 1 cup lukewarm water (see headnote) and mix well. Stir in the salt and vegetable oil. Add the flour and mix well with a wooden spoon for about 1 minute, until the dough comes together.

2. Cover and let the dough rise at room temperature for 1½ hours, until doubled in volume.

3. Deflate the dough and knead it by hand for about 3 minutes, until smooth.

MAKE THE HOTTEOK

1. Put the 2 tablespoons vegetable oil in a small bowl. Set aside the seed mixture in another bowl.

2. Heat the 1 cup vegetable oil in a large skillet over medium-high heat for 3 to 4 minutes, then reduce the heat to medium. Put a tiny amount of dough in the oil. If it bubbles briskly, it's the right temperature.

3. Dip your fingers into the bowl of vegetable oil. Pinch off about one-fifth of the dough. Shape it into a ball with your oiled fingers (it will be sticky). Flatten the ball slightly and spoon about 2 tablespoons of the sugar into the center. Lift the edges of the dough up over the sugar and pinch together firmly so that the sugar is completely enclosed in the dough.

4. Put the filled hotteok in the hot oil, sealed side down. Cook until the bottom turns light brown, about 1 minute. Flip it over with a spatula, then press it down in the oil to shape a 5-inch disk. Reduce the heat to medium-low and cook for 4 to 5 minutes, turning the hotteok over and pressing it down from time to time, until the sugar inside has melted into a syrup and the outside is brown and crispy on both sides. Take care not to allow the surface of the pancake to burn. The syrup might ooze out, and that's fine—it will make the hotteok crunchy on the outside.

5. With tongs, transfer the hotteok to a plate. Hold the hotteok with the tongs, and with your other hand, cut it open along the edge with scissors, to make a pouch. Spoon about 2 tablespoons of the seed mixture inside. Transfer the hotteok to a small plate and serve, or do as the Korean street vendors do and fold the hotteok lengthwise using tongs, put it in a paper cup, and serve.

6. Make 4 more hotteok with the remaining dough, sugar, and seeds.

Bread Rolls

ROLL-PPANG 롤빵

Makes 6

"Maangchi, I make these for my children to eat when they come home from school! They love them!"

Millions of my fans tell me this. These hot, fresh, slightly sweet bread rolls are not traditionally Korean. My good friend Jeongjin introduced me to them when my children were in elementary school. It was a great snack to tide them over until dinnertime, and I served them with strawberry jam and milk.

This is a small-batch recipe, but I often make larger batches so I'll have extra in the freezer.

3 tablespoons unsalted butter

½ cup whole milk

2 tablespoons sugar

¼ teaspoon kosher salt

1 large egg, lightly

beaten, plus 1 large egg white, lightly beaten

2¼ teaspoons active dry yeast (1 packet)

1½ cups all-purpose flour, plus more for dusting

MAKE THE DOUGH

1. Melt the butter in a small saucepan over medium heat. Remove from the heat and add the milk, sugar, and salt. Stir well until the sugar has dissolved. Add the whole egg and stir. Cool to lukewarm.

2. Test the mixture with your finger, and when it is lukewarm, add the yeast and let stand for 5 minutes, or until the mixture is cloudy and a little foamy. Transfer to a large bowl, add the flour, and mix with a wooden spoon for about 1 minute, until the dough comes together. It will be sticky.

3. Cover the dough and let it rise at room temperature for 1 to 1½ hours, until doubled in size.

4. Uncover and deflate the dough. Knead for a few minutes in the bowl, until smooth.

5. Cover and let rise again for 30 minutes, until doubled. Deflate the dough and knead for 1 minute.

SHAPE THE ROLLS

1. Transfer the dough to a generously floured work surface and divide into 6 equal pieces. Cover the dough pieces with plastic so that they won't dry out.

2. Flour your fingers so they don't stick to the dough. Take a piece of dough and shape it into a ball. Using your hands, roll the ball into a rope about 8 inches long, moving your hands up and down the dough so that it rolls out evenly. Starting from one end, coil the rope, then tuck the end under and up through the middle (see photo). Transfer to a nonstick baking sheet.

3. Repeat with the remaining dough pieces. Be sure to leave about 1 inch between the rolls on the baking sheet to give them room to expand. Cover and let rise for 1 hour.

BAKE THE ROLLS

1. Preheat the oven to 350 degrees F, with the rack in the middle.

2. Lightly beat the egg white and gently brush it on the rolls. Bake for 15 to 17 minutes, until the tops are light brown.

3. Remove the pan from the oven and turn on the broiler.

4. Brush the rolls again with the remaining egg white. Broil for 1 to 2 minutes, until the rolls are golden brown and shiny. Remove from the heat and serve hot. Leftover rolls can be frozen for up to 1 month in an airtight container or zipper-lock plastic bag. They take about 10 minutes to thaw at room temperature, or 40 seconds to a minute in the microwave.

Doughnut Twists

KKWABAEGI 꽈배기

Makes 16

In high school, we used to go to a kkwabaegi place that was crowded with people waiting to eat these doughnut twists hot from the pan. They were crunchy outside and fluffy inside, with a heavenly yeasty and cinnamon aroma.

Years later, when I was a mom, my friend Jeongjin taught me her kkwabaegi recipe and showed me her technique for making them pretty. Even if you don't shape and twist them perfectly, they will taste incredible.

2 tablespoons unsalted butter

1 cup whole milk

5 tablespoons sugar

2¼ teaspoons active dry yeast (1 packet)

½ teaspoon kosher salt

1 large egg, lightly beaten

3 cups all-purpose flour, plus more for dusting

Vegetable oil

½ teaspoon ground cinnamon

MAKE THE DOUGH

1. Melt the butter in a saucepan over medium heat. Remove the pan from the heat. Add the milk and 2 tablespoons of the sugar. Stir well and add the yeast. Let sit for 5 to 10 minutes, until the yeast is dissolved and creamy. Add the salt and stir. Transfer the mixture to a large bowl, add the egg, and stir well.

2. Add the flour and mix well with a wooden spoon until the dough comes together. Knead the dough for 2 to 3 minutes in the bowl until smooth. Cover and let rise at room temperature for 1 to 1½ hours, until the dough is more than doubled in size.

3. Deflate the dough and knead in the bowl for a few minutes, until very smooth and soft. Cover and let rise for 1 hour.

SHAPE THE DOUGHNUTS

1. Deflate the dough and knead for 1 minute. Divide the dough evenly into 16 pieces. Put them on a large baking sheet, leaving space between the pieces. Cover with plastic wrap to prevent the dough from drying out while you work.

2. Place a piece of dough on a floured work surface. Roll the dough into a rope 10 to 12 inches long and ½ inch thick. As you roll it, move one hand upward and the other downward so there is some tension in the rope. Lift up the dough and bring the ends together. The tension in the dough will twist it around itself as it hangs. If it's not twisted much, turn it with your hand to twist it a little so you get three or four twists.

3. Place the twist on the floured work surface or baking sheet. Repeat with the remaining pieces of dough, leaving space between them as they sit. Let the twists rise for about 30 minutes. After 15 minutes, gently flip each piece over with your hands so the bottoms don't get flat and all sides rise nicely.

FRY THE DOUGHNUTS

1. Heat 3 inches vegetable oil in a large, deep skillet over medium-high heat until the temperature reaches 350 degrees F. Lower the heat to medium. Working in batches, gently lower a few twists into the hot oil. Fry until the bottoms turn light brown, 2 to 3 minutes. Gently turn them over with tongs and fry for another 3 to 5 minutes, turning over with tongs occasionally, until all sides are an even golden brown. Transfer to a strainer set over a bowl to drain the excess oil.

2. When all the doughnuts are fried, combine the cinnamon and remaining 3 tablespoons sugar in a paper bag and shake it to mix well.

3. A few at a time, put the doughnuts in the bag and shake to coat. Transfer to a large platter and serve right away. You can freeze leftover doughnuts in a zipper-lock plastic bag for up to 1 month. Thaw at room temperature for 10 minutes.

Fish cakes at a street market in Seoul.

BASIC KOREAN COOKING TECHNIQUES

How to Shell and Skin Fresh Chestnuts

1. Lay the chestnut on the flat side and slice off the flat end, then slice off the pointed end.

2. Using a paring knife, slice down both of the narrower sides, removing the dark skin inside the shell.

3. Peel off the remaining shell with your fingers. Trim away the dark skin on the outside of the chestnut so that it is a uniform creamy color.

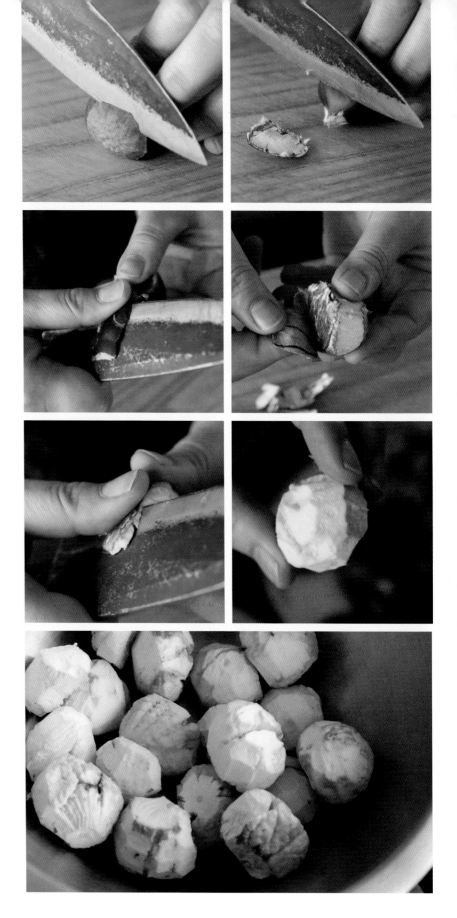

How to Shell and Cook Ginkgo Nuts

I usually buy ginkgo nuts already shelled, but if you can only find them in the shells, here's how to shell them. It's important to gently crack the shells on the edges where they come together. I usually press the nut between the handles of my kitchen scissors to gently crack the shells. You can also press them between the handles of a can opener, or any tool that will let you get a purchase on the nut. As soon as you hear the nut crack, release your pressure so you don't crush the soft nut inside the shell. Using your fingers, gently remove the shell and discard.

You can either stir-fry the nuts in a little bit of oil or blanch in boiling water to remove the skins.

TO STIR-FRY

Heat about 2 teaspoons vegetable oil in a skillet over medium-high heat and add the shelled ginkgo nuts. Add some kosher salt and stir-fry until the skins loosen and the color of the nuts changes to golden or bright green. Transfer to paper towels, fold the paper towels over the nuts, and gently massage the nuts to remove more skin.

TO BLANCH

Bring a pot of water to a boil, add the nuts, and boil for 2 minutes. Drain and remove the skins when cool enough to handle.

How to Make Scallion Threads

1. Cut the root ends off the scallions.

2. Holding your knife on a very sharp diagonal, cut the scallions into very thin slices, 2 to 3 inches long.

3. Place the slices in a bowl and cover with cold water. Soak for 5 minutes, then drain in a strainer. Rinse with cold running water, tossing the scallion threads with your hand.

How to Clean Soybean Sprouts

Pick out and discard any brownish beans and place the sprouts in a large bowl. Fill with cold water. Grab a handful of sprouts and swish them around in the water, then transfer to a colander. Any bean skins should come off in the water. Repeat until you have transferred all the sprouts. Change the water and repeat until there are no more skins remaining on the sprouts. Discard the water and the skins.

How to Remove the Tips of Pine Nuts

Since the tips are darker than the rest of the pine nut, the pine nuts are prettier when you remove them. Simply snap off the tips with your fingers.

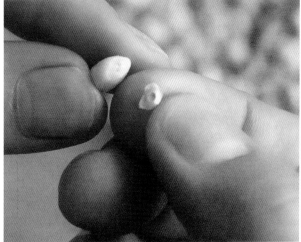

How to Soak and Prepare Dried Fernbrake for Cooking

1. Rinse 1½ ounces dried fernbrake and place in a 6-quart or larger pot. Add 5 quarts water and bring to a boil over medium-high heat. Cover and cook for 1 hour.

2. Remove from the heat and let sit, covered, for 3 hours.

3. Drain the fernbrake and rinse in cold water, changing the water several times. Drain.

4. You will end up with about 1 pound of soaked fernbrake. Use it right away or freeze it in a zipper-lock plastic bag. Do not squeeze out the water before freezing or it will be too stringy when you thaw it.

How to Pit Dried Jujubes

Holding the jujube in one hand and your knife in the other, carefully cut into the fruit lengthwise until you feel the blade against the pit. Turn the jujube a bit and work the knife blade around the pit, until you've cut away all the flesh.

How to Soak and Prepare Dried Taro Stems for Cooking

After soaking what looks like a small amount of taro stems, the stems will expand to about ten times their original weight. You can freeze what you don't use. This will save you a time-consuming step when you need them for another recipe. Don't squeeze out the water before freezing or the stems will be too stringy when you thaw them.

1 (2.82-ounce) package dried taro stems

¼ cup all-purpose flour

1. Wear rubber gloves to handle the dried taro stems. Take the dried taro stems out of the package and put them in a large bowl. Cover with warm water and soak for 1 hour. Wash the stems vigorously, rubbing them well and kneading to remove any dirt. Rinse in several changes of cold water.

2. Transfer the clean stems to a large, heavy pot. Add the flour and rub into the stems vigorously until well mixed. (The flour acts as an abrasive and helps clean the stems.) Add 3 quarts water. Cover and place over medium-high heat until the mixture begins to boil over, about 15 minutes. Uncover and cook for another 15 minutes, stirring occasionally with a wooden spoon. Drain.

3. Wearing your rubber gloves, rinse the stems under cold running water until they are very clean. Wash the pot thoroughly and put the clean stems back in. Fill with cold water and soak the stems for 24 hours, changing the water a few times. Drain and rinse well. Your taro stems will weigh about 1¾ pounds.

How to Toast, Crush, and Shred Seaweed Paper

TO TOAST

Hold one edge of a sheet of gim between your thumb and forefinger and wave it over a low flame or electric burner. Keep it moving so it doesn't burn. As it toasts, it will become crisp and go from almost black to green. Turn the gim periodically to toast it evenly. It should take just seconds. You can put it right into the flame. If it catches fire, just blow it out and continue until the color changes and the gim is very crisp. Now you can either crush it or shred it.

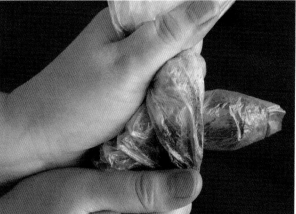

TO CRUSH

Put the toasted gim in a plastic bag and crush it into small pieces.

TO SHRED

Using scissors, cut the toasted gim sheet in half. Stack the halves and cut into 4 equal pieces. Cut the quarters into thin threads.

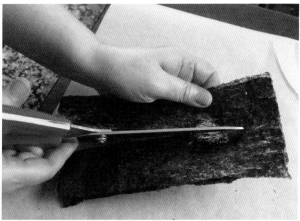

How to Clean and Fillet Spanish Mackerel

You will need a 2½-pound whole Spanish mackerel to yield 1½ to 2 pounds fillets.

1. Place the fish on a cutting board and cut off the head. Discard.

2. Slit open the belly and remove the intestines. Discard. Wash the fish under cold running water, along with the cutting board and knife. Pat the fish dry with a paper towel.

3. Cut open the top of the fish by sliding in the knife next to where the head was, as close to the backbone as possible along the top edge. You should feel the backbone under the blade a little bit. Cut all the way to the tail.

4. Flip the fish over and make a slit along the belly from the tail to the head end of the fish.

5. To fillet the fish, insert a sharp knife at the tail end between the backbone and the ribs and, holding the tail, cut the flesh away from the ribs along the backbone from one end to the other. Then flip the fish over and cut the other side away from the bones. Pull out the backbone and discard.

6. Carefully remove the rib bones remaining in the belly flesh with your knife, leaving as much flesh as possible on the fillet.

7. Open the fillet with the skin side down. You will see small pin bones all along the center. Cut them out by making two parallel cuts lengthwise, all the way down the fish, making a shallow "V" so you lose a minimum of flesh. Be sure not to cut all the way through to the skin. Pull out this strip of flesh with the pin bones inside and discard. Your fish is now ready for cooking.

How to Clean Large Dried Anchovies

Break off the head. Pull out and discard the dark entrails around the belly. Sometimes bones will come out as you clean the anchovies, but it is not necessary to pull them out.

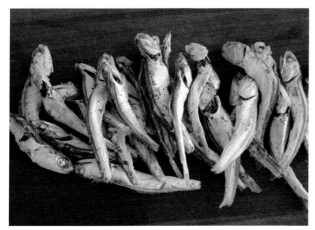

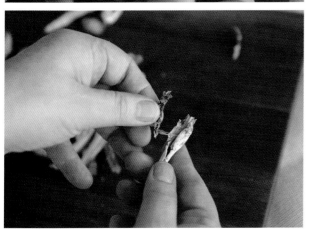

How to Devein Shrimp

Peel the shrimp. Using the tip of a knife, make a slit down the length of the back, approximately ¼ inch deep. Open and, using the tip of your knife, lift and remove the dark string. Rinse the shrimp under cold running water.

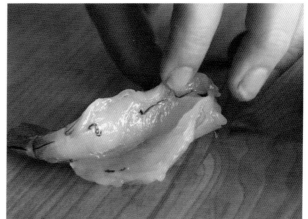

How to Clean Live Clams

1. Tap on each clam and discard any that do not close. (If a clam stays open when you tap on it, it's dead.)

2. Place the clams in a bowl and cover with cold water. Brush each clam and rinse a few times with cold water. Drain.

3. Rinse the bowl. Add 2 quarts cold water and ¼ cup kosher salt and stir to dissolve the salt. Add the clams and cover. Refrigerate for 2 hours. The clams will spit out any remaining grit, mud, and sand. Rinse and drain.

How to Open Live Clams

I'm not strong enough to open clams with a clam shucker; I find it easier to use the back of my heavy 6½-inch Korean knife to create a small opening in the shell.

1. Knock on the bump of the shell, just above the hinge, with the back of a knife to make a small break in the shells where they come together. Insert the tip of the knife into the break between the two shells. Press down and ease the shells apart.

2. Pull out the knife, turn the clam around, and work the shell open from the other side. Insert the knife into the hole again, no more than ½ inch in so that the blade doesn't go into the clam meat. Move the knife along the edge between the shells, taking care not to insert the blade more than ½ inch in.

3. Once the two halves have been separated, spread the shells wide enough to use the tip of your knife to nimbly detach the meat. It's attached to the shell in two spots near the edges of the top and bottom shells.

How to Soften Dried Sea Cucumbers

4 ounces dried sea cucumbers (3 to 4½ inches long)

Kosher salt, as needed

1 (1-inch) piece peeled ginger, sliced thin

¼ cup soju or mirim

1. Wash the dried sea cucumbers and put them in a large, heavy pot. Add 5 quarts water. Cover and bring to a boil. Remove the pot from the heat. Let the dried sea cucumbers soak in the hot water, covered, for 6 hours. Drain, add 5 quarts fresh water, and bring to a boil. Remove from the heat and soak again for 6 hours. Repeat two or three more times.

2. The next day, the sea cucumbers will be slightly soft. Drain, wearing disposable gloves, if you want, and cut off both ends of each one with kitchen scissors. Cut all the way up along the belly. Remove the intestines, put some salt in the belly, and rub it around to clean it. Rinse in cold water a couple of times.

3. Wash the pot and put the cleaned sea cucumbers back in. Add 5 quarts water and bring to a boil. Remove from the heat, cover, and soak for 6 hours. Repeat this step two more times over the next 24 hours, until the sea cucumbers are soft. Add the ginger and soju just before boiling the final time and leave them for the final soak. This will reduce the fishy aroma.

4. On the third day, the soaking is done. Drain the sea cucumbers and rinse in cold water. Use what you need and freeze the rest for up to 3 months.

How to Clean Whole Large Squid

1. Cut off the head with the tentacles where they join the body. Slit down the entire length of the body.

2. Using both hands, open up the body. Grab the entrails, along with the long bone that looks like a quill, and lift up and out. Discard.

3. Take the head, and with a large knife, cut in half between the eyes. Remove and discard the eyes and beak.

4. Open out the body flat on your cutting board, white (inside) side down, skin side up. Sprinkle about ¼ teaspoon kosher salt on one corner. (This will give you some traction, so your fingers won't slip when you pull off the skin.) Grab the corner of the outer skin and pull it away from the body. You can also use paper towels to give you traction. Pull all the skin away. Use the same technique—salt or paper towels—to pull the skin away from the tentacles. The tentacles don't need to be as white as the body, just a little cleaner than they were.

5. Rinse thoroughly and pat dry.

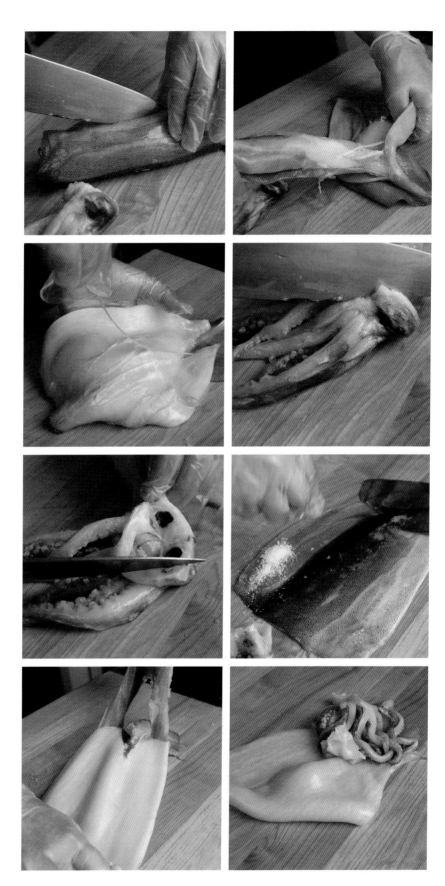

How to Clean and Cook Octopus

MUNEO-SONJILBEOP 문어손질법

In Korea it's common to see live octopus, freshly caught, sold in an aquarium in the market. We love our seafood as fresh as possible, preferably right off the boat, and when it comes to octopus, the larger and thicker the better. In many markets you can choose an octopus from the tank and they will clean and cook it for you right there.

I used to be afraid to clean octopus. I'd watch my mom handle a live octopus, one meter long, with no fear or hesitation at all. She quickly turned its head inside out, cleaned it, and put it in a huge pot of boiling water. Then we'd have fresh octopus for breakfast.

Koreans like their octopus a little chewy but not rubbery, so we're careful not to cook it very long. Basically, once it's opaque, we stop cooking. When I went to Mexico, I had octopus cooked in tomato soup and the octopus was very tender. They had cooked the octopus for a long time, until it was soft, like long-cooked beef brisket. I'm not sure many Koreans would like that texture.

I've bought freshly caught octopus and cleaned and cooked it in Nice, in the south of France. But here in New York City, where I live, there are no aquariums selling octopus. Unfortunately, all I can get in the local fish markets are frozen, or frozen and thawed. So this is my method of cleaning, tenderizing, and cooking the frozen octopus I buy here. If it were fresh, I'd need to remove the guts inside the head, too. I'd do this by flipping the head inside out, then removing anything attached to the inside, including the ink sac, until it's smooth.

1 (5-pound) octopus, fresh or frozen and thawed

¼ cup kosher salt

1. Place the whole octopus in a large bowl and sprinkle the salt all over the surface. Wearing disposable gloves, if you want, rub and scrub vigorously for 5 to 6 minutes, until the octopus is very foamy, to tenderize the meat and clean the suckers. Rinse and drain several times under cold running water until the octopus is no longer slippery. Drain and set aside.

2. In a large pot, bring 5 quarts water to a boil over medium-high heat.

3. Grab the head and gradually lower the octopus, arms first, into the boiling water. Press the octopus down into the water with a wooden spoon to submerge it. Using tongs, lift each arm one by one and let them curl up. Cook for 4 to 5 minutes, until all the arms are nicely curled up and set in a pretty shape, like a crown.

4. Using tongs and a spatula, turn the octopus over and cook for another 10 to 15 minutes, turning it over from time to time so that it cooks evenly. The octopus and the cooking liquid should now be red, and the octopus should be opaque. To check to see if the octopus is cooked sufficiently, insert a wooden skewer into the thickest part of one of the arms. If the wooden skewer is easily inserted, it's cooked. If not, cook a little longer. It usually takes about 4 minutes per pound.

5. Remove from the heat. Fill a large bowl with ice water. Transfer the octopus to the ice water. This process will help set the red color, and also keep the skin from peeling off. Reserve some of the red octopus broth to make Octopus Porridge (page 60) if you wish.

6. Drain the octopus and transfer to a large cutting board. Cut off the head and remove the eyes and translucent beak. (Discard the eyes and beak.) The octopus can be frozen, wrapped in plastic wrap and in a plastic bag, for up to 1 month.

What to do with the cooked and frozen octopus arms

1. Slice thinly and serve with sesame oil dipping sauce (Octopus Slices with Sesame Dipping Sauce, page 187). This makes a great accompaniment for beer or soju.

2. Chop it up and make Octopus Porridge (page 60) with the reserved octopus broth.

How to Bone a Whole Chicken Leg and Prepare It for Marinating

1. Pat dry a whole chicken leg (both thigh and drumstick) and put it on a cutting board, skin side down. The thigh and drumstick are separated by a fatty yellow line. Cut along that line, find the joint, and cut it to separate the two.

2. Find the bone in the center of the thigh and insert the tip of your knife on one side of it. Cut down along this bone without going all the way through the thigh. Then insert the tip of your knife on the other side of the bone and cut along that side. Push the knife under the bone and cut through, lifting the bone as you cut. Remove the skin if desired.

3. Use the same technique with the drumstick, inserting the tip of your knife on one side of the bone and cutting down along the bone without going all the way through the drumstick. Then insert the tip of your knife on the other side of the bone and cut along that side. Push the knife under the bone and cut through, lifting the bone as you cut. Remove the skin if desired.

4. With your knife, score a crosshatch pattern on both sides of the chicken pieces to help them absorb the marinade.

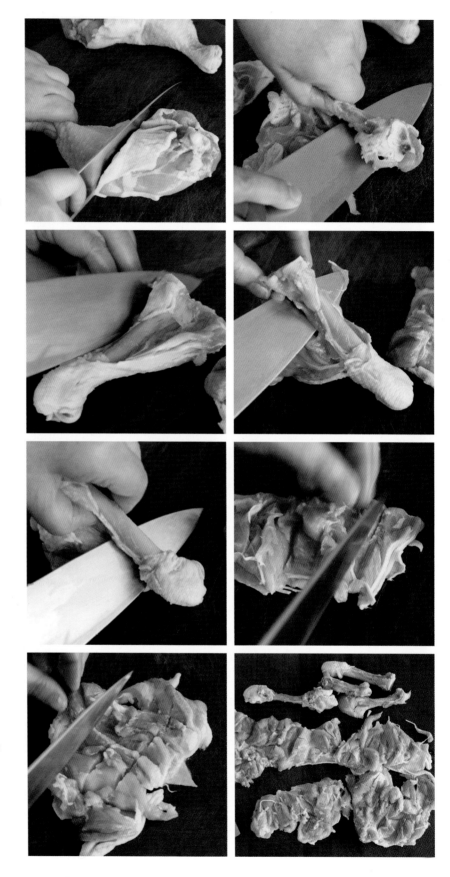

INDEX

NOTE: Page references in *italics* refer to photographs of finished recipes.